CW00584627

David Lyons is one of the preeminent philosophers of law active in the United States. This volume comprises essays written over a period of twenty-two years in which Professor Lyons outlines his fundamental views about the nature of law and its relation to morality and justice.

The underlying theme of the book is that a system of law has only a tenuous connection with morality and justice. Contrary to those legal theorists who maintain that no matter how bad the law of a community might be, strict conformity to existing law automatically dispenses "formal" justice, Professor Lyons contends that the law must earn the respect that it demands. Moreover, we cannot, as some would suggest, interpret law in a value-neutral manner. Rather, courts should interpret statutes, judicial precedents, and constitutional provisions in terms of values that would justify those laws. In this way officials can promote the justifiability of what they do to people in the name of law and can help the law live up to its moral pretensions.

Moral aspects of legal theory

Moral aspects of legal theory

Essays on law, justice, and political responsibility

DAVID LYONS

Susan Linn Sage Professor of Philosophy &
Professor of Law and Philosophy
Cornell University

CAMBRIDGE
UNIVERSITY PRESS

Published by the Press Syndicate of the University of Cambridge
The Pitt Building, Trumpington Street, Cambridge CB2 1RP
40 West 20th Street, New York, NY 10011-4211, USA
10 Stamford Road, Oakleigh, Victoria 3166, Australia

© Cambridge University Press 1993

First published 1993

Printed in the United States of America

Library of Congress Cataloging-in-Publication Data
Lyons, David, 1935–
Moral aspects of legal theory : essays on law, justice, and
political responsibility / David Lyons.
p. cm.
Includes bibliographical references.
ISBN 0-521-43244-8 (hc). – ISBN 0-521-43835-7 (pb)
1. Law and ethics. 2. Justice. 3. Justice, Administration of.
I. Title.
BJ55.L954 1993
340'.112 – dc20 92-28985
CIP

A catalog record for this book is available from the British Library.

ISBN 0-521-43244-8 hardback
ISBN 0-521-43835-7 paperback

To the memory of
ROBERT NEMIROFF

Contents

Preface

The essays in this volume were written over a period of twenty-two years. The first six essays reflect the traditional concern of legal philosophy with the nature of law, especially law's relation to moral principle. The remaining essays address problems and emerging issues of legal interpretation.

If this volume has a dominant theme, it is a *lack* of reverence for the law. The law to which I refer is not some sanitized ideal but rather what counts as law in real legal systems. As far as I can see, those bodies of law have merely contingent, indeed fragile, links with justice.

My attitude toward law is not derived from theory. It was kindled by a clash between reasonable ideals and harsh realities. Growing up during a war against fascism, one naturally acquired ideals of democracy and political decency. But it was dangerous to act on those ideals in the succeeding decade, when law was placed in the service of political repression while it continued to sustain practices of racial and sexual domination.

My sense of law's fallibility was confirmed by some knowledge of its record. Far more often than not, law has served oppressive, unjust, inhumane social arrangements.

Of course, American law has also served as a means of emancipation. In recent decades, law has helped to honor the constitutional promise of justice and liberty. That is why law should be seen not as inherently evil but as available for service to injustice as well as justice.

Despite the historical record, we have reason to think of law as bound to justice, for law has moral pretensions. Judges and others who speak for the law typically contend that what they do in its name is justifiable and just. That posture seems deeply rooted in legal practice and may well be essential to it. The claim invites the demand that law live up to its moral pretensions. As I suggest in the last two essays, this provides a reason for interpreting law so as to maximize the justifiability of official decisions.

When I first encountered legal theory, I thought that the tradition called "legal positivism" embodied a fitting lack of reverence for the law. That seemed the spirit of its so-called "separation of law and morals." I am not so sure anymore.

I can best explain my uncertainty by referring to a feature of positivist writing that is exemplified by a passage from Bentham's *Fragment on Government:*

Under a government of Laws, what is the motto of a good citizen? *"To obey punctually; to censure freely."*[1]

This might be taken to imply that disobedience to law cannot be justified. But Bentham's motto is misleading.[2] He presumably means that there is a moral presumption in favor of following law. Bentham seems to mean that disobedience to law requires justification, but obedience does not, even when law fails to satisfy the standards by which it is properly appraised.

Now consider a passage that reflects Bentham's root conception of law:

No law can ever be made but what trenches upon liberty: if it stops there, it is so much *pure* evil: if it is good upon the whole, it must be in virtue of something that comes after. It may be a necessary evil: but still at any rate it is an evil. To make a law is to do evil that good may come.[3]

In other words, law has inevitable costs but only contingent benefits. One need not accept Bentham's analysis of law to agree. But this truism seems at variance with his idea that there is a moral presumption in favor of following law. Bentham's presumption and the truism are not strictly incompatible. But if one accepts the truism that law has inevitable costs and only contingent benefits, then the presumption favoring obedience needs justification.

It is often suggested that law normally does enough good on the whole to support a presumption favoring obedience, if not a full-fledged moral obligation to obey the law. It may be suggested, for example, that law makes social life possible or that life without law would be nasty, brutish, and short. The trouble is that life has been like that for most people living under law. But it is not uncommon for positivists to assume a moral

---

[1] Preface, par. 17: in Jeremy Bentham, *Comment on the Commentaries* and *A Fragment on Government,* ed. J. H. Burns and H.L.A. Hart (London: Athlone Press, 1977), p. 399.

[2] See, for example, ibid., chap. IV, §21; p. 483f.

[3] Jeremy Bentham, *Of Laws in General,* ed. H.L.A. Hart (London: Athlone Press, 1970), chap. VI, § 4; p. 54.

presumption in favor of following law. This aspect of positivism is considered in several of the essays.

The past two decades have witnessed a remarkable turn in legal philosophy. Prior to Dworkin's work,[4] the subject of legal interpretation largely consisted of theories denying its possibility. The later essays in this volume address problems of interpretation. Beginning with familiar issues in constitutional theory, they go on to embrace elements of Dworkin's approach but also suggest its limits.

Another ground of my worry about legal positivism concerns interpretation.[5] To interpret law is not merely to assign it meaning but to discover its meaning. Some positivists maintain that judges do not interpret law when their reasoning involves moral judgment. We are told that, even when moral reasoning is needed because the law contains explicit moral language, this clarification adds to law and does not count as interpretation.[6]

This view of the matter depends on a theory of linguistic meaning. The positivist recognition that law is morally fallible does not require it. For moral language can be incorporated into law without ensuring that the law satisfy minimal standards of moral decency. Moral language can be found in unjust law.

If we do not consider the explication of moral language in law as interpretation, we may not assume, as we should, that sound principles should provide the basis for applying explicit moral requirements that are laid down by law; and we cannot criticize as unsound interpretation the use of unsound moral principles when officials explicate moral language in law.

Using sound principles presumably serves justice better than explicating moral requirements by reference to, say, the values embraced by groups that dominate society. Justice may be served even more effectively if one generally approaches interpretation by reading constitutions, statutes, and precedents in terms of values that provide their best justification. The last two essays in this volume consider merits and demerits of such an ap-

---

4. See Ronald Dworkin, *Law's Empire* (Harvard, 1986); for an earlier version, see his " 'Natural' Law Revisited," *University of Florida Law Review* 34 (1982) 165.
5. This volume's essay "Legal Formalism and Instrumentalism" examines assumptions – associated with positivism as well as legal "realism" – that deny the possibility of legal interpretation when it is most often needed.
6. I have not seen evidence that positivists embraced such a view before it was attributed to them by a critic; see Ronald Dworkin, *Taking Rights Seriously* (Harvard, 1978), pp. 345–50. For one positivist's concurrence, see Joseph Raz, *The Authority of Law* (Oxford, 1979), pp. 37–52.

proach to legal interpretation. It does not ensure that judges can in good conscience apply law as they find it. That is the problem with which these essays leave the reader.

A judge's commitment of fidelity to law may be stronger than any comparable obligation on the part of ordinary members of a community. But we have no reason to assume that a judicial obligation of fidelity to law is absolute. That is a lesson from our past – from judicial involvement in chattel slavery and other crimes against humanity. It is a painful issue that legal theory tends to avoid.

Acknowledgments

I had the good fortune to be introduced to legal philosophy by Herbert Hart, first by studying his then–recently published *Concept of Law* in a graduate seminar at Harvard, then by attending his seminar and lectures in Oxford. When I later began to research theories about rights, Hart's helpful suggestions led me deeper into legal theory. I am grateful for his generous support in these and in other, more important ways.

During the period in which these essays were written I have been a member of the Sage School of Philosophy at Cornell University. By the time the third essay was composed, I was a member of Cornell's Law School faculty as well. I am grateful to both sets of colleagues for friendship and encouragement, and to students in both schools for continual challenges.

Some of these essays were written, in whole or part, during leaves from teaching, in which I received support from Cornell, the John Simon Guggenheim Memorial Foundation, and the National Endowment for the Humanities, for all of which I am grateful.

The essays in this volume are presented in the order of their composition. Original publishing information is provided at the bottom of the first page of each essay. The last essay was written for another collection, which has not yet appeared.

The essays are reprinted here with only a few minor corrections, confined mainly to notes. Unnumbered footnotes and bracketed material in numbered footnotes have been added.

1

The internal morality of law

I

The distinctive doctrine of Natural Law theory often seems to be that an unjust law is not a law at all. An unjust law is like counterfeit currency, which causes trouble because it so closely resembles and may be taken for the real thing. But unjust law is not genuine law. And thus it deserves no respect.

Unfortunately, law can be, and much too often is, bad or unjust. What seems distinctive about Natural Law, therefore, is false – but so plainly false that the doctrine deserves a new reading.

Other ways of understanding natural law may be inferred from the obvious concerns of many Natural Lawyers. One is that law be subject to moral assessment. This turns the doctrine around. Laws are not necessarily right or morally neutral but can be good or bad, just or unjust. There are moral standards independent of the law that can be applied to judge it. Another concern is that the obligation to obey the law be recognized as having limitations. Natural Lawyers may be taken as saying that no one has any valid and binding obligation to obey an unjust law. But views like these, while avoiding the paradox, also seem to lack the spirit of Natural Law. For they do not imply that law and morals are essentially connected in a special way.

Perhaps Natural Lawyers have really wanted to press only such claims on us – none that would seem philosophically unrespectable to-day. What has gone under the label "Natural Law", indeed, is not always controversial or even clearly philosophical. Nevertheless, one might ask: Is there any sort of philosophic view that captures the spirit, without the blatant paradox, of Natural Law?

I shall construct and consider one such view. I call it Natural Law because it maintains that moral standards are implicit in or intrinsic to the law (in a sense to be explained). It is suggested by passages in Lon

"The Internal Morality of Law," *Proceedings of the Aristotelian Society* 71 (1970–71): 105–19. Presented at the meeting of the Aristotelian Society at 5/7 Tavistock Place, London WCI, on Monday 25th January 1971, at 7:30 p.m. In writing this paper I have benefited from discussions with Nicholas Sturgeon, Norton Batkin, Bernard Katz, William Nelson, Eileen Serene, Jerrold Tannenbaum, and John Turner.

Fuller's book, *The Morality of Law;*[1] though the argument I shall construct cannot safely be attributed to him, and it shall not employ all the interesting suggestions he makes. The general idea I find in Fuller is that one need not go beyond the law itself to find the basis for assessing it. One need not appeal to principles that have no necessary connexion with the law. But we are not required to say that unjust law somehow fails to exist. We may say instead that concepts of the law itself imply principles to be used in calling the law good or bad, just or unjust. When we understand what the law is then we see – not that all law is necessarily good and just – but *how to judge it.* The law thus carries within it principles for its own evaluation.

This Natural Law theory is more modest than its putative ancestors; but that is what any plausible theory must be. Indeed, following Fuller, our theory shall be even more modest. The argument shall not concern what might be called the main substance of the law – the particulars of what the law requires or allows and of how its straightforward application would affect the interests of individuals. It shall concern what Fuller calls "procedural" aspects of a legal system. Let us suppose for the moment that the law is a system of rules, or laws, that are administered, applied and enforced by public officials. We can then draw upon the common-sense distinction between the justice of a law and of its application or enforcement. Our theory shall not concern the "substantive" justice of the legal rules themselves. It shall be limited to "procedural" justice in the administration of the law.

There are various reasons for considering this type of view. One is that it might make some distinctive sense out of the Natural Law tradition. It might explain what does not seem implausible to suppose, that there are significant conceptual connexions between law and morals, connexions manifested, for example, in their shared vocabulary of rights and obligations, responsibility and justice. Another reason is that this "procedural" Natural Law could be a common ground for Natural Lawyers and their traditional opponents. For this type of theory does not threaten what many critics of Natural Law have sought to defend. It allows the standard distinctions between law and morals and between "law as it is" and "law as it ought to be". It does not imply that moral standards necessarily determine the content of existing legal rules. It leaves room for moral criticism of "positive" law.

It should be noted, however, that these virtues have nothing to do with our restriction of the theory to "procedural" questions. They result from the sort of connexion claimed between law and morals. One might be

[1] New Haven and London: Yale University Press, 1964.

more ambitious and claim that all the applicable principles of justice, including those concerning the "substance" of the law, are implicit in the law in the same sense. And a theory of this type could avoid the paradox of traditional Natural Law. But I shall not attempt to do this, for I do not know how to make a reasonably tempting argument with so strong a conclusion – and also because I think the more modest version we shall consider is itself mistaken.

II

Let us begin by assembling some of Fuller's claims. He says that public officials, those who make and enforce the law, are committed to ideals of legal excellence – eight ideals concerning not the substance of the law but whether its requirements can be understood, followed, and met, and how they are to be applied. There ought to be general rules, first of all, and these ought to be clear, consistent, publicized, prospective, satisfiable, constant, and "scrupulously" enforced.[2]

It is not entirely clear, however, why we should suppose that there is such a commitment. One reason that sometimes is suggested by Fuller does not yield the sort of view we seek and so must be discarded. In accepting positions "of public trust" (as we say), public officials may be construed as tacitly promising to behave properly. But if the commitment of public officials is explained in terms of promising, we are led away from problems of justice. For the breakings of promises are not necessarily acts of injustice, which violations of procedural justice should be. Moreover, why should we suppose that such a promise is a necessary consequence of making and enforcing the law? Could there be no legal system without it? And, if so, does the necessity of the tacit promise follow from the nature of law itself? These two questions require affirmative answers for our purposes, but we as yet have no grounds for so deciding. Finally, even granting that public officials make some such promise, its content remains indeterminate. To what specific standards do public officials commit themselves? Are they always, and necessarily, the same? Why should they include the particular ones listed by Fuller?

We need a different way of understanding the commitment by public officials to such ideals of legal excellence.

Fuller also writes: "To embark on the enterprise of subjecting human conduct to the governance of rules involves of necessity a commitment to the view that man is, or can become, a responsible agent, capable of understanding and following rules, and answerable for his defaults".[3]

---

[2] Op. cit., chapter II. [3] Op. cit., p. 162.

3

This passage is suggestive, though it hardly solves our problem. Why should we say there is this commitment? And what has it got to do with justice? I shall not try to say what Fuller really means. I shall sketch an argument designed to show that certain principles to be used in assessing the law are implicit in it. I shall concentrate my attention on the claim that the law ought to consist of rules that can be understood, followed, and met, and that only these ought to be applied. Later I shall say a word about Fuller's interesting but difficult suggestion that making and enforcing the law commits one to the view that man is or can become "a responsible agent".

III

Fuller lists eight kinds of legal defect corresponding to the eight kinds of legal excellence. These include, a failure to make general rules; rules that cannot be understood, that are inconsistent, not made known to the parties affected, retroactive, or frequently changed; rules that "require conduct beyond the power of the affected party"; and "a failure of congruence between the rules as announced and their actual administration".[4] Of what interest are such factors to us?

The defects listed (to which others could probably be added) may be divided into several types. It should be noted first that some have moral significance beyond the scope of the present argument. For example, the last factor listed – a failure to apply the rules faithfully, equally, uniformly and impartially – is often thought to constitute a special kind of injustice, sometimes called "formal". This is closely related to the "procedural" kind we shall consider, even in the respect that it could be construed, along similar lines, as a branch of Natural Law. But formal justice deserves separate treatment and I shall say no more about it here.[*] For our purposes, we are interested in the last factor listed by Fuller only as it affects the *followability* of legal rules and requirements. If officials administer rules erratically, a person to whom they apply might find it difficult to know what they require of him. He may be unable to use the rules in deciding what to do and to know when he runs the risk of legal sanctions.

Several of the factors listed by Fuller are significant in this way. They make it difficult to learn or be reasonably certain what the law requires, as when rules are secret (or difficult to discover) and frequently changed. Two things may be true in this first type of case that are not true in the others: At the time of behaviour for which one is later penalized the legal

[4] *Op. cit.*, p. 39. [*] See Chapter 2 in this volume, "On Formal Justice."

requirement actually exists; and it requires something one is able to do. The trouble is that the law makes it difficult for a person to know what is required of him and that he runs a greater risk of penalties for acting one way rather than another. And to the degree that the law is responsible for this, it is *unfair* to penalize him for failing to meet the legal requirements.

A second type of case is that in which the law "requires" something one can't do. The requirement may be clear and determinate and known, but this is little help. For the law is impossible to satisfy and can't be used in the appropriate way for deciding what to do. It seems unfair when the law penalizes a person for failing to meet such a requirement too. A third type of factor is found in Fuller's list. When there are gaps in the law or rules that are unclear, inconsistent or retroactive, no relevant legal requirement may exist at the time of behaviour for which one is later penalized. Failing special circumstances, one cannot learn what the law — as it shall later say — now "requires" of him. There is, in fact, no requirement for him to be guided by. Again, it seems unfair to penalize someone in these circumstances.

Allowing for the special character of the third type of case, we could summarize by saying that the defects listed by Fuller are cases in which the putative requirements of the law are not followable. And it is unjust to penalize a person for failing to meet unfollowable requirements.

But sometimes the law is like that. It can be difficult or even impossible to do what the law requires or to know what it requires (or what it shall retrospectively "require" by filling in the law, making it determinate, eliminating inconsistencies, and so on). And later the law says, in effect, that one has failed to do what it required — when that really cannot be true, when one could not have known, or when one could not have done it anyway. The law then adds injury to insult by penalizing one for failing to meet its putative requirements, even though it did not provide a fair chance to avoid the penalties. But it seems unfair to punish a person, to make him lose or suffer, even to blame or criticize him, in such a case. And yet this treatment is just what the law dispenses when there are defects of the sort that Fuller lists.

Before we use these materials to construct an argument for Natural Law, one point should be made. The legal defects that interest us are not limited to the criminal (as opposed to the civil) law. In fact, there may sometimes be a great temptation to tolerate such defects in the civil law. The injustice to one person of invoking an unfollowable requirement may be ignored in the desire to compensate another innocent victim for his losses. In any case, the relevant kind of loss, for our purposes, need not be imposed as punishment but can be, say, in the form of civil damages. This should be kept in mind when I speak of a person's being *penalized,* which covers all types of loss imposed and blame imputed by the law.

IV

Legal rules are characteristically supposed to regulate behaviour; and this seems no accident. The law may do more than this, but it can hardly do less. Part of the very idea of systems of social control like the law is that they set standards and lay down guide-lines for behaviour, which, it is hoped, will be followed by those to whom they apply. Now legal rules can be used for various purposes, but in light of what has just been said, one of their main purposes is to determine legal requirements. And a legal requirement is something that is *supposed* to be followable – something a normal, competent adult, at least, should be capable of meeting and of using to guide his own behaviour. This is not merely to say that the normal point of laying down legal requirements is to provide guidelines for behaviour. It is to say that part of the very concept of a legal requirement is, not that it actually is followable, but that it is supposed to be and may be presumed to be. The idea of law includes that of regulating behaviour in a certain way – by setting standards that people are to follow. And this idea is incorporated in the notion of a legal requirement. If so, from the notion of a legal requirement it might seem to follow that, to the degree a putative legal requirement cannot be used by one to whom it applies to guide his own behaviour, that requirement is *defective.*

Furthermore, someone who makes or enforces the law understands that requirements are supposed to be followable. And since that is built into the very notion of a legal requirement, a public official is logically committed to viewing unfollowable requirements as defective.

This is one way of taking Fuller's claims. There is a necessary connexion between law and principles to be used in criticizing it. From the very concept of a legal requirement – in view of what law essentially is (which is something functional) – we can derive standards for calling putative requirements defective.

However, we have not yet made a clearly moral judgment. One is generated as follows. When a person is penalized for failing to meet an unfollowable requirement, he is treated unjustly. This step of the argument seems uncontroversial (at least with minor qualifications). I have explained it informally already and shall not attempt to prove it.

Let us suppose, then, that it is unjust to penalize a person for failing to meet an unfollowable requirement. This occurs when the law can and should be criticized on grounds that are intrinsic to it – that follow from what it is for something to be a legal requirement. These grounds show that the putative legal requirement is defective. And this adverse judgment corresponds to the judgment of morality. It is precisely because the requirement is unfollowable and hence defective that penalizing someone for failing to meet it is unjust. So it appears that a moral claim about the injustice of such treatment is warranted by standards implicit in the law.

V

The argument just sketched could, perhaps, be strengthened. My purpose is, in part, to invite such reconstructions. But I think there is an unbridgeable gap within it. Let us consider some complications first.

In some cases, when a person is penalized under an unfollowable rule the result does not appear unjust. This may happen, for example, in war crimes trials where rules are established retroactively. But the rules could have been justified earlier so that they would have had prospective effect, and the agent is thought to have been competent enough to know that he should have acted otherwise. If someone is punished under such conditions the outcome might not be unjust on the whole – although it could be held that there is *some* injustice in the proceeding, due to the unfollowable character of the rules. We can, I think, ignore such complications. But they remind us that the moral judgments we are entitled to make in this context must generally be qualified by *"ceteris paribus"*.

The example of retroactive legislation raises more serious questions, however. One might deny that the relevant legal requirements are truly "supposed" to be followable. Unless someone thought we could change our past behaviour, he would not imagine that a rule we call "retroactive" was designed by its creators to serve as guidance for behaviour that retrospectively falls under it. In the relevant cases, then, we could say that any general presumption to the effect that legal rules of the sort that lay down putative requirements are supposed to be followable cannot extend to *ex post facto* laws. As far as the makers and probably the enforcers of such laws are concerned, that presumption is rebutted. Consequently, retroactive laws cannot be criticized for failing to be what they are supposed to be, since they are not supposed to be followable. The defects they have must be explained in other ways.

But if we can go this far we can go much further. The same objection holds for rules that are deliberately made unfollowable in other ways too. And in most of the remaining cases, a judge, say, must realize that the rules or putative requirements could not have been followed by the person subject to the penalties. So the fact that he invokes the penalty is no sure sign he thinks them followable. In most of the cases to which the

7

argument is intended to apply, then, we find grounds for rebutting the initial presumption that putative legal requirements are supposed to be followable.

I am uncertain what to think of this objection. The problem is whether there is a sense in which we still can say that putative legal requirements, by their very nature, are supposed to be followable. The objection does not seem to exclude this. For the argument we constructed did not turn upon any contingent, actual aims or intentions of law makers and enforcers. It had to do with the nature of the enterprise in which they are engaged and the view of it to which they are logically committed. It is important to see that an argument for Natural Law could not rest upon contingent aims or intentions. An ineffective argument would work like this: "*If* law makers want to lay down guide-lines for behaviour, *then* they are committed to making their requirements followable". The claim seems true enough – trivially so. But it allows the possibility that actual law makers lack that aim and thus are not committed logically to the idea that their requirements are supposed to be followable. An argument for Natural Law must show a necessary connexion between the standards to be used in criticizing the law and the law itself. The supposition of followability must come directly from the enterprise of making or enforcing the law, at least within a limited area.

Our argument claims that the idea of something can incorporate or imply a standard to be used in judging things of that kind, even when things of that kind do not live up to the standard. This much seems quite plausible. One might contend that the idea of a knife implies the standard of efficiency in cutting. From this it does not follow that a knife cannot be misused, that a badly-made knife cannot be used, or even that a knife cannot deliberately be made in such a way that it will not cut well. The argument claims the same sort of thing about legal requirements: they are essentially supposed to be followable, since it is their essential function to give guidelines for behaviour. But this supposition survives the discovery that legal rules or requirements can be made unfollowable, even deliberately.

VI

The more serious difficulty for this attempt to prove a kind of Natural Law must now be considered. If the argument uncovered any standards implicit in a legal system, these warrant calling requirements that can't be followed *defective*. But to say this is not to make a moral judgment. Nor is it, I think, to imply one.

What is it we judge to be unfair or unjust here? In the first instance, it is the way individuals who run afoul of unfollowable requirements are treated. Were they not penalized we would not call their treatment unjust. If we call the rules under which they may be penalized unjust, that is because individuals are, or are likely to be, penalized unjustly under them. But this kind of treatment is not essential to or inevitable in a legal system – not even one that contains defective requirements. (And defective requirements probably cannot be avoided entirely.) From the fact that a legal system contains rules or requirements that cannot be understood or followed or met, it does not follow that anyone *shall* be penalized under them or even that the system requires or *allows* such treatment. Such practices may be so deeply entrenched or rationalized on other grounds that it may be hard to imagine legal systems without them. But nothing logically requires this treatment. And so the judgment that some actual rules or requirements of a system are *defective* to the degree that the law makes them hard to understand or follow or meet is not the same as the judgment that an actual practice of penalizing individuals under such rules or requirements is *unjust*. For there need not be that practice in the system even when the rules or requirements have the relevant defects.

My explanation of this point carries with it a moral plea. The law may not hesitate to penalize a person who is "found" to have failed to meet a requirement that did not exist or was not made known to him or that he could not have met in any case. But we could stop that – and if the practice is unjust we have a good reason to do so. We could deliberately refrain from penalizing in these cases or make adjustments as justice requires. This would involve modifying legal procedures. It would be decided whether the law was followable. If not, punishments and other "penalties" could be waived, and steps could be taken even to compensate those who otherwise would have been penalized unjustly to make sure they suffer no undeserved burdens or losses. We could even apologize and try to remove any lingering stigma. (We could also compensate other parties in civil cases for their undeserved losses by a system of social insurance.) Judges would not make changes in the law without admitting it, pretending to find their newly corrected law in the old. They could make changes as appropriate – by rendering unclear requirements more determinate, eliminating conflicts, and so on – so that others would be better able to follow the law in the future; or they could refer defective portions of the law to legislative bodies for correction. There seems no inconsistency in describing such changes in procedure, so penalizing individuals under unfollowable rules and requirements would not seem

9

logically inevitable. There may, of course, be obstacles to making these reforms, but there seems a *prima facie* moral case for introducing them.

It must be emphasized that these points apply as well to laws that are deliberately made in such a way as to be unfollowable, including retro-active laws. It is one thing to make such law, another to enforce it. The enactment of such rules does not entail their unjust application. Their application is not logically inevitable. And if it would be unjust, there is a *prima facie* moral case against it.

It seems clear, then, that the judgment that legal requirements are defective is not the same as, and does not entail, a judgment that an actual practice is unjust – since the practice need not exist even when require-ments are defective. If so, the principles alleged to be implicit in the law are not principles of justice. They seem, in fact, *a*moral.

It could be argued, however, that the judgment that a requirement is defective entails, not the judgment that an actual practice is unjust, but rather a hypothetical or conditional judgment to the effect that the prac-tice of penalizing persons under the defective requirement *would be* un-just. For this claim seems compatible with the previous objection.

But what ground can we find for saying this? The temptation to sup-pose that standards of justice are implicit in the law is given by the com-mon coincidence of defective requirements and the unjust practice of penalizing persons for failing to meet them. We were led to suppose that in judging the requirements to be defective we were *thereby* judging the practice of invoking them to be unjust. But we see through this now, and we are left with no further reason for drawing such an inference.

Moreover, the standards that may seem implicit in the law, conceived at least in part as a system of guidelines for human behaviour, would seem to say nothing about what *counts as* an *injustice*. They tell us only that a certain kind of requirement or rule is defective – and only because it is not followable. But this does not tell us that the application of such a rule would be unjust.

Another rebuttal may be suggested by the passage from Fuller in which he claimed that "To embark on the enterprise of subjecting human con-duct to the governance of rules involves of necessity a commitment to the view that man is, or can become, a responsible agent, capable of under-standing and following rules, and *answerable for his defaults*". At this juncture one might try to show that the idea of law includes much more than I have been willing to grant. In view of what Fuller says about public officials' being committed to the view that humans are (or can become) responsible agents, answerable for their defaults (as well as capable of understanding and following rules), one might claim that penalties, or at least sanctions, are built into the very notion of law (or at least the notion of one essential part of it, that is, the criminal law). Just as legal requirements, by their very nature, are supposed to be followable, so the failure to meet them is supposed to be punished. The law is not a set of rules that neutrally allow or disallow certain "moves". A person who breaks the rules is supposed to have defaulted. Legal requirements are not conceived of as, nor are they supposed to be or to function like, lotteries or guessing games. A person is supposed to have a chance to avoid the penalties. If so, the very concept of a system of requirements such as those found in the criminal law implies that punishing a person for failing to meet unfollowable requirements – not giving him a chance to avoid the penalties – is what? a defective practice, I would suppose.

A simple way of meeting this rebuttal would be to show that legal systems can exist without including sanctions. And this seems true. If those to whom the rules apply are motivated sufficiently to use them voluntarily as guidelines for their own behaviour, sanctions will be unnecessary. But if they are not needed, then it may be rational to exclude them. And then they can't be logically inevitable in such a system.

Imagine that a group of utopian socialists was able to isolate itself and construct a society along co-operative lines. They establish rules by procedures that are agreed upon by all and that seem fair to every member of the group. Each member also thinks the resulting requirements just. So we have a kind of legislation, which is needed since the shared morality of the members of the community will not suffice to cover all details of social and economic life that they think need regulation. The legislated rules can be changed or repealed as circumstances seem to demand. But for certain reasons sanctions are never provided (and therefore never invoked) in this community. In the first place, the views of its members on psychological and social questions incline them strongly to regard the use of sanctions, even as deterrents, as undesirable and to be avoided if possible. Secondly, each member of the community is strongly committed to making it a success and so is highly motivated to do his part. He needs no threats to goad him. And each member knows the same is true of all the others. Here is a system of general rules, then, that closely resembles law and yet excludes legal sanctions. We could elaborate the story in many ways, allowing or disallowing informal (extra-legal) sanctions, for example. But the conclusion seems clear. Sanctions are not essential to a system of rules deliberately laid down as guidelines for behaviour, rules that are supposed to be followable. If so, in criticizing legal requirements as unfollowable, we would seem to imply nothing at all about the use of sanctions.

11

But the main point could be made more directly. The argument we have constructed out of materials provided by Fuller claims that a principle like the following is implied by the notion of a legal requirement:

1. If a putative legal requirement is not followable, it is defective.

But this is not to say that the notion of a legal requirement entails a rule of justice like this:

2. If a person is penalized for failing to meet an unfollowable requirement, he suffers an injustice.

(1) does not seem to entail anything like (2). (2) rests on considerations that we have no reason yet to believe are implicit in the law. It really makes no difference whether sanctions are essential to the law. The point is that we cannot learn what use of sanctions is (or would be) unjust simply by understanding what the law is. We need to know what constitutes an *injustice*. And so far, our understanding of what the law is tells us nothing about that.

One might argue – as Fuller sometimes seems to do[5] – that a citizen or public official is committed to the view that the law of his land is just. And from this claim it might seem to follow, somehow, that one is also committed to criticizing certain practices as unjust. But we have no reason yet for saying that any such commitment is determined by the law itself. We have no reason to say, for example, that one cannot possibly "embark on the enterprise of subjecting human conduct to the governance of rules" without supposing either that those rules are, or even that they ought to be, just. At least, we have no reason yet for saying that such a commitment follows from the concept of law – which is what the Natural Lawyer needs to show. For there could, of course, be said to be a kind of "commitment" to justice on the part of law makers and enforcers, among others, in the sense that principles of justice apply to them, regardless of their contingent aims or intentions. But this could be true if, for example, these principles of justice were independent of, and not determined by, the law itself. In a similar way, it may be said to be *necessarily* the case that penalizing a person under an unfollowable law is unjust. But the reason for this could simply be that the applicable moral principle is supposed to possess a kind of necessity, without there also being any necessary *connexion* between law and morals. These possibilities may be at the root of some Natural Lawyers' theories, but they suggest no interestingly intimate connexion between law and morals.

---

[5]   See also Fuller's "Positivism and Fidelity to Law – A Reply to Professor Hart", *Harvard Law Review*, vol. 71 (1958), 630–672, *e.g.*, at 639.

2

On formal justice

A number of legal and political theorists have suggested that public officials who fail to act within the law that they administer act unjustly. This does not mean that injustice is always likely to be done merely because it often happens to be done when officials depart from the law. Some writers have held that injustice is done whenever an official fails to act within the law, regardless of the circumstances.[1] I shall call this type of view "formal justice."

Such a view may be considered "formalistic" because it places value, in the name of justice, on adherence to existing legal rules without regard to "substantive" factors such as their contents, the consequences of obeying them, their defects or virtues, or any other circumstances of their application. The only condition imposed is that an official must by law follow the rule in his official capacity. Furthermore, those who attempt to account for this view believe that the requirements of formal justice rest directly on such notions as "proceeding by rule" or "treating like cases alike," which are thought to be at the heart of our shared concept of justice. The basic requirements of formal justice are thus supposed to be exempt from the controversy over substantive principles of justice and their possible justification. It is believed that one can embrace formal justice without committing oneself to "ideological" positions. The arguments seeking to ground formal justice on such notions also make circumstances irrelevant to its requirements, which accounts for their formalistic character.

"On Formal Justice," *Cornell Law Review*, Vol. 58, No. 5 (June 1973): 833–61. Copyright © 1972–73 by Cornell University. All rights reserved. This article was begun during the author's tenure as a Guggenheim Foundation Fellow at University College, London, and completed while he was a Fellow of the Society for the Humanities at Cornell University. The author would like to thank Professor Robert S. Summers of the Cornell Law School for his help and encouragement.
    [1]   See, e.g., S. Benn & R. Peters, *The Principles of Political Thought* 128–29 (1965); H. L. A. Hart, *The Concept of Law* 155–57 (1961); H. Kelsen, *General Theory of Law and State* 14 (A. Wedberg transl. 1949); C. Perelman, *The Idea of Justice and the Problem of Argument* 1–87 (J. Petrie transl. 1963); A. Ross, *On Law and Justice* 273, 280 (1959).

I

THE THEORY OF FORMAL JUSTICE

Formal justice is the latest in a line of legalistic theories. One often mentioned view, ascribed to some famous writers, identifies justice with conformity to law. Hobbes, for example, is noted for stating that "no law can be unjust,"[2] and for suggesting that justice and injustice apply only to acts under the law, never to the laws themselves.[3] This view fits nicely with his claim that the word "just" is "equivalent" to the expression "he that in his actions observes the laws of his country."[4] Austin has said, "By the epithet *just,* we mean that a given object, to which we apply the epithet, accords with a given law to which we refer to it as a test. . . . By the epithet *unjust,* we mean that the given object conforms not to the given law."[5]

These statements suggest a radical conception of justice. First, if they are correct, then we must be utterly confused when we describe laws as unjust – perhaps even when we call them just. Hobbes and Austin seem to be saying that moral appraisal of law in terms of justice exceeds the logical limits of the notion. Second, the suggested view has alarming moral implications, for an unjust act is wrong, morally wrong, unless it can be justified by overriding considerations. Other things being equal, injustice should not be done. But the idea that justice consists in conformity to law then implies, on the one hand, that deviation from the law is always wrong, unless it can be justified on other grounds, and, on the other hand, that no such justification could be based on the injustice of the law, since a law cannot be unjust. This does not mean that noncompliance must always be judged morally wrong, for one who believes that justice consists in conformity to law may recognize other moral considerations that support noncompliance. But the view nevertheless does seem to stack the moral cards in favor of conformity.

Few contemporary legal theorists would accept this identification of justice with conformity to law, and it is doubtful if any legal theorist ever meant it literally. One might be tempted to mouth such slogans when "law" is understood to cover the so-called "moral law," for this includes

---

[2] T. Hobbes, *Leviathan: Parts I and II,* ch. 30, at 271 (H. W. Schneider ed. 1958). H. L. A. Hart cites this quotation as evidence that Hobbes was tempted by the view in question. *See* H. L. A. Hart, *supra* note 1, at 251.

[3] T. Hobbes, *supra* note 2, ch. 13, at 108.   [4] *Id.* ch. 4, at 39.

[5] J. Austin, *The Province of Jurisprudence Determined* 262 n.23 (I. Berlin, S. Hampshire & R. Wollheim eds. 1954) (emphasis in original). Edgar Bodenheimer cites this quotation as evidence that Austin holds the view in question. *See* E. Bodenheimer, *Treatise on Justice* 13–14 (1967).

those extralegal principles that determine when a law is just or unjust. Discussion of formal justice in these terms may cause some confusion, but if so understood the view clearly loses its distinctness and bite. If the view is not watered down, it has an obviously unacceptable implication, namely, that a law cannot be unjust – that it makes no sense to speak of an unjust law. But the appraisal of laws as just or unjust seems as intelligible and legitimate as the appraisal of official actions in administering the law, and no one denies that the latter can be just or unjust.

It is worth noting that Austin apparently never held such a view, and it is doubtful that Hobbes did. Austin argues in Hobbes's defense and thereby provides his own: Hobbes's statement that "no law can be unjust" should not be taken as the "immoral and pernicious paradox" it superficially seems to be.[6] In context, Austin claims, it may be seen that Hobbes meant only that "no *positive* law is *legally* unjust," which Austin regards as "merely a truism put in unguarded terms."[7] The evidence is, however, somewhat equivocal. As Austin reminds us, Hobbes also wrote that laws are not always good since they do not always serve the people's needs.[8] It does not follow, however, that Hobbes believed that such laws should be called "unjust." He might subject laws to utilitarian appraisal while refusing to regard the appraisal as a measure of the peculiar virtue of justice. However, Hobbes also states that justice consists fundamentally in the "performance of covenants."[9] A full explication of his theory would, I think, show that he regarded conformity to law as only a derivative requirement of justice within civil society, and even then within the limits of the social contract. The evidence is clear enough in Austin's case, for Austin was, of course, no legalistic skeptic but a utilitarian who maintained that valid moral principles have divine sanction. Ironically, his defense of Hobbes begins with the very passage that is sometimes quoted to show that he identifies justice with conformity to law.[10] The context of the passage makes clear that Austin defined "law" as any general rule, legal or extralegal, that is applied as a standard of appraisal, including "the ultimate measure or test: namely, the law of God," which when applied to law "is nearly equivalent to general utility."[11] Such a theory may not generate much enthusiasm today, but it would be closer to Austin's true sentiments than the view sometimes ascribed to him.

At any rate, the idea that justice consists in conformity to law (in the ordinary sense of the word "law," meaning what Austin calls "positive

[6] J. Austin, *supra* note 5, at 260 n.23.   [7] *Id.* at 261 n.23 (emphasis in original).
[8] T. Hobbes, *supra* note 2, ch. 30, at 272; see J. Austin, *supra* note 5, at 261 n.23.
[9] T. Hobbes, *supra* note 2, ch. 15, at 119; *id.* ch. 26, at 212.
[10] J. Austin, *supra* note 5, at 260 n.23.   [11] *Id.* at 263 n.23 (emphasis omitted).

law") is not easily subdued. Something like it is implicit in various current conceptions of justice and legal ideals. It may even be found incorporated in the seemingly innocuous claim that justice in the administration of the law consists in impartial application of the law to particular cases. The result is what I call formal justice. This view identifies conformity to law not with justice overall but with justice in the administration of the law, and thus with justice in the conduct of public officials.

It is important to separate formalistic tendencies from other tendencies among recent writers, especially from the trend toward moral skepticism, for this particular combination results in extreme positions, and a formalist need not be a moral skeptic. Extreme variations on the formalistic theme are suggested by Kelsen, Ross, and Perelman. Whereas the early "legal positivists," Bentham and Austin, regarded certain extralegal principles as rationally defensible and thus valid for appraising legal institutions, the more recent writers maintain a skeptical view of ethics that has been associated with philosophical positivism in this century ("logical positivism"). They see disagreement about extralegal principles to be used for judging law as evidence of subjectivity in such judgments because they assume that "objective" questions can be settled by "empirical" means which have no place in ethics except when questions of principle are begged. Thus, Kelsen despairs of finding any rational way of choosing among alternative resolutions of conflicting interests and declares that "[j]ustice is an irrational ideal."[12] However, he does believe that a rationally defensible element can be salvaged, although it concerns only the application of the laws, not the laws themselves. This element he identifies with "legality," which requires adherence to the law without exception.[13]

Ross regards the idea of justice as "a demand for equality,"[14] but he maintains the impossibility of finding any rational way of deciding among competing criteria of like treatment and like cases. He settles for "[t]he ideal of equality as such," or "justice in [a] formal sense," which stands for "regularity."[15] He concludes that "the idea of justice resolves itself into the demand that a decision should be the result of the application of a general rule. Justice is the correct application of a law, as opposed to arbitrariness."[16] Ross's reason for supposing that this conclusion requires official conformity to law is similar to Kelsen's: so far as the laws are given, decisions made by applying them can at least be based upon "observable facts."[17]

---

[12] H. Kelsen, *supra* note 1, at 13.   [13] *Id.* at 14.
[14] A. Ross, *supra* note 1, at 269.   [15] *Id.* at 273.
[16] *Id.* at 280.   [17] *Id.* at 284; *cf.* H. Kelsen, *supra* note 12, at 13.

Perelman expressed similar views in his early writings.[18] He based the
requirement that officials conform to the law upon the precept "treat like
cases alike," which he held to be the kernel of our shared concept of
justice and thus something common to all substantive standards, however divergent or indefensible.[19] This precept was understood by Perelman to require scrupulous adherence to law by public officials as the sole
rationally defensible requirement of justice.[20] The result is a formalistic
view of justice in both content and ground.

These views are comparable to the theory ascribed to Hobbes and Austin. Kelsen, Ross, and Perelman recognize that laws may be judged just
or unjust only by reference to extralegal standards; the law cannot be the
measure of its own morality. Thus, they acknowledge a distinction between the justice of laws and justice in their administration, which suggests the possibility of arguing against official compliance with the law
when, for example, the laws to be applied are substantially unjust. But
they exclude this possibility by regarding extralegal standards as arbitrary and indefensible. They recognize valid judgments about justice in
the administration of the law, but none about the justice of the laws
themselves. Because they are skeptical of moral principles generally (except for the requirements of formal justice, which are conceived of as a
special case), they must believe that no sound moral arguments could
favor official deviation from the law when formal administrative justice
opposes it. Thus, they seem committed to the view that official departure
from the law cannot possibly be justified under any circumstances. Although emotional outbursts may be made to that effect, respectable arguments can be marshalled only for obeying the law.

This position seems extreme, but this is partly a consequence of moral
skepticism, not of formal justice alone. The arguments for discounting
moral appraisal of the law are unimpressive; indeed, it is difficult to identify any clear arguments at all. But this need not detain us. I shall later
examine Perelman's suggestion that formal administrative justice rests on
the precept that like cases be treated alike.[21] For the present, one may
simply observe that formalists could develop more moderate positions;
some in fact have done so. Many seem to accept the idea that administrative justice always requires adherence to the law, while acknowledging
that it might conflict with other respectable principles of justice. For example, Patterson does not reject the notion of "justice according to law"
(that is, the application of "established rules and principles of law"), but

[18]   See C. Perelman, *supra* note 1, at 15–16, 25–26, 36–45, 50–56.
[19]   *Id.* at 16, 29, 36–41.   [20]   *Id.* at 20, 25, 41, 43, 62.
[21]   *Cf.* notes 40–48 and accompanying text *infra*.

17

only notes that it may conflict with and may be outweighed by "social expediency and justice."[22] Fuller believes that

there lies in the concept of justice itself a hidden conflict or tension between opposing conceptions of the end sought by justice. On the one hand, there is what has been called *legal* justice, a justice which demands that we stick by the announced rules and not make exceptions in favour of particular individuals, a justice which conceives that men should live under the same "rule of law" and be equally bound by its terms. On the other hand, there is the justice of *dispensation,* a justice ready to make exceptions when the established rules work unexpected hardship in particular cases, a justice ready to bend the letter of the law to accomplish a fair result.[23]

This sort of view is given formalistic underpinnings and developed further by Benn and Peters, who believe that "[t]o act justly . . . is to treat all men alike except where there are relevant differences between them."[24] They insist upon "a distinction between unjust administration of the law and an unjust law."[25] But when the law speaks clearly, they maintain that justice in its administration requires adherence to it. They do not shrink from the formalistic consequences, acknowledging, for example, that

we should have to admit that a South African judge applying racial discriminatory laws was doing justice, so long as he decided according to the law and nothing else. . . .

. . . .

. . . The judge may act justly in denying a man the vote because he has a black skin, if that is the law; but we can still question whether the criterion established by the law is itself defensible.[26]

Perelman now falls into this camp; he remains a formalist but accepts the possibility of rational argument about substantive standards.[27] He thus opens the door to arguments against official compliance based on extralegal considerations. The most important development of a moderate formalistic view has been suggested by H. L. A. Hart, who does not seem skeptical of moral appraisal of laws or of moral considerations generally.[28]

I do not claim that all these writers would insist upon the view that I

---

[22] E. Patterson, *Jurisprudence: Men and Ideas of the Law* 104–06 (1953).

[23] L. Fuller, *Anatomy of the Law* 38 (1968) (emphasis in original). Fuller quotes Freud as holding that justice "demands that a law once made will not be broken in favour of an individual." *Id.* at 64.

[24] S. Benn & R. Peters, *supra* note 1, at 128.   [25] *Id.* at 129.

[26] *Id.* at 128–29.

[27] *See* C. Perelman, *supra* note 1, at 85–86. *See also* C. Perelman, *Justice* 53–87 (1967).

[28] Hart's views are discussed in notes 39–56 and accompanying text *infra.*

call "formal justice." I wish to emphasize, however, that the view I am constructing and criticizing is not my own invention. Some of the arguments for it[29] have been gleaned from discussions,[30] but the chief ones[31] exist more or less whole in the literature, although they need some sympathetic reconstruction. I have also refined the view under discussion to eliminate extreme implications that seem inessential. My purpose is to expose a clearly discernible tendency in legal and political theory, and I would not want formal justice rejected for inadequate reasons, only to reappear later in more presentable garb.

The task seems worth the effort, for both theoretical and practical reasons. Formalistic notions of justice misplace value by valuing mere form, thereby obscuring the essential connection between justice and the treatment of persons. Acceptance of formal justice interferes with our attempts to understand justice and to determine whether there are, after all, any intersubjectively valid principles.[32] I have also suggested what is morally at stake. At minimum, a formalist maintains that acting within the law is a necessary condition of justice in its administration, and thus that any official deviation is an injustice. Formal justice thus implies that there is always a real moral objection to official deviation from the law – however iniquitous the laws may be, whatever they require or allow, however horrendous the consequences of official obedience, and regardless of all other circumstances. Formal justice holds that this objection cannot be diminished even by full knowledge of all the relevant facts. In other words, formal justice maintains that official departure from the law is like the breach of a basic moral principle.

This point should not be exaggerated. Claims of formal justice do not absolutely condemn official disobedience under all circumstances. It may

---

29 *See* notes 33–38 and accompanying text *infra*.
30 In discussions of earlier versions of this paper, which were read at several universities in England (London, Oxford, Sussex) and America (Cornell, Maryland, Virginia, Rockefeller, Wisconsin), I heard formal justice defended so often that I am persuaded the published claims are but the tip of a generally unarticulated iceberg of hunches and convictions. I am grateful to the many discussants on those occasions for their stimulating and helpful comments.
31 *See* notes 39–56 and accompanying text *infra*.
32 This work has already received fresh impetus from the appearance of John Rawls's long-awaited book, *A Theory of Justice*, in 1971. It is interesting to note that Rawls appears at first to accept formal justice (*see* J. Rawls, *A Theory of Justice* 58–60 [1971] but later seems to reject the concept. *See id.* at 348–49. In the former place, Rawls cites Henry Sidgwick, who comes close to endorsing formal justice himself, for Sidgwick sometimes seems to identify justice with treating like cases alike. See H. Sidgwick, *The Methods of Ethics* 209, 267, 379–80, 496 (7th ed. 1962). But Sidgwick's view is unclear, for he does not seem to regard this kind of justice as an independent moral value – one that might conflict, for example, with other non-equivalent values. Thus, the sort of concern that Sidgwick manifests about the possible conflict of Egoism and Benevolence (*see id.* at 497–509) is not exhibited here.

be said, however, that formal justice always argues for official compliance with existing laws under all circumstances. Therefore, if formal justice claims are unsound, they serve to mount invalid objections to official disobedience, and thus they foster excessive reverence for existing law. For example, formal justice principles make it seem easier than it really is to argue soundly for official compliance with unjust laws, and more difficult to justify official noncompliance. This result is particularly objectionable when injustice could be avoided by official departure from the law, for those who would be wronged by its application are refused relief on the basis of a spurious requirement of justice, perhaps by officials or others who, by virtue of their own social positions, are likely to be beneficiaries of the unjust arrangements.

I do not contend that officials should always *diso*bey unjust or otherwise defective laws. This conclusion does not follow from a denial of formal justice. Factors exist favoring official adherence to the law, even when injustice will result – factors which may outweigh those favoring noncompliance. My point is that justice, even administrative justice, depends upon the circumstances.

Formal justice is, then, the view that official deviation from the law is a kind of injustice, regardless of the circumstances. I say "a kind of injustice" because the most plausible formalist position would allow for recognition of other kinds of injustice, such as injustice in the laws themselves, in legal or other institutions, and in social systems. I am concerned here only with justice in the administration of the law, and my discussion is meant to be neutral with respect to a variety of views about the other branches of justice.

One may allow the formalist to say that official deviation from the law, while always a kind of injustice, may sometimes be justified. Such conduct need not be wrong, all things considered. As I have already mentioned, some formalists have suggested the contrary; but we should allow for the more plausible position. Thus, the formalist can acknowledge other moral factors which have a bearing upon official conduct and maintain that those favoring deviation may outweigh those favoring adherence (including formal justice) in specific cases. Moreover, since he can also recognize other kinds of justice, such as that of the laws themselves, he may hold that worse injustice may sometimes be done by following than by departing from the law, for example, when the law itself is unjust. For this reason, he may wish to balance the various factors that relate to justice in a given case, and although he regards official deviation from the law as a kind of injustice, he may sometimes decline to characterize an official deviation as "unjust" *overall*. But the formalist nevertheless does believe something like the following: justice in the adminis-

20

tration of the law fundamentally requires official adherence in all cases. Any official departure from the law is like the breach of a basic principle – it may sometimes be justified, but it always requires justification, for there is an ineradicable moral objection to the departure.

Three further preliminary points should be made. First, as has already been mentioned, we are concerned here only with the behavior of persons acting in an official capacity. Formalists might maintain that injustice is done whenever *anyone* breaks the law. This position would be more difficult to defend, and formalists do not take it. I shall criticize the more modest and less vulnerable contention.

Second, distinctions may be made among different ways of "administering" the law (for example, enforcing, interpreting, and applying the law) and among different spheres of official conduct (for example, the administration of substantive and procedural law), but formalists employ none of these distinctions; they are clearly irrelevant to the basic points at issue here and may therefore be ignored.

Third, I assume that laws are morally neutral in the sense that a given law can be either just or unjust. It is not that laws are immune from moral appraisal, but rather that laws are not necessarily either all just or all unjust. This may seem to beg a central question, for if one assumed that all laws were just (and also that injustice would always be done by departing from them), then the claims of formal justice would be harder to deny. I have two reasons for not making this assumption. First, it is implausible. Second, formalists do not rely upon it. They regard laws as morally neutral in the relevant sense and indeed insist upon the independence of justice in the law and justice in its administration. In omitting this unreasonable assumption, one does not deny any of the formalists' premises.

II
APPLICATION OF FORMAL JUSTICE CLAIMS

One route to formal justice proceeds as follows. If one considers any law, one can imagine some applications of it that are unjust and others that are invulnerable to such criticism. This can be done whether the law in question is just or unjust. For example, a rent administrator might be biased toward landlords and always settle disputes in their favor, without seriously considering the merits of the tenants' cases; a judge might discriminate against blacks in his sentencing and rulings; a prosecutor might be gentle with his friends and harsh with his enemies. These examples may seem to involve injustice, but they do not turn upon the justice or injustice (or more generally the morality or immorality) of the particular

21

laws being administered. The respective injustices appear rooted not in the laws but in the way they are administered. In particular, injustice seems to arise simply because the laws have not been followed by officials. The rent administrator, for example, is supposed to base his decisions on the merits of the cases, as determined by the applicable laws or regulations, and not on whim, prejudice, or personal interest. The judge who discriminates against blacks without official sanction exceeds his lawful authority. This is not to deny that injustice could *also* be done if the judge simply followed a law which required such discrimination; but that is another point entirely. Similar considerations apply to the prosecutor in the third example. These considerations suggest that mere failure by officials to follow the laws they administer constitutes an injustice.

Another example might run as follows. You and I commit similar unlawful acts, and there are no grounds for treating us differently. But you are accused, tried, convicted, and punished for your act, while I am left alone, even though my conduct was not secret. You might complain that injustice has been done,[33] the cause of which appears to be officials' failure to follow the law. I shall now change the example slightly to show that this difference in treatment can occur even under an unjust law. Suppose that a law is established only after we have acted, so that what had been lawful conduct when we did it is now unlawful. Other things being equal, any penalties imposed pursuant to this ex post facto law would be unjust. But, even here, injustice can result from the way in which the law is administered. For example, imagine that we are both tried and convicted, but while I am punished within the limits of the law, you receive exceptionally harsh treatment, not authorized by the law. We could then both complain of injustice because of prosecution under a retroactive criminal law. But you would seem to have additional ground for complaint, based on the manner in which the law was administered.

Such examples suggest that the justice of laws is independent of justice in their administration. Formal justice readily explains this observation by saying that laws, either just or unjust, are the basic standards of administrative justice, at least in the sense that acting within the law is a necessary condition of justice in its administration. By this view, whatever standards of justice apply to laws cannot be identical to the standards that apply to official conduct. The examples given above also suggest that a premium be placed upon official adherence to the law, since

---

[33] This position may be maintained even if it is agreed that there were independent, valid, and sufficient reasons for selective prosecution. To agree, for example, that sometimes a small injustice may legitimately be done to prevent a greater evil is not to deny that the small injustice would be done.

injustice seems to be done precisely when officials fail to follow the law. Formal justice accounts for this condition directly. It may appear, therefore, that formal justice has explanatory power, accounting for the data observed in such examples. One is tempted to conclude that formal justice is *needed* to account for the relevant moral phenomena.

But these conclusions would be hasty, for, upon reflection, it becomes quite clear that formal justice is not mandated by such examples. One can understand, for example, how administrative justice can be independent of the justice of laws without supposing that official deviation from the law per se must be disvalued. When laws themselves are judged, we either consider how they have actually worked in practice or else assume some predictable degree of compliance by officials. But when we judge how laws are administered, we judge official behavior itself. These two branches of justice can be conceived of independently even if similar factors are relevant to the appraisal of both. For example, both branches concern certain ways in which people are affected by the law, but each concerns them differently. In the appraisal of one, we would consider the effects that can be attributed to the laws themselves, while in the other, we would consider the effects ascribable to public officials. Thus, we need not conclude that administrative justice is formalistic in order to account for the independence of these two types of moral appraisal.

The examples given do, in fact, support the conclusion that administrative injustice concerns not merely official departure from the law but also the ways in which people are treated under it, such as the relative disadvantages they suffer at the hands of administrators. In some cases, it was hypothesized also that the offending officials were moved by certain attitudes, such as bias or self-seeking. It seems clear that factors such as the treatment of individuals and the attitudes of administrators will enter into any satisfactory and complete account of justice in the administration of the law. Formal justice, however, has absolutely nothing to say about such factors, which go well beyond the mere idea of official departure from existing law. In other words, nonformal factors are available to account for the administratively inflicted injustices of our hypothetical cases. Furthermore, it is difficult to imagine a case in which injustice seems intuitively to be done by official deviation which has no adverse effect upon anyone at all. When such nonformal factors are present, it seems that they, rather than mere official departure from the law, are morally relevant.

So much for the notion that formal justice is required to account for the independence of the justice of laws from justice in their administration. What about another point suggested by the examples – a general presumption favoring official adherence to the law? The strategy of offering alternative explanations that I have just employed would seem to work here also.

The examples show that official deviations often threaten to cause injustice of the nonformal variety. These injustices are a serious matter. Any risk of them should be undertaken reluctantly. In the normal case in which individuals are likely to be affected by official action, the danger of injustice being done by departure from the law may always be assumed present, and this danger can help to explain a kind of presumption favoring official adherence. But the relevant injustices turn upon the ways individuals suffer under administrators; their actual occurrence, even when officials fail to follow the law, always depends upon the circumstances of such deviation. Complete knowledge of a case might show that official departure would not cause a relevant injustice. In other words, one can understand the temptation to suppose that there is always a moral objection to official disobedience, but one need not agree that such an objection always exists.

This point may be reinforced in at least two ways. First, public officials are usually thought to have special obligations to uphold the law that they are charged with administering. Such obligations should not be confused with formal justice, but belief in them can illicitly lend credibility to formal justice claims, for their requirements are similar. An official deviation could, for example, seem to count both as the breach of such an obligation and as the breach of a formalistic principle of administrative justice. Nevertheless, one may acknowledge such obligations while denying formal justice claims, and belief in the former also commits one to a kind of presumption favoring official adherence to the law.[34]

Second, official deviations, as is often pointed out, are very likely to have some disutility.[35] For example, if we rely upon officials to act within the law, then we are likely to suffer (or at least to be inconvenienced) when they fail to do so. Other disadvantages may attend the inability to rely on officials to follow the law. Considerations such as these apply to an enormously wide and varied range of cases and circumstances, under both just and unjust laws, and thus tend to support another kind of presumption favoring official adherence. They rest, however, upon contin-

---

[34] *See* section IV *infra.*

[35] *Cf.* B. Barry, *Political Argument* 97–105 (1965). Analogous points about the value of excuses and limitations on punishment are made by H. L. A. Hart. *See, e.g.,* H. L. A. Hart, *Punishment and Responsibility* 22–24, 44–49, 181–83 (1968). Hart elsewhere suggests a nonformalistic treatment of justice in the administration of the law. *See* Hart, "Philosophy of Law, Problems of," in 6 *The Encyclopedia of Philosophy* 274 (P. Edwards ed. 1967). But such considerations are absent from this discussion of the topic in "The Concept of Law." *See* notes 39–56 and accompanying text *infra.*

gent and circumstantial factors, for official deviations do not necessarily cause disutility. Thus, they do not support a presumption that is unaffected by the circumstances. Full knowledge of a case might show that no disutility would result from official deviation.

In short, the factors enumerated thus far tend to favor official adherence to the law, but they are distinct from and cannot support formal justice claims. An argument for formal justice cannot rely on contingent or circumstantial factors.[36]

These objections to the first argument for formal justice do not, of course, completely discredit the entire notion. But they do eliminate one possible reason for believing that official deviation from the law per se must be disvalued in the name of injustice, regardless of the circumstances. And if this appeal to the explanatory power of formal justice were the only argument in its favor, its attraction would undoubtedly be quite limited. Radically different sorts of arguments have also been advanced, however, which seek to ground formal justice upon the concept of justice itself.[37] Before examining them, I shall note the limits of an objection to formal justice that is also based upon examples.

One might try to present a real or hypothetical (but not implausible) counterexample to formal justice. Suppose that a morally indefensible law prescribes extermination for all members of a certain group. Under this law, a judge is presented with information so that he may decide a question of fact, such as whether the person in question belongs to the designated group. Let us imagine that a particular judge has remained on the bench in desperate hope of somehow doing some good, believing that he could do none elsewhere, and knowing that he would be replaced by a zealous racist if he resigned. Suppose further that he follows this law until one day a supervisor is absent from the court, and our judge has the chance to save a single person from the deadly net. To do this, he must fail to follow perfectly clear provisions of the law, for example, the rules of evidence. He does this, and the one life that he is able to save while acting in his official capacity is thereby saved.

---

[36] I am prepared to admit that it may be *useful* – and may even serve the interests of justice – to inculcate in lawyers and officials a deep conviction that official deviation from the law is always unjust or otherwise wrong, for this might help dissuade some from official misconduct. But this does not make such a conviction true, nor does it clearly justify the required deliberate oversimplification of moral issues. One must also consider the disadvantages of dogmatic and conservative attitudes on the part of those who may be called upon to administer unjust and inhumane laws, policies, and directives, with their consequent failure to face the difficult moral issues squarely. Unfortunately, such issues are often regarded much too crudely, as if the choice were simply between "the rule of law" and "anarchism." Formal justice may encourage just such blindness in officials.

[37] See notes 39–56 and accompanying text *infra*.

Has this judge acted wrongly? All things considered, I would suppose that he does right in breaking the law and saving the life he is able to save.[38] It is not clear that any case could be made for saying that this judge acted unjustly in failing to follow the law. Who, for example, is to be regarded as the victim of the judge's injustice? Surely the person who is saved is not the victim. Nor does it seem plausible to maintain that those he had already sent to the extermination camps are victims of an injustice done by the act in question, because a new murder has been averted. However, someone may grasp upon the obvious difference in treatment accorded those who pass before the judge. For example, one may assume that those already sent to the camps deserved no worse treatment than the one who fared better. But even if this argument seems to be a ground for saying that injustice is done by the judge's failure to follow the law in the instant case, the argument does not show that his mere failure to follow the law constitutes an injustice, which is what the formalist contends. The charge of injustice here rests on the differences in treatment dispensed by the judge. It should be emphasized that failure to follow the law does *not necessarily* result in such differences of treatment; it does not even mean that anyone will be affected.

Despite this analysis, the formalist may continue to insist that the judge has acted unjustly in departing from the law. He believes this because he thinks that there are general arguments for formal justice. He also regards this case as parallel to others in which it seems more obvious that injustice is done simply by departing from the law. To deal with formalism, therefore, one must undermine its entire rationale.

Moreover, while insisting that injustice has been done, the formalist can readily agree to our overall judgment in this case. He can, consistently, admit that for the judge to save the life is the right thing to do, because he can agree that an injustice may be justified when all factors are considered. Under the theory of formal justice I have constructed, a formalist can maintain that official deviation from the law, though in itself unjust or the breach of a basic principle, may sometimes be justified by overriding considerations. A small injustice, for example, which could help to save many innocent lives, might not be wrong, all things considered. The failure to follow an unjust law may also result in less injustice than adherence to it and might thereby be justified. The formalist can accept these points, but since he maintains that justice in the administration of the law is independent of other branches of justice and fundamen-

[38] It should be noted that my question concerns the judge's failure to follow the law this once, not his following the genocidal law before. Neither am I judging his decision to remain on the bench. These questions, while important, are also separable, as the formalist must agree, and they need not be decided here.

tally requires adherence to the law, regardless of circumstances, he counts even these justified departures from the law as injustices. They may be small departures, but they are regarded as injustices nevertheless. This classification is the distinctive claim of formal justice. However, although the requirements of formal justice are not supposed to depend on circumstances (including under this head the morality of the laws to be applied), other moral factors do depend on circumstances, and so the formalist can agree that what is right or wrong for a public official to do, all things considered, depends upon the circumstances. It follows that formal justice cannot be discredited merely by our conclusion that the judge's departure from the genocidal law was morally justifiable. With this the formalist could agree. Formal justice thus resists quick and easy refutation. Likewise, it is not wildly implausible. But these are not, of course, arguments for formal justice. To the chief ones I now turn.

III
ARGUMENTS FOR FORMAL JUSTICE

The arguments to be considered are recognizable as arguments for formal justice because they do not turn at all upon contingent factors. They present a noncontingent connection between administrative injustice and official deviation from the law.

H. L. A. Hart offers the most important formalist propositions in *The Concept of Law*. In fairness, one should note that Hart is at least as much concerned with refuting old-fashioned legalism as with promoting formal justice. He argues, for example, that justice cannot consist in "conformity to law," because laws themselves are judged to be just or unjust, and not simply by reference to other laws.[39] Although acknowledging justice, the old formula ignores such criticisms and even seems to exclude the possibility of an unjust law. However, Hart concedes too much to legalism by endorsing a formalistic account of justice in the administration of the law.

My discussion will center upon three points in Hart's brief treatment of the topic. The first bases administrative justice on the precept "treat like cases alike"; the second grounds it on a notion with which the first is often confused, namely, following a rule; the third is rooted in the idea of impartially applying the law to particular cases. These notions are worth examining closely because suggestions of formal justice are often expressed in such terms.

---

[39] H. L. A. Hart, *supra* note 1, at 157.

A. *Treating like cases alike*

Hart believes that "a central element in the idea of justice" is expressed by the precept "treat like cases alike and different cases differently."[40] This bare precept, however, "cannot afford any determinate guide to conduct"[41] and must be supplemented. "This is so because any set of human beings will resemble each other in some respects and differ from each other in others and, until it is established what resemblances and differences are relevant, 'Treat like cases alike' must remain an empty form."[42] The *bare* precept requires neither more nor less than uniform treatment. Of course, there are innumerable ways of treating cases uniformly, depending upon which features of persons, acts, and circumstances one considers relevant. There are as many possible interpretations for the precept "treat like cases alike." But justice requires more than mere uniformity of treatment. Some systematic ways of dealing with cases are just and others are unjust, and the bare precept does not help us to distinguish one from another. Hart concludes that there are two parts to the idea of justice, "a uniform or constant feature, summarized in the precept 'Treat like cases alike' and a shifting or varying criterion used in determining when, for any given purpose, cases are alike or different."[43]

I am not persuaded that this approach to analyzing the concept of justice is very promising, for the idea of treating like cases alike does not appear to have any special connection with justice. This seems true, at least, if we agree that justice does not consist simply in treating cases systematically; it requires certain kinds of treatment for certain classes of persons. But the same notion obtains for other aspects of morality, such as the requirement that one fulfill promises or that one come to the aid of those in need; these likewise require "treating like cases alike" according to specified patterns. For present purposes, however, this qualm can be suppressed. One may agree that justice requires *some* kind of uniform behavior. But what kind? Of what classes of persons? And in what circumstances?

Hart does not attempt to answer these traditionally contested questions in discussing the justice of the laws themselves. But he finds no difficulties when he turns to justice in the administration of the law:

In certain cases, indeed, the resemblances and differences between human beings which are relevant for the criticism of legal arrangements as just or unjust are quite obvious. This is preeminently the case when we are concerned not with the

[40] *Id.* at 155.   [41] *Id.*
[42] *Id.*   [43] *Id.* at 156.

justice or injustice of the *law* but of its *application* in particular cases. For here the relevant resemblances and differences between individuals, to which the person who administers the law must attend, are determined by the law itself. To say that the law against murder is justly applied is to say that it is impartially applied to all those and only those who are alike in having done what the law forbids; no prejudice or interest has deflected the administrator from treating them "equally."[44]

Hart's claim seems to be that the law provides the basic standard to be followed by a public official. He implies that an official who departs from the law thereby acts unjustly, regardless of the rules, the consequences, and other circumstances.

From the parts of Hart's discussion considered so far, it may appear as if he believes that this conclusion follows from a direct application of the requirement that like cases be treated alike. Hart realizes, however, that the bare precept "treat like cases alike" is "an empty form,"[45] and as the argument for using it seems so obviously invalid, I am hesitant to impute it to him. Nevertheless, it is the main basis that Perelman, for example, suggests for his own formal justice claims,[46] and it should therefore be considered. I believe, moreover, that this is the main theoretical prop ostensibly supporting formalistic tendencies among philosophers.

From the premises that justice fundamentally requires a uniform treatment of cases and that the law prescribes *one* way of uniformly dealing with them, we are asked to conclude that justice in the administration of the law requires officials to follow the law. But this argument begs the question at issue, which is whether the pattern of treatment prescribed by law is identical (or even compatible) with the pattern required by justice. Once we realize that the justice of a law is not determined by the law, or in other words that the resemblances and differences between persons, acts, and circumstances which the law tells us to consider are not necessarily the ones that justice says we may consider, the error of the formalist becomes obvious.

A formalist might object that his claim is only supposed to account for justice in the administration of the law; it is not supposed to exhaust all of justice, including that of the laws themselves. But this really makes no difference. Why should we suppose that the pattern of treatment prescribed by the law is the same as (or even compatible with) that prescribed by *any* principle of justice? An argument based on the idea of treating like cases alike gives us no reason at all.

The argument could be valid if certain assumptions were true. One might imagine, for example, that the only *possible* way for officials to

[44]   *Id.* (emphasis in original).   [45]   *Id.* at 155.
[46]   *See* C. Perelman, *supra* note 1, at 16, 29, 36–41.

deal with cases uniformly would be by following the law, as if failing to follow the law somehow guaranteed that cases would not be dealt with in a uniform manner.[47] But such an assumption would clearly be false. An official *can* deal with cases uniformly without following the law; that is, his conduct may fit another pattern, which does not perfectly follow the law, but requires some unauthorized actions. Corrupt officials who take bribes or who for some other reason act systematically in a partial or prejudiced manner, although breaking legal rules, can sometimes act with permanent legal effect. Such actions are a kind of uniform behavior, implemented according to a uniform pattern. Thus, appeal to the bare precept "treat like cases alike" is not sufficient to show that justice requires following the law.

At this point, formalists may say that they are not invoking merely the bare precept "treat like cases alike"; appeal is also being made to something special about the law. But what is this unique characteristic? I have mentioned that the possibility of construing legal rules as prescribing a way of "treating like cases alike" is of no help, for such rules prescribe only one of many possible patterns.

I have also given some reasons why injustice can be linked with official deviation from the law.[48] But these connections are contingent; they depend on the circumstances of each case. Arguments appealing to them cannot possibly give aid or comfort to the formalist. It should also be obvious that arguments for such connections make appeal to the precept "treat like cases alike" entirely unnecessary.

B. Following a rule

Hart suggests a second argument for formal justice when he observes:

> The connexion between this aspect of justice and the very notion of proceeding by rule is obviously very close. Indeed, it might be said that to apply a law justly to different cases is simply to take seriously the assertion that what is to be applied in different cases is the same general rule, without prejudice, interest, or caprice.[49]

This is a new argument, for the notion of applying a rule is clearly not equivalent to that of treating like cases alike. The precept "treat like cases alike" makes no reference to rules at all. It can be followed by devising a uniform treatment of cases even when no relevant rules exist, for ex-

---

[47] This is not the same as saying that the only *just* way for officials to deal with cases uniformly is by following the law, for this would again simply beg the question.

[48] *See* pp. 21–27 *supra*.

[49] H. L. A. Hart, *supra* note 1, at 156–57. *See also* C. Perelman, *supra* note 1, at 36–45.

ample, by comparing current cases among themselves. When a judge does this, he cannot be construed to be *following* an existing legal rule, even though he may create a new one. It is also possible to apply an existing rule *without* treating like cases alike, for example, by applying a rule for the first time to the case at bar.

Hart's suggestion may be elaborated into an argument along the following lines. From the premise that an official should apply a given rule, it follows that his behavior is subject to adverse criticism if he fails to do what the rule prescribes. The mere notion of applying a rule to particular cases might therefore be said to generate a principle by which behavior can be judged. This principle takes no account of what the rules require or allow, of what their effects are likely to be, or of particular circumstances. When there are rules for officials to apply, this principle is necessarily operative, and they are bound by it. It requires that the rules be applied exactly, without deviation in any respect.[50]

Such an argument does not necessitate an extreme legalistic position, nor does it mean that public officials must always follow the law. It can be taken as an account of one principle of justice, which can conceivably be overridden.

But is the outcome really a principle of *justice?* The argument turns entirely on the notion of applying a rule to particular cases; it contains no further restrictions. If the result were a principle of justice, then any deviation from any rule that one is supposed to apply would be, in itself, an unjust act. Nothing restricts this mode of argument to the conduct of public officials, or even to the law. For that reason, it seems clear that the argument must fail, for either it works for all kinds of rules, regardless of the circumstances, or it works for none. And it clearly does not work for some. To see this, one need only select a rule the breach of which has no necessary moral significance, regardless of the circumstances. The charge of injustice carries moral weight, and if the breach of some rule does not automatically carry such weight, then it cannot be an unjust act. Suppose, then, that when I speak ungrammatically I can be said to break a rule of language. The argument would have it that I thereby commit an unjust act. But this is implausible. Of course, I can do wrong by misusing language, but whether what I do is not only grammatically

---

[50] If this argument were sound it would be of special interest for supporting a traditional natural law contention, namely, that there is a significant, necessary connection between law and morals because the principle requiring adherence to legal rules would seem to be implicit in the law by virtue of the fact that every legal system contains some rules. For another attempt to show such a connection, see L. Fuller, *The Morality of Law* (1964). I have discussed Fuller's suggestions elsewhere. *See* Lyons, "The Internal Morality of Law," 71 *Proc. Aristotelian Soc'y* 105, 105–19 (1970–71) [Chapter 1 in this volume].

incorrect but also morally wrong, some kind of injustice, or the violation of a basic moral principle, would seem to depend on contingent circumstances.

A formalist might agree that departures from some rules are not always unjust, but insist that departure from existing law, at least by officials responsible for administering it, is always a kind of injustice – that there is something *special* about that kind of rule breaking. This is an intelligible contention, but one has been given no reason to accept it. Another argument is needed.

The problem is as follows. Insofar as official nonconformity to law is regarded merely as the failure to follow rules, it is implausible to regard it as a kind of injustice. Is there anything else essential to official noncompliance that would provide the required link? It must be something *essential* to this kind of rule breaking, that is, something independent of all circumstances. Otherwise, a formal justice claim cannot be supported, for formal justice maintains that official disobedience is always morally objectionable, regardless of the circumstances. If one invokes considerations linking deviation with injustice in a contingent manner, that is, dependent on the circumstances, one has no argument for formal justice.

I cannot think of anything to fulfill the formalistic requirements, but it is worth emphasizing what will *not* work. It can be argued, as I have shown, that official deviation from the law is likely to cause injustice involving, e.g., mistreatment of individuals. But these are risks; actual injustices depend upon the concrete circumstances. Sometimes it can be certain that injustice will result from misadministration of the law, but this sort of argument also suggests that sometimes no injustice will be done at all. When such cases arise, there can be *no* objection, based on injustice, to official deviation from the law.

C. Impartially applying the law to particular cases

Each of the direct arguments for formal justice that I have considered can be criticized in yet another way, namely, that they lead to the conclusion that following the law is *sufficient* as well as necessary for administrative justice. This conclusion, however, seems much too simple a conception. Even if one agrees that justice in the administration of the law cannot be done unless the law is followed, one may still wish to say that justice requires more than merely acting within the limits laid down by the law.

In his remarks on justice, Hart suggests a much more plausible view, namely, that administrative justice consists in applying the law *impartially* to particular cases. For example, while invoking the idea of treating like cases alike, Hart maintains:

32

To say that the law against murder is justly applied is to say that it is *impartially* applied to all those and only those who are alike in having done what the law forbids; *no prejudice or interest has deflected* the administrator from treating them "equally."[51]

A similar qualification seems indicated when Hart appeals to the notion of proceeding by rule:

Indeed, it might be said that to apply a law justly to different cases is simply to take seriously the assertion that what is to be applied to different cases is the same general rule, *without prejudice, interest, or caprice.*[52]

Although the standard of impartiality is invoked by Hart when he suggests the first two arguments for formal justice, it plays no apparent role in either of them. Moreover, appeal to impartiality goes beyond the ideas of proceeding by rule and treating like cases alike. This point should be emphasized. Impartiality is not implicit in the ideas of treating like cases alike or proceeding by rule. Although impartiality may require *some* kind of uniform behavior, *merely* to deal with cases in a uniform manner is not to be impartial. An official might systematically favor one group over others as a consequence of personal prejudice or interest, and get uniform results. Likewise, impartiality is not implicit in proceeding by rule, because rules leave areas of discretion.

What difference can considerations of impartiality make to the formalist's position? In answering this question, it is useful to contrast formalists who have different conceptions of a legal system. Suppose, first, that a formalist conceives of the law as a set of rules that officials can apply "mechanically" to cases as they arise, in the sense that officials can actually follow the law only in one way. If they do one thing, they follow the law; if they do anything else, they fail to follow it. This means that there is only one way for officials to administer the law justly, for formalists maintain, at the least, that official departure from the law is an injustice. Such a "mechanical" formalist is therefore obliged to embrace the overly simple formal justice claim that justice in the administration of the law consists in following it; deviation from the law would then be seen as both a necessary and a sufficient condition of administrative injustice.

How would this kind of formalist conceive of and value impartiality? He could not regard it as an essential element of administrative justice; it could not enter into his basic position. He could value it, however, in at least two other ways. On the one hand, its absence could be seen as

[51] H. L. A. Hart, *supra* note 1, at 156 (emphasis added).
[52] *Id.* at 156–57 (emphasis added).

33

one possible, contingent cause of deviation from the law and thus of injustice. On the other hand, he could value it as a cast of mind that is intrinsically fitting for a public official. But, either way, impartiality would add nothing of relevance to the formalist's position. It would not repair the defects of the views that we have already considered.

The appeal to impartiality can make a substantial difference to the formalist's position – a difference relevant to our concerns – only if he does not accept a "mechanical" conception of the law but believes instead that officials sometimes face alternative lines of lawful behavior and must often make significant choices in administering the law. If the formalist also believes that the choice of lawful alternatives is subject to criticism in the name of justice, then he must qualify his formal justice claim accordingly, because the simple requirement that officials act within the law does not enable the formalist to differentiate between the lawful alternatives. To evaluate them, the formalist must supplement that requirement with some other extralegal standard. For when officials have such "discretion," strictly speaking, the binding guidance of the law has been exhausted. Impartiality may then be invoked as a supplementary standard, to be applied when officials must exercise discretion. The resultant view would be that, given the understanding that the law itself does not fully determine what constitutes its own impartial application, administrative justice consists in applying the laws impartially to particular cases. Although incorporating extralegal standards, such a view would still be formalistic in the original sense because it holds that adherence to existing law is a necessary condition of administrative justice.

Hart himself argues that officials have discretion.[53] No legal rule or set of rules completely determines in all relevant respects how an official is to deal with cases that arise. Legal rules cannot be applied "mechanically"; there is always room for the exercise of official judgment. Lawmakers often deliberately allow for discretion in particular cases, as when judges are authorized to fix punishments. But occasions for exercising discretion also result from conflicts between laws, problems left untouched by laws, and vague or ambiguous laws, which cannot entirely be eliminated.

An official's choice among lawful alternatives is subject to criticism in the name of justice. Thus, the discretion that judges have in sentencing convicted offenders may be exercised impartially or partially; police and prosecutors may ration their time and attention in a partial or impartial manner. If these officials fail to act impartially, they may be charged with injustice.

[53] *Id.* at 121–50.

34

The claim that administrative justice requires impartial application of the law to particular cases is not inherently formalistic. One might agree, for example, that the just way of applying the law is the impartial way, while believing that justice may sometimes require that officials *not* apply the law. The formalistic version of the claim maintains that impartial application of the existing rules of law *fully embodies* administrative justice, with the understanding that this claim fundamentally requires officials to act within the limits laid down by law. I wish to discredit the latter version.[54]

This formula clearly may be thought to exhaust the topic of administrative justice because what an official essentially does is administer the law. If one goes beyond this formula, beyond the requirement of impartial application of existing rules of law, it will be argued, one is necessarily changing the topic, since one is no longer confining oneself to justice in the administration of the law.

I believe this to be a mistaken notion. I have already observed that it is possible for an official to overstep the legal boundaries while acting in his official capacity. The question remains whether such conduct must always be unjust, or the breach of a basic principle. In giving this reply, however, I am assuming that the question of justice in the administration of the law is identical to or at least co-extensive with the question of justice in official conduct. The formalist might deny this for some reason. I see no way of arguing this particular point directly, so I shall take a different tack.

Let us assume that officials should, to do justice, be impartial; this does not imply adherence to any particular set of rules, such as the rules of law. Again, suppose that the only just way of applying the law is the impartial way; it does not follow that an official who fails to follow the law acts unjustly. Let us agree that an *application* of the law which is *not* impartial is *un*just; it does not follow that all *deviations* by officials from the law are unjust. For not every such departure could be described as an application of the law that fails to be impartial. An official might deliberately refuse to follow the law; this is not the same as applying it in, for example, a biased or prejudiced manner. This distinction is important, for the official may refuse to follow the law on principled grounds, precisely in order to prevent an injustice of which he would be the instrument.

Is it possible for this to happen – for an official to prevent an injustice

---

54   The formalistic version can be ascribed to Hart because he offers the formula within unquestionably formalistic arguments. For him, impartiality is required by administrative justice, but only within the limits laid down by the law. *See* text accompanying notes 51–52 *supra*.

by refusing to follow the law, while avoiding other injustices? If so, then mere deviation from the law by a public official does not by itself constitute a kind of injustice. If one can give an affirmative answer to this question, it will imply that the formula, "administrative justice requires the impartial application of the law to particular cases," has only conditional force. It does not exhaust the topic of administrative justice, for if it did, and if the law were broken, then injustice would be done.

An affirmative answer may be suggested by an example. Suppose that Jones is an official responsible for administering a law that is unjust because it discriminates against blacks by depriving them of certain benefits conferred upon whites. Jones realizes that he is in a position to distribute benefits more equitably by using his office but without following the law. Let us imagine that Jones so acts, thus exceeding his official discretion. *Must* an injustice have been done? If one examines the situation and finds no one wronged, then one should look for some other sign, mark, or symptom of injustice. If none is found, one is left with no ground for confirming the claim that official deviation from the law is inherently unjust.

None of those directly affected by the distribution made by Jones, acting in defiance of the law, would seem to be wronged as a necessary consequence. Some, indeed, are treated justly only because Jones refuses to follow the law; they are surely not wronged on that account. Nor are those in whose favor the law discriminates necessarily wronged, for one can suppose that they receive the same benefits they would have enjoyed had the law been followed; the class formerly discriminated against is simply not given less. Can any other basis be found for saying that Jones's behavior is unjust? It would seem that *all* potential arguments similarly turn upon contingent circumstances. For example, Jones might expose others, such as official subordinates, to risks without their knowledge and consent. This may seem to be a kind of injustice, or at least some kind of moral wrong, but this complication is not inevitable; he might protect others or he might act alone, assuming all the risk himself. Again, he might find it necessary to deceive others in order to carry off his plan successfully. But this fact — which has uncertain ties to the charge of injustice — also turns upon contingencies, for deception might not be necessary.[55]

There are many possible grounds for the charge of injustice or some other kind of wrong when officials fail to follow the law. Benefits or burdens may be distributed unjustly as a consequence, or someone may

---

[55] Once again, one may wish to note an official's special obligation of allegiance to the law, which Jones has presumably incurred by accepting and retaining his position. I shall discuss this point shortly.

fail to receive something that he deserves. But formal justice cannot rely upon any such "substantive" considerations since it maintains that an official can act unjustly by simply failing to follow the law. Injustice seems, however, to depend upon the surrounding circumstances.[56] At least, one has no reason at all to think otherwise.

IV
OFFICIAL OBLIGATIONS

Considerable illicit support for formal justice may derive from the widespread conviction that officials have special obligations to uphold the law. This conviction, properly qualified, is not implausible. But the support it affords formal justice, even were it not illicit, would in any case be insufficient.

Official obligations of allegiance to the law may readily appear to bolster formal justice claims. Officials have a special relation to the law, unlike ordinary citizens, for they are responsible for administering it. This relation is part of what it is to be a public official. If those in public office undertake and reaffirm obligations of fidelity to law, they thereby provide a basis for criticism of their deviations from the law, for any such deviation would seem to amount to the breach of such an obligation. The case for formalistic requirements is strengthened because it may appear that any official *must be* under such obligation by virtue of his acceptance of and continuation in a position of public trust. If so, the obligations always require official conformity to the law, regardless of the circumstances.

The first difficulty with this line of reasoning arises from the fact that formal justice pretends to give an account of what constitutes *justice* in the administration of the law. The argument demonstrating that there are special obligations incumbent on officials has nothing to say about such matters. The vice of an official who strays from the law is not depicted as an injustice but rather as an infidelity or breach of faith. What justice requires of him is something else.

[56] One might construct less serious examples. Suppose a law prescribes a useless ritual, for example, that a county clerk is required to spit twice out of the left side of his mouth when certifying that a will has been witnessed in the required way. An official might well be tempted to rebel, save for the fact that wills are regarded as invalid unless this ritual has been performed. But suppose the official is *certain* that no one will know if he performed the ritual, and he merely pretends to have done it. He thus fails to follow perfectly clear provisions of the law. Has an injustice been done? Would the answer be any different if the ritual were required *of the clerk* but not required for the validation of the will? Suppose the clerk refused to do it under those circumstances. Would he be acting unjustly? Or perhaps only imprudently, assuming there were penalties for official noncompliance?

Second, it is doubtful whether such obligations always give a reason for official conformity, regardless of the circumstances. Consider, for example, the suggestion that a public official must always be under such an obligation. This cannot be correct, for there may be circumstances in which no such obligations can be incurred or sustained.[57] One should not confuse the obligation in question with institutional requirements; the question is whether a basis for *moral* criticism of officials who deviate from existing law is always present. It would seem that the requisite conditions may be lacking. Suppose, for the moment, that such an obligation arises when a person voluntarily accepts and retains official responsibility; it does not follow that all officials have such obligations, for one might be coerced into accepting or retaining this position. It would then be highly questionable whether such an obligation had been incurred. The very existence of such obligations therefore depends upon the circumstances, and another argument for formalistic conclusions dissolves.

Even if voluntary acceptance and retention of official responsibility are necessary to give rise to such an obligation, they may not be sufficient. One recognizes similar limits when arguing, for example, that certain contracts are void *ab initio* because of their nature or subject matter. Similarly, there may be circumstances in which no morally binding commitment can be made, even if made of one's own free will, or in which certain conduct could not be required. One might argue, for example, that the judge in our earlier example[58] was under no moral obligation to follow the genocidal law he was charged with administering – and mean it *strictly*. This argument can be understood in one of two ways, depending on the circumstances: either any obligation of fidelity to his nation's laws that he had incurred was entirely extinguished, or such matters fall outside the scope of that obligation, in which case he would still be obligated to follow other, innocuous laws.

A formalist who wishes to salvage as much as possible from a sinking ship may be tempted to object that the official obligation argument is unaffected even in such cases, for he can admit that such obligations can be overridden, and he may say that this has happened. The obligation persists, even in the extreme case, but is simply outweighed. If so, a formalist objection to official deviation from the law in such cases remains.

However, this response will not save formal justice or even the weaker claim that there is always *some* kind of moral objection to official deviation from the law, regardless of the circumstances, for, as I have men-

---

[57] Even if a person *willingly* accepts responsibility for implementing his government's genocidal policies, it is doubtful that he thereby incurs a *morally* binding obligation to discharge his official duties.

[58] *See* text preceding note 38 *supra*.

tioned, officials are not always under such obligations, as, for example, when they are coerced into serving.[59] The reasoning behind that point can be applied to my last. To say that voluntarily undertaking and retaining responsibility is a necessary condition of an obligation to uphold the law is not to draw a conclusion from conventional rules; it is to make a moral judgment. The very idea that a person who voluntarily accepts and retains a position of public trust incurs an "obligation" rests upon a moral conception of what constitutes a valid and binding agreement, for the institutional rules do not necessarily recognize such limitations. Moral considerations are relied upon in claiming that there is such an obligation, and the substance of such obligations – what they are obligations to do or to refrain from doing – can likewise be the subject of a moral judgment. Furthermore, by saying that someone who undertakes to administer the law incurs an obligation to uphold it, one is surely not bound to say that he is to be regarded as under an obligation to do whatever the law requires of him, regardless of the particular requirement, the effects of following it, and all other circumstances. A moral judgment is required here. Some acts, perhaps, are beyond an official's special obligation of allegiance to the law. In other words, it is doubtful that a sound moral reason for a public official to abide by the law that he administers always exists, even when he has voluntarily undertaken to uphold the law.

CONCLUSION

I have been appraising the notion that injustice is done whenever an official fails to follow the law that he is charged with administering, regardless of the circumstances. This notion, which I call "formal justice," appears to have several sources, but no firm foundations.

It is sometimes suggested that formal justice is required to account for the distinction between justice in the administration of the law and the justice of the laws themselves, as well as for the moral premium placed on official adherence to the law. But I have shown that other explanations are readily available. It has also been suggested that formal justice derives from the precept, at the heart of justice, that like cases be treated alike, or from the notion of following a rule, which is central to the law. But I have shown that these slender reeds cannot support the weight of formal justice. I have considered the idea that justice in the administra-

---

[59] One might be coerced into serving or remaining in office by threats to oneself or one's family. A government might wish to do this to exploit the skills or prestige of certain individuals. It should be noted that, although examples of such coercion may be found in recent history, the mere *possibility* of such cases is sufficient for the present point.

tion of the law involves the impartial application of the law to particular cases. This idea seems unobjectionable, when understood to mean that the law should be impartially applied, if and when one is justified in following it. But an appeal to the notion of impartiality cannot show that deliberate refusal to follow the law is unjust. Finally, I have taken account of the conviction that officials are under obligations of allegiance to the law, deriving from their positions of public trust. These convictions are distinct from formal justice claims. Moreover, the arguments for such obligations would not show that there is always a moral objection to official deviation from the law, regardless of the circumstances.

Formal justice therefore seems theoretically unfounded. It appears to be an exaggerated expression of otherwise legitimate concern for justice in the administration of the law. But since it exaggerates the case to be made for compliance with unjust and inequitable laws, it is morally objectionable.

3

Legal formalism and instrumentalism – a pathological study

Holmes and those who followed in his wake believed they were rejecting a rigid and impoverished conception of the law (often called "formalism") which had, in their view, adversely affected judicial practice. They spawned a collection of doctrines that Professor Summers dubs "pragmatic instrumentalism"[1] – fittingly so-called both because they viewed the law as an eminently practical instrument and because they were so strongly influenced by the philosophical pragmatists William James and John Dewey.

This essay has two parts. The first and longer part identifies and examines the basic doctrines of formalism and instrumentalism. The arguments offered by instrumentalists against formalism suggest that both schools generally agree on two fundamental points. First, the law is rooted in authoritative sources, such as legislative and judicial decisions (a "source-based" view of law). Second, legal judgments that are justifiable on the basis of existing law can be displayed as the conclusions of valid deductive syllogisms the major premises of which are tied very tightly to the authoritative texts (a "formalistic model" for legal justifications). The difference between the schools concerns the question of whether law is complete and univocal. Formalists are understood to argue that existing law provides a sufficient basis for deciding all cases that arise. This belief, in combination with the formalistic model for legal justifications, leads the formalists to conclude that the authoritative texts are logically sufficient to decide all cases. In denying this, instrumentalists appear to have the better of the argument. I shall go further, however, to argue that the formalistic model for legal justifications, which is shared by formalists and instrumentalists alike, is subject to serious question.

The second part of this essay examines criticisms by instrumentalists of "formalistic" judicial practice. I argue that these criticisms appear ill-

"Legal Formalism and Instrumentalism – A Pathological Study," *Cornell Law Review,* Vol. 66, 5 (1981): 949–72. Copyright © 1980–81 by Cornell University. All rights reserved.
  [1] Summers, "Pragmatic-Instrumentalism in Twentieth Century American Legal Thought – A Synthesis and Critique of Our Dominant General Theory About Law and Its Use," 66 *Cornell L. Rev.* 861 (1981). Professor Summers's Article is assumed here as a guide to these doctrines.

41

founded and that the doctrines of formalism provide little, if any, basis for the sort of practice to which instrumentalists have objected.

I

FORMALISM AND INSTRUMENTALISM COMPARED

A. Legal formalism

Legal formalism is difficult to define because, so far as I can tell, no one ever developed and defended a systematic body of doctrines that would answer to that name. We have no clear notion of what underlying philosophical ideas might motivate its conception of the law. It is sometimes tempting to suppose that there has never been any such thing as a formalistic theory of law, but only pregnant pronouncements by some legal writers which lack any coherence or theoretical foundation, combined with judicial practices that are thought (soundly or unsoundly) to embody the attitudes of those writers. Although the instrumentalists were distressed by a variety of judicial and juristic errors, their reactions must be our principal guide to formalism.

Part of what is meant by formalism is this: The law provides sufficient basis for deciding any case that arises. There are no "gaps" within the law, and there is but one sound legal decision for each case. The law is complete and univocal. According to Summers, formalists hold that law is "traceable to an authoritative source."[2] This leads one to inquire, however, about what counts as an authoritative source. One must assume that authoritative sources include legislative and judicial decisions or authoritative records of them. But what else might they comprise?

The question is crucial because some of those who have been called formalists have also been understood to argue that law is determined not just by such mundane human actions and decisions, but also by what is sometimes called "natural law." Natural law has never been laid down as law in any ordinary way, so far as our ordinary legal records show. One jurist who suggests this view is William Blackstone, who, although sometimes called a formalist,[3] wrote in his *Commentaries* that "no human laws are of any validity, if contrary to [the law of nature that is dictated by God]; and such of them as are valid derive all their force and all their authority, mediately or immediately, from this original."[4]

---

[2]   *Id.* at 867 n.4, item 6.
[3]   *See* Hart, "Positivism and the Separation of Law and Morals," 71 *Harv. L. Rev.* 593, 610 (1958).
[4]   1 W. Blackstone, *Commentaries on the Laws of England* 41 (8th ed. 1783).

Blackstone's position is usually understood as follows: Nothing counts as law unless it derives from, or at least accords with, God's dictates. If we assume that Blackstone was a formalist and that formalists believe law is complete, then we must understand him as arguing that human law is not only rectified by divine command but also completed by it. In other words, some of our law comes only from *extra*ordinary authoritative sources. This last point is important because it suggests the shape formalism might have to take in order to secure the formalists' claim that law is complete, without surrendering any of their other fundamental claims. Because formalism is assumed to tie law very closely to authoritative sources, the class of sources must be expanded into the supernatural realm in order to supply sufficient law to close all the gaps left by authoritative, mundane sources.

The idea of a "natural law that is dictated by God" functions in theories like Blackstone's as a specific conception of a more general concept which an atheist, for example, would interpret differently: that of "moral law." Blackstone thus suggested the more general view (which exposed him to biting comments from Bentham and others) that nothing counts as law unless it is morally acceptable, and there is as much law as morality requires. Law is not only thought to have moral sources but is regarded as morally infallible as well. The instrumentalists, however, knew better than that.

This reading of Blackstone stresses a kind of authority at the base of law and, hence, might be credited as formalism. Despite the possibility of such an interpretation, I think we should follow Summers, who I take it conceives of a "source-based" conception of law in narrower and more mundane terms, excluding the supernatural. This renders formalism more plausible and more deserving of serious critical attention. Straw men impede the progress of legal theory.

This understanding of formalism is compatible with Blackstone's remarks on another, more faithful reading. Blackstone can be understood to say not that morally objectionable law does not exist, but rather that there is no automatic moral obligation to obey it. "Natural law" is relevant to determine when ordinary human law "binds in conscience." This is not an uncommon view among natural lawyers. It was developed most clearly by Aquinas,[5] who argued that human laws are either just or unjust, and that one has an obligation to obey just laws, but not all unjust laws. Human laws are unjust when they fail to serve the common good, when they exceed the lawmaker's authority, when they distribute bur-

---

[5]   2 T. Aquinas, *Basic Writings of Saint Thomas Aquinas* 794–95 (A.C. Pegis ed. 1945).

dens unfairly, or when they show disrespect for God. One is morally bound to obey such an unjust law only when circumstances demand it, in order to prevent scandal or disturbance.

If we understand Blackstone (who was not so clear) along the lines suggested by Aquinas, then Blackstone may be interpreted as saying that "natural law" provides a standard for determining when human law merits our obedience. Under this sympathetic interpretation, Blackstone could be credited with an ordinary source-based view of law. Thus, he would qualify as a formalist – provided, of course, that he also espoused certain other doctrines, to which we now turn.

Our sketch of formalism amounts so far to this: First, the law is rooted in authoritative sources, like legislative and judicial decisions; second, it is complete and univocal. But what makes it "formalistic"? That label turns on a third doctrine – namely, that law decides cases in a logically "mechanical" manner. In other words, sound legal decisions can be justified as the conclusions of valid deductive syllogisms. Because law is believed to be complete and univocal, all cases that arise can in principle be decided in this way. This is the *formalistic model* for legal justifications. These three doctrines capture the essence of formalism when it is viewed as a type of legal theory.[6] They do not, however, explain what may be called the "formalistic method" in judicial *practice,* which will be discussed below.

B. Instrumentalism

Ironically, it is more difficult to pin down the doctrines of instrumentalism, because this school of legal thought is determined by the writings of a variety of jurists. They do not always agree and, indeed, are not always self-consistent. Consider, for example, the instrumentalists' attitudes towards what Summers calls "valid law."[7] One finds three views in unhappy aggregation. Summers claims that instrumentalists share with formalists a source-based conception of law, but that they also embrace the predictive theory. Some instrumentalists, however – the radical fringe on the edge of legal realism – are "rule skeptics." The rule skeptics claim that real law consists only of past judicial decisions, which are understood as limited to their specific holdings, without any further binding implications. No two of these views are compatible.

What is a "source-based" view of law? Presumably, it means that courts are bound by certain authoritative texts or decisions. If the relevant texts

[6] Moreover, they seem to cover all of Summers's twelve points. *See* Summers, *supra* note 1, at 867 n.4.
[7] *Id.* at 896.

or decisions are entirely neglected, judicial decisions or their justifications are that much in error. Authoritative sources establish legal limits or constraints upon judicial decisions. This is not to say they are sufficient to determine a uniquely correct decision in each case or that they must be applied syllogistically. Instead, they must be given their due weight, however that is to be understood.

Rule skepticism clearly does not square with a source-based view of law, for it implies not just that judges are liable to decide cases as they please, but that they are legally free to do so. Furthermore, the idea that laws are "predictions" of what courts will probably decide sits well with neither of these other instrumentalist notions of law. The prediction theory is advanced as a conception of law that goes beyond past decisions. It is meant to perform a task that rule skepticism avoids, but it cannot possibly do that job. A prediction of judicial decisions is not the sort of thing that can bind a court; it cannot serve as a normative standard with which a judge might or might not comply. If a decision accords with a prediction, it may confirm the prediction, but it does not demonstrate that the decision is legally sound. The fact that a decision falsifies a prediction is in no way indicative of judicial error.

Radical rule skepticism can be understood as a way of trying to cope with a puzzling legal phenomenon. If a court acts when existing law seems to provide insufficient guidance, its capacity to help shape the law may not be puzzling. A court's departure from the literal reading of a statute or from a binding precedent, however, may be puzzling if its decision effectively establishes new legal doctrine. It may seem as if one cannot account for the efficacy of such decisions except by holding that *all* law actually is made by courts. Courts themselves cannot be seen as laying down *general* standards, however, for this would only introduce the same problem all over again. Hence, the logical extension of this argument is rule skepticism, which claims that there never is any determinate law aside from specific holdings in past cases.

The question is whether it is more reasonable to conclude that (1) there are legally binding standards from which courts can sometimes effectively depart, even if they do so erroneously, or (2) there are no legally binding standards, which excludes the possibility of judicial error. The following observations may be useful. To acknowledge the possibility of judicial error is to assume neither that law provides a unique answer to every legal question nor that when law provides one, it does so with logical conclusiveness, excluding all argument to the contrary. Judicial error may be the failure to follow the *best* legal arguments or the *strongest* legal reasons, as is usually assumed when judicial decisions are criticized on one legal ground or another. Furthermore, one who believes that courts can err is not committed to the view that such cases have no effect on the law. One might believe that judicial decisions pronouncing new legal doctrines do not always succeed in entrenching those doctrines into the law. Such entrenchment occurs when subsequent courts follow the decision. A novel decision, however, is not always followed – not even by the same court. If a court fails to follow its own previous decision, then, according to the radical realist, it has nothing to explain. The court cannot be regarded as changing either the law or its interpretation of the law, because that would imply that there is law beyond specific holdings. The opposing view maintains that a court might fail to follow its own previous decision either by mistake or because it believes it made an error that it wishes to rectify. This seems to fit our usual ways of thinking when we are not spinning theories about the law, and it is incumbent on legal theories to account for any divergence from these legal phenomena. It may also be admitted, however, that it is incumbent on the opposing theorist to explain how and when judicial mistakes become entrenched within the law.

Despite the excesses of its skepticism, the theory of the radical realists represents a clearer and more consistent overall legal philosophy than its instrumentalist competitors. It can be understood as suggesting that a judicial decision is justified when, but only when, it serves (perhaps to the maximum degree possible) the interests of those who will be affected by the decision. Although many other instrumentalists endorse this normative theory, their views are inconsistent with it, because they believe that past legislative and judicial decisions serve as constraints upon the decisions that can be justified in a particular case. Thus, these nonradical instrumentalists are committed both to the view that courts are bound by past legislative and judicial decisions and that they are not so bound. Their official normative theory does not conform to their understanding that courts are bound by other authoritative decisions. One cannot consistently maintain that those past decisions must have some influence on the decision in the present case – that they provide authoritative standards to be followed – while arguing that the case at hand must be decided solely by consideration of the likely consequences.

To see what is wrong with the normative theory of radical realism, one must ask what would make it right. Two conditions must be satisfied. First, there must be no basis for supposing that past legislative and judicial decisions are properly regarded as binding. Second, the proper basis for judicial decisions must be simple, direct utilitarianism. Hence, we must ask why others assume that past legislative and judicial decisions properly guide judicial decisions.

One nonutilitarian explanation is that judges have morally committed themselves to being bound by such decisions and to deciding cases in light of whatever law there is. They have accepted this public trust, as everyone understands. This is not necessarily an absolute obligation; one can find examples in which deciding a case according to the law conflicts with a judge's more salient nonjudicial obligations. The judicial obligation of fidelity to law is limited in other ways as well. It is conditional upon being voluntarily undertaken; a judge coerced into serving on the bench under a brutally corrupt regime is, if bound at all, not bound in the way that judges are ordinarily bound by the public trust they willingly assume. Furthermore, there may be limits on the moral scope of such obligations. Just as it makes perfectly good sense to hold that soldiers in wartime are not legally or morally bound by certain orders – such as those clearly and openly intended to have the soldiers commit atrocities – so it makes perfectly good sense to hold that some law may be so morally corrupt as to lie outside the limits of a judge's obligation of fidelity to law.

For such reasons, we might infer that the law must satisfy some moral minimum if judges are to be regarded as bound by past legislative and judicial decisions. The procedures must satisfy minimal conditions of fairness, the outcomes must satisfy minimal constraints of justice, or both. Without such assumptions, the idea that judges are "bound" to follow the law or that judges are expected to render "justifiable" decisions is unintelligible. We merely play misleading and possibly pernicious games with serious and important ideas like obligation and justification unless we suppose that they are linked significantly to factors such as those we have just listed. The alternative is a mindless sort of authority-worship – the notion that mere "legal" authority (in the narrowest sense), which is compatible with the worst sorts of abominations the world has suffered under law, is somehow capable of creating a real "obligation" and is capable of "justifying" what it does to innocent victims. Legal positivists sometimes seem to employ such a desiccated conception of "legal" authority, obligation, right, and justification, though they truly have no need for it. The upshot is confusion about the relations between law and morals. Just as we need not suppose that law and morals are completely divorced in order to recognize that law is morally fallible, we need not suppose that law automatically possesses any genuine authority in order to analyze its structure, systematize its restrictions, or appreciate that it is something to contend with in practice.

It is reasonable to suppose that the more moderate instrumentalists make such relevant assumptions about the law they see themselves as bound by and that such considerations explain why past legislative and judicial decisions bind courts and limit the scope of their decision-making power. As Summers observes,[8] nonradical instrumentalists seem to accept a source-based view of law, as do all instrumentalist judges in practice, whatever they may say when writing about the law.

C. Moderate instrumentalism and formalism compared

How do these moderate instrumentalists diverge from formalism? Surprisingly, not by very much. They too have a source-based view of law, which distinguishes them from the radical realists. They reject, however, the "formalistic" notion that law is complete and univocal. Unlike the radical realists, the moderate instrumentalists believe that there are laws between the gaps; unlike the formalists, they believe that there are gaps between the laws.

This does not address the third aspect of formalism – the formalistic model for legal justifications. It is tempting to suppose that instrumentalists reject this doctrine as well; after all, they attribute much less significance to the role of formal logic in the law than do the formalists. It is worth asking, however, what is meant by the instrumentalists' complaints about the formalists' excessive use of formal logic. One factor that complicates matters is that these issues are sometimes framed in terms of the logical character of "judicial reasoning." But "judicial reasoning" is ambiguous; it can refer to the logical relations between premises and conclusions, or it can refer to the thought processes of judges. The former is something logicians study, while the latter is a field for psychologists. Although psychologists concerned with the logical character of thought processes require training in logic, logicians need no training in psychology. Claims about the role, or lack thereof, of formal logic in judicial reasoning are correspondingly ambiguous. One who has a formalistic conception of logic, or of legal justifications in particular, assumes that all good arguments are deductive. One who has a formalistic conception of thought processes, or of judicial thinking in particular, assumes that our thoughts run along deductive lines. These ideas are quite independent. One might deny, for example, that judges' thought processes always proceed along straight deductive paths before they arrive at a tentative decision, yet believe that sound judicial decisions can be presented as the conclusions of valid deductive syllogisms with true legal propositions as the major premises and factual assumptions as the minor premises. Thus, an instrumentalist who maintains that formalists have exaggerated the role of logic in adjudication might simply mean that judicial *thoughts* do not run along syllogistic lines.

[8] *Id.* at 900.

This point is innocent enough, but it is often misunderstood. It is sometimes suggested, for example, that if judicial thought processes are not syllogistic, then later presenting the corresponding judicial opinion in syllogistic form is hypocritical and involves some form of rationalization (in the pejorative sense). The recognition that judicial thought is not always shaped by syllogistic reasoning may lead to the conclusion that formal logic has no real role in "judicial reasoning." But this would be mistaken. Entertaining hypotheses in a variety of ways is compatible with the justification by rigorous argument of those that survive systematic criticism, and this combination is indispensable as well as routine in all spheres of inquiry and all respectable disciplines. Indeed, it is sometimes a virtue for judicial thought to be relatively unfettered, but the justified decision must take account of all relevant considerations, verify the premises adopted, and include only sound reasoning. If opinions generally did that, we should have no instrumentalist complaints of excess logic.

Another factor that complicates the instrumentalists' attitudes towards formal logic is their emphasis on factual considerations in judicial decisions. Their innocent and innocuous point is that law applies to cases only in relation to factual assumptions that are made. In other words, law's actual implications for cases depend on the facts, while its de facto applications depend on presumed facts. The determination of the facts, however, cannot be solely a matter of deductive reasoning. The basis for the latter claim is the familiar point that factual statements about what has happened or is likely to happen in the natural world are always established by evidence that is logically insufficient to entail those statements. This does not reflect badly on logic, but is merely a symptom of two phenomena. First, empirical conclusions logically outstrip the evidence that confirms them. Second, the confirmation of empirical conclusions is therefore necessarily *non*deductive. This is hardly central to legal theory, and formalists are without reason to deny it. Moreover, it concerns the preliminary arguments needed to establish factual premises used in the justifications of judicial decisions. It should be emphasized that formalists cannot be understood to deny that factual considerations play a decisive role in legal decisions. No one in his right mind believes that law dictates decisions in particular cases independently of the facts; one cannot even classify a case without making factual assumptions about what goes on in the world. Formalists assume that facts need to be established in order to justify judicial decisions. Their idea that legal justifications are deductive concerns the arguments for judicial conclusions only *after* factual premises have been established.

Even after consideration of these elementary points, something clearly remains of the instrumentalists' concern about formalism's dependence on logic. They seem to argue that formalists make a pretense of deducing decisions from the law when the law does not, in fact, support those deductions. Alternatively, formalists are deluded by their theory into thinking that they can rely solely on law, and they stretch the law in order to do so. But concepts are not so precise and legal norms are not so wide as to cover every case that does arise. According to instrumentalists, there are gaps within the law that formalists do not recognize.

This is not only a complaint about "formalistic" adjudication, but also a reflection of the differences in legal theory previously discussed. It is partly definitive of formalism that it regards law as complete and univocal, and partly definitive of instrumentalism that it regards the law as, at best, incomplete. This brings us back to the differences between formalism and instrumentalism, which first led us into this thicket of logical theory. Now that we have emerged from the undergrowth, what can we say about the third aspect of formalistic theory? Do instrumentalists reject the formalistic model of legal justification, as their complaints about formalism's excess use of logic might lead one to suspect?

The instrumentalists might be interpreted as maintaining that deductive, syllogistic argument is fine, as far as it goes. Unfortunately, it won't take us far enough to reach the conclusion that formalists desire – namely, that law is complete and univocal. The law, instrumentalists would say, simply does not extend so far. If we are faithful to the texts provided by the authoritative sources, we find that they are vague and sometimes conflicting, subject to alternative interpretations, and therefore incapable of supporting logically adequate, conclusive arguments for judicial decisions in all cases.

There is some reason to interpret instrumentalist criticism in this way, even though it commits the instrumentalists to questionable philosophical assumptions. One reason is that these assumptions are quite commonly made, especially within "tough-minded" legal theory, such as instrumentalists claim to possess. This interpretation also makes moderate instrumentalism parallel to legal positivism, just as philosophical pragmatism, which seems to underlie instrumentalism, is parallel to the traditional empiricism that seems to underlie positivism.

The general picture of these two theories we then get may be stated as follows. Moderate instrumentalists and positivists alike embrace a source-based conception of the law as well as a formalistic model for legal justification; partly *because* of this combination, they reject the formalistic notion that law is complete and univocal. Instrumentalists, like positivists, emphasize that because the interpretation of authoritative legal texts and their application to cases are often controversial, reasonable arguments are often possible on both sides of a legal issue. Since there are no hard and fast rules for adjudicating such disputes, positivists conclude that law in such cases is indeterminate – not yet fully formed, needing judicial legislation. Instrumentalists most likely have a similar view of the law. They assume that law is determinate on an issue at a given time only if its identification and application are, roughly speaking, mechanical. Hence, law is gappy and incomplete, and judicial discretion must be exercised and law created in hard cases. Thus, rather than rejecting the formalistic model of legal justification, they merely insist on its limitations.

This sort of view is so widely accepted today that it is important to understand its presuppositions and limitations. The instrumentalists make the decisive assumption that law is not determinate if it is controversial, for law is thought to be gappy and indeterminate only when reasonable legal arguments are possible on both sides of a legal question. That occurs, however, just when the content of law is controversial – when competent lawyers can reasonably disagree about it. It relates to the formalistic model of legal justification in the following way: When law is controversial in the sense that reasonable legal arguments are possible on both sides of a point of law, then the law *cannot* be identified and interpreted mechanically by means of deductive, syllogistic arguments. Considerations must be weighed on both sides of the issue, and there is no rule fixing how that must be done. Hence, deductive logic cannot govern the justificatory arguments that are then made.

This reasoning exposes a more fundamental assumption of formalism, instrumentalism, and positivism: Nondeductive reasoning is incapable of adequately establishing any conclusion. Perhaps the assumption should instead be articulated as follows. If, in principle, it is impossible to prove a proposition by presenting it as the conclusion of a sound deductive argument – that is, where true premises absolutely entail the conclusion – then there is no such fact as the one ostensibly represented by the proposition. Taken as a general claim, this is either an idle philosophical prejudice or else represents very radical doubt about the possibility of knowledge. For, as we have already observed, the most respectable conclusions of the "hardest" of the sciences always logically outstrip the evidence and other considerations used to establish them. Such conclusions are never decisively proven in a logically water-tight manner. Therefore, when we claim to know what they assert, it is conceivable that we are mistaken. The view under consideration takes this to imply that in such cases there is no natural fact corresponding to the scientific conclusion. It is not that we are liable to be mistaken, but that there is nothing to be mistaken about.

This reading of instrumentalism is supported by the similarity between its underlying philosophical empiricism and the philosophical views that appear to underlie legal positivism. Empiricism can be understood to claim that what we can know about the world must be discovered by the use of our ordinary senses. But both British Empiricism, which is the dominant influence behind legal positivism, and American philosophical pragmatism generally assume a particular version of this theory that regards what goes on in the world as ultimately "reducible" to "hard" observable facts by means of rigorous entailments or deductive logical relations. Applied to physics, for example, this version of empiricism has led some philosophers to maintain that there "are" no sub-atomic particles such as electrons, at least not in the full-blooded sense in which there "are" particle accelerators such as synchrotrons. This is so because only the latter are perceived "directly." Therefore, sub-atomic particles have no more substance than the physical evidence for them, such as configurations on a photographic plate taken from a cloud chamber.

This version of empiricism is compatible with a source-based conception of law combined with a formalistic model for legal justifications. The "hard data" are the authoritative texts and their literal implications. The "four corners" of such texts, stretched only to include their most literal implications, represent the limits of real, determinate law. All the rest is mere "theory."

D. Does law go beyond the texts?

If the preceding discussion is accurate, formalism and instrumentalism share two out of three central doctrines, and we can account for the instrumentalists' contention that formalism stretches the law to create implications where no clear implications can honestly be found. Given their mutual assumptions, the instrumentalists seem to have the superior position. If we conceive of law as so thoroughly determined by authoritative texts, as both schools of legal thought appear to do, it seems implausible to suppose that law is complete and univocal, for the texts are not collectively univocal, and are often unclear.

We need not rest on the above assumptions, however; instead, we need to ask why we should conceive of law in such a way. Perhaps it is inescapable. After all, the texts are taken as authoritative, and the texts admittedly have somewhat uncertain implications. But we can move too quickly here. We cannot derive such significant conclusions about *law* from such innocent facts about *texts* unless we make certain assumptions about what law is. In other words, we can jump from the verbal limits of authoritative texts (such as statutes and records of judicial decisions) to the gappiness of law *only if we assume that law is fundamentally a lin-*

guistic entity, that law is exhausted by the formulations of such texts and their literal implications.

This assumption may be questioned once it is identified. After all, the law is not just a collection of words. Why must we limit ourselves to thinking about the substantive content of the law in terms of its authoritative words and their literal implications? The obvious explanation is that law is a human artifact, fashioned with words like those in the authoritative texts. The words are not the beginning and end of the law – law is a social institution, too – but they represent its normative content. Whatever content the law has, it has because of what we have put into it.

It is important to recognize that this theory represents not just a source-based conception of the law, but one that is bound by the formalistic model for legal justification. Its general appeal rests to some extent on the tacit assumption that nondeductive arguments are somehow suspect, so that we cannot derive law from authoritative texts using anything but literal readings and strict implications. This opinion hardly comports with our most respected intellectual practices outside the law, but doubt about the theory need not rest entirely on such analogies.

The question we must face is whether it is reasonable to maintain that law goes beyond the authoritative texts and their strictly deduced implications. The following argument suggests that this position is tenable.[9] The point is not to establish an alternative conception of the law, but rather to show that alternative conceptions are feasible and that the doctrines we have found embedded in both formalism and instrumentalism are themselves just theories about the law which are neither self-evident nor self-certifying, but require substantial justification.

One need not unqualifiedly endorse the following argument to recognize its point. It involves what are sometimes called "vague standards" in the law. The due process clause is an example. Calling it a "vague standard" suggests that the due process clause is mainly an empty vessel waiting to be filled with doctrines supplied by covertly legislative activities of courts. This is the view I wish to challenge. In so doing, I shall ignore the complication that decisions based on the clause today must take into account past judicial treatments of it. The point of ignoring such authoritative interpretations is that it provides the central reading around which other factors must be understood to turn. For example, it may be customary to read the due process clause in terms of the "intentions" of the Framers. This would have to be acknowledged in any final decision about how to interpret and apply the clause today. That partic-

---

[9]   This argument is adapted from R. Dworkin, *Taking Rights Seriously* 131–37 (1978).

ular approach, however, is to be considered here *only* as a direct reading of the clause itself. The due process clause is most naturally read to prohibit the government from doing certain things to a person in the absence of fair procedures. Once this is agreed, we can focus on the requirement of fair procedures.

Why should we think the due process clause vague? Perhaps because it does not tell us what is fair. The criteria of fairness are not to be found within the four corners of the text, nor can they be inferred from it. We must go beyond the text to determine what the clause prohibits, if indeed it can be understood to prohibit anything – if it is determinate enough to do that.

One thing is certain. The clause concerns fairness, not something else, such as economic efficiency. That it requires fair procedures is all but explicit – what else could "due process" mean? Only a wild theory could support the claim that the clause requires procedures to be economically efficient. Hence, the clause must have some meaning – at least enough to tell us what it is about, thus excluding some other possibilities.

Let us pursue the analogy with economic efficiency. Imagine a law that requires some activity to be "economically efficient" without defining economic efficiency. How could a court apply it? First, the text would have to be understood as assuming that there is such a thing as economic efficiency; that it makes sense to suppose that certain activities are economically efficient and that some are not; that some judgments about efficiency are true and others are false; and that criteria of efficiency are determinable in principle, at least in specific contexts. A court applying such a requirement must therefore identify appropriate criteria of economic efficiency. It will soon discover that there are alternative conceptions of efficiency; it must weigh the relative merits of those alternative conceptions as well as their relevance to the specific context at hand. It must then proceed on the assumption that in each context, some conception is most appropriate. But the court might find this assumption indefensible. It might find that there is absolutely no reason to prefer one specific conception of efficiency to another in the particular context. If so, assuming the two equally tenable conceptions are not practically equivalent, the court must make an arbitrary selection.

Suppose, however, that did not happen. Suppose the court concludes that some specific conception of economic efficiency is the most appropriate, at least for the specific context in question. It must then attach that conception to the law, providing the law with more content than it had originally, but not so that it would be legislating freely. That is, if there really are reasons for preferring one conception of economic efficiency to others in a given context, the assumption of the law in question would be true; if the court correctly identifies and applies that conception, it is simply carrying out its legal mandate. It would be faithful to the text, but it would not be limited to the four corners of the text and its literal implications.

To reach a preferred interpretation, the court must consider economic theory. If economic theory provides a correct answer to the court's question, it cannot be arrived at mechanically. Therefore, the court's justificatory argument for its interpretation cannot be mechanical. This leads us to the main point of the argument: A judicial decision need not be limited to the words of the authoritative texts and their literal implications in order to be based firmly on those sources.

Moreover, a court could make a mistake in such a case. If, in a given case, a single best criterion of economic efficiency exists, but the court instead adopts another, its reading of the law would be mistaken, for it would have incorrectly applied the economic efficiency requirement. There is, however, nothing problematic in the idea that even the highest court within a jurisdiction can make a legal mistake (or so we must agree if we do not swallow the most extreme rule skepticism of the radical realists).

Let us return to the due process clause example. Just as a court in the preceding hypothetical would have to defend a particular conception of economic efficiency, a court applying the due process clause must defend a particular conception of fairness suitable to the case in order to ensure fidelity to the clear meaning of the text at hand. No such conception, no principle of fairness, is implicit in the clause. But it does not follow that a court that goes beyond the four corners of the text and its literal implications is not doing precisely what the Constitution requires – no more, and no less.

If the due process clause requires that certain procedures be fair, courts cannot adhere to it if there is no such thing as a fair procedure. It makes no sense to require that procedures be fair unless one believes that such procedures exist – that is a presupposition of the clause. The only plausible reading of the clause, judging from the text, is that this is what the Framers must have assumed. Anyone who takes seriously the task of applying that part of the law must share this assumption.

One could not follow the law literally if its presupposition were false – that is, if there were no such thing as a fair procedure. We are in no position, however, to assume that there is no such thing as a fair procedure. We seem quite capable of distinguishing clearly fair procedures from clearly unfair procedures. It may be difficult to articulate fully the criteria by which we make such judgments, but much has been written on the subject, and one could begin there for help.

Some theorists profess to believe that there is really no such thing as a fair procedure because moral judgments are inherently, inescapably, unavoidably, and irremediably arbitrary. It is not just that people can easily make mistakes in this area, or that people tend to "rationalize" their prejudices in the pejorative sense. Instead, the very distinction between sound and unsound moral judgments is untenable. Such thought represents the most radical kind of moral skepticism.

Some instrumentalists have flirted with this notion, though it hardly comports with their own notions of what judges ought or ought not to do, which they present as defensible. In any event, radical moral skepticism seems an unsuitable attitude for a judge, because it requires both cynicism and hypocrisy. It is questionable what significance a moral skeptic can attach to an undertaking of fidelity to law or to the idea that a judge must justify his judgments. Of course, most if not all of those who regard themselves as "tough-minded" moral skeptics limit this to abstract theoretical pronouncements, which are dissociated from their reasoned use of moral concepts in other contexts and their acceptance of responsibilities.

If we do not approach the due process clause encumbered by the burdens of moral skepticism, how must we understand it? The general approach is clear: One must defend a particular conception of fairness and apply it. One might get it right and then be faithful to the law, not only in aspiration but also in decision. Alternatively, a court might get it wrong because it has committed a significant error of moral theory. Assuming that there is a right answer to the moral question, there is a correct reading of the clause. This reading is faithful to the text even though it is not limited by the four corners of the document and the literal implications of the text. Because such an answer could not be arrived at by deducing it from fixed premises, a court's justificatory argument for its interpretation of the clause cannot be mechanical.

This method of understanding the due process clause and other "vague standards" may be contrasted with two others. One is to assume that the clause must be understood in terms of certain examples of fair and unfair procedures that the Framers accepted or would have been prepared to accept upon reflection. Another is to interpret it in terms of current popular conceptions of fair procedures. There may, of course, be good reasons for adopting such approaches to understanding legal provisions. One must recognize, however, that if the due process clause literally requires fair procedures, then these approaches are theory laden in very significant ways. Adopting either approach involves either a departure from the text or a theory of what fair procedures are or how they can be determined.

Take the latter case. The due process clause requires that certain procedures be fair. To apply it by asking what procedures the Framers would have considered "fair" requires the assumption that fair procedures *are* whatever the Framers believed them to be. To apply it by asking what procedures would popularly be credited as fair amounts to the assumption that fair procedures *are* whatever popular opinion suggests they are. Such criteria of fairness are implausible. The due process clause assumes that there is such a thing as fairness; this is not the same as some particular individuals' conception of fairness, which might be mistaken. We therefore cannot use one of these approaches to such a clause without a powerful theory to support it.

The original approach suggested, which involves the application of an appropriate conception of justice, does not avoid theory. It proposes that courts must engage in theoretical deliberations in order to be faithful to the text and carry out its legal mandate. If that is right, then a source-based conception of the law does not commit one to the formalistic model of legal justification; it is, in fact, incompatible with that narrow view of legal reasoning. It follows that the formalistic model, which seems fundamental to both formalism and instrumentalism, is untenable. What the law has to say about a legal matter is not limited to the literal reading of and strict deductions from authoritative texts. Only a radical moral skeptic can avoid this conclusion, but such a skeptic would have no clear understanding of judicial responsibilities.

Finally, consider the issue of completeness – the one that seems most directly to divide this pair of legal theories. We have no clear idea why formalism regards law as complete, but we do have some idea about instrumentalism's opposite conclusion. So far as instrumentalism regards the law as gappy because it interprets legal sources by means of a formalistic model, its conclusion is unwarranted. If law is incomplete, it is not simply because we must go beyond the texts. For the law sometimes mandates, in effect, that we go beyond the text not only to find the facts, but also to unveil those further considerations that help make up the law on a particular subject.

II
INSTRUMENTALISM AND JUDICIAL PRACTICE

One of the preoccupations of instrumentalists has been judicial practice. According to Summers, "their critique of formalist legal method may be their most important single achievement."[10] I shall conclude with a brief review of this critique and its relations to theoretical doctrines like those we have discussed.

---

[10] Summers, *supra* note 1, at 909.

Summers mentions several charges of judicial malpractice that instrumentalists lay at the door of formalists. They abuse logic, overgeneralize case law, artificially distinguish cases, introduce legal fictions instead of facing up to the need for judicial legislation, and fail to decide cases in light of community policy.[11] These charges have varying connections with general theory – connections that the instrumentalists appear to have exaggerated. Several, but not all, seem related to differences of doctrine. If we are correct that formalists believe the law provides a complete decision procedure, while instrumentalists deny it, then this disagreement underlies some of the charges of judicial malpractice. For instrumentalists believe there is sometimes insufficient legal basis for decisions when judges they regard as formalists purport to find such bases in the law. Thus, it is natural to expect the instrumentalists' criticism that formalistic judges overgeneralize case law and otherwise overextend the law by introducing fictions and ignoring community policy.

The latter point reminds us that instrumentalists embrace a particular normative theory, which they do not always balance successfully against their acknowledgement of existing law. If instrumentalists believe that decisions unsupported by existing law should be made in light of community policy, then they have two bases for disagreement with judges who decide cases differently. First, others may believe that the law provides sufficient basis for deciding cases that instrumentalists believe require judicial legislation. Second, they may believe that grounds other than community policy legitimate decisions that the law does not adequately determine. Instrumentalists, with a naive utilitarian outlook, seem to assume that no other normative theory is rationally tenable – all other views reflect either a disguised consideration of the consequences of decisions on the interests of those affected, or some superstitious form of valuation. Such an attitude, however, leads inexorably to the extreme realism of the radical fringe of instrumentalism, because it leaves no room for the notion that past legislative and judicial decisions demand some measure of respect even if their guidance is not optimific. To insist on maximum promotion of satisfactions and on deference to past authoritative decisions only when that deference could reasonably be expected to have such optimific consequences is to deny that courts are bound in the slightest degree by statutes or precedent. One cannot have it both ways; one must either go with the radical realists or drop such naive utilitarianism. But if naive utilitarianism is surrendered, the charge of failure to decide cases in light of community policy is limited to cases in which the law provides insufficient basis for decision. "Community pol-

11   *Id.* at 910–13.

icy" thus becomes shorthand for "whatever standards are properly applied in such a case." Hence, the issue between formalists and instrumentalists reduces once again to that of completeness or incompleteness in the law. The question thus becomes whether and when the law provides no basis for decision, and what standards then properly apply.

Instrumentalistic criticism of "formalist legal method" sometimes does reflect theoretical disagreement, but not always very clearly. For example, consider, in light of Summers's imaginary example,[12] the criticism that formalistic judges "abuse logic." The majority of a court holds that a child cannot collect damages from negligent individuals as compensation for injuries received during its period in utero. The court's argument is elegant: (1) this child had no rights that could have been violated, because (2) the capacity to possess legal rights presupposes the capacity to have legal duties, and (3) an unborn child cannot have legal duties. The instrumentalist judge argues in dissent that (4) an unborn child can have legal rights without legal duties, because (5) "we as judges can alter these concepts as we desire to serve useful goals";[13] since there was a negligently caused injury, room can and must be made within the law for compensation through civil liability.

Before we examine the specific charge that logic is "abused" by the majority's decision, we should note that if we take these arguments at face value, they *agree* that the law speaks clearly about this particular case. The majority supports its decision with an argument that the dissenter does not dispute. Instead, *the dissenter advocates changing the law*. There is no need to "alter" the relevant legal concepts unless they lead to a decision that the dissenter believes should not be reached. Therefore, at least on the surface, the disagreement concerns whether to change the law by judicial legislation. Before addressing this issue, let us analyze these opinions more closely.

The majority claims that capacity for legal rights presupposes capacity for legal duties, which it characterizes as a kind of "symmetry." This is supposed to represent a "formalistic" attitude, because formalists are supposed to prize such aesthetic values and read the law as embodying them.[14] That sounds silly; perhaps we can make it seem a bit more plausible.

First, formalists are supposed to regard the law as complete. If, as we have argued, this means going beyond the authoritative texts and their literal implications, it must involve elaboration of the law on the basis of some theory of how to understand it. Constraints that any such theory

---

[12] *Id.* at 910–11.   [13] *Id.* at 910.
[14] *Id.*

would have to respect include precisely those that Summers mentions, namely "coherence, harmony, and consistency with existing law."[15] However law is read beyond the four corners of the texts, as an elementary matter of theory-construction it must respect those texts and develop systematically. In other words, these values are not vices but virtues once it is agreed that law extends beyond the four corners of the texts. Unfortunately, this way of working out the implications of the law does not adapt itself to the formalistic model for legal justifications. Formal logic alone will not generate such theory-based extensions of the texts. Therefore, logic must be abused if it is made to serve the illusion that the texts can be so stretched.

Second, the alleged symmetry exemplified in the majority's second claim is a familiar extension of a real symmetry embedded in normative systems. It is often asserted that rights and duties (or obligations) are "correlative," and there are cases in which this appears undeniable.[16] If Alex owes Basil five dollars, then (1) Basil has a right to payment of five dollars from or on behalf of Alex and (2) Alex has a duty (is under an obligation) to pay Basil five dollars. The corresponding right and duty are two sides of a single normative relation; they stand or fall together. Thus, it is plausible to claim that some pairs of rights and duties are logical or conceptual correlatives, and it would not be misleading to refer to this as a kind of "symmetry" in the law.

But not all alleged relations between rights and duties are like that. It may be contended, for example, that Alex himself cannot have rights without duties, in the sense that one has no valid claim against others unless one respects others' claims on one. Alex cannot legitimately claim any rights unless he lives up to his obligations and responsibilities. This could be characterized as a kind of "symmetry," but it is significantly different from the one discussed above. This sort of claim represents a substantive proposition of fairness, not a mere logical or conceptual correlation. This proposition is distorted, however, in the opinion of the majority on the court. Those who are incapable of assuming obligations or responsibilities cannot be regarded as irresponsible and, thus, to have forfeited any claim to have their rights respected. Hence, mental incompetents and new-born infants, for example, presumably possess rights that we are bound to respect, despite their inability to reciprocate. The law apparently respects this moral proposition, because both mental incompetents and new-born infants presumably possess, for example, the right not to be deprived of life without due process of law, although they

[15] *Id.* at 867 n.4, item 5.
[16] This idea is discussed in Lyons, "The Correlativity of Rights and Duties," 4 *Nous* 45 (1970).

lack the capacity for legal duties. If that is correct, then the majority's decision is based on a false principle – an imaginary symmetry – and its conclusion cannot be sustained.

If the argument thus far is right, and the majority's "symmetry" proposition is mistaken, is the majority guilty of "an abuse of logic"? That charge seems misleading or confused. Given the court's assumptions, its conclusion follows by the strictest logic. The dissenter is in no position to claim it is an abuse of logic, because he accepts both the majority's assumptions and its reasoning and only wishes to circumvent the proceeding by changing the law. If the decision is wrong, it is wrong either because its premises are false, as suggested above, or, as the dissenter urges, the decision is so objectionable that a responsible court should take the law into its own hands and change it. Logic itself, however, is neutral with respect to all these issues. Of course, it might be imagined that the very quest for "symmetry" involves an abuse of logic. But that would be mistaken – logic argues only for such symmetries as logic guarantees. Because the sort of symmetry predicated by the majority involves a substantive point of fairness, which it overextends, logic is silent on the matter.

Moreover, formalism as we understand it cannot be blamed for the specific decision of the court in this case. Formalistic judges assume that the law is determinate in all cases, and if they are mistaken, they will read the law as determinate when in fact it is not. Formalists, therefore, may stretch the legal facts, but this leads in no particular direction. If one is going to discover illusory "symmetries" in the law, there is no telling what one might claim to find. The quest for symmetry is too vague a basis for fixing formalistic judges in any particular direction.

One might contend that the clash between formalist and instrumentalist judges is more social than theoretical. Formalism is often characterized as politically and economically "conservative." It has been associated with judicial decisions that secure the interests of the economically powerful against those who suffer at their hands. The trouble with this interpretation of formalism is that it has no causal connection with the type of theory we have described. Some aspects of our law tend to favor the powerful against those who would encroach on their established rights, but other aspects tend to favor those whose rights are violated by the rich and powerful. If formalism systematically favors one side over the other, that is not because it favors symmetries or imagines the law to be more complete than it actually is. Rather, it is because the individuals who compose that group are biased and possibly dishonest, though perhaps as dishonest with themselves as with the community at large. This is not to deny that legal battles reflect economic struggles, or that legal theory can be politically motivated. What the critics of formalism fail to demonstrate, however, is that formalism is especially related to one side of these battles, or that instrumentalism is especially related to the other side.

The instrumentalists' criticism of the imaginary decision discussed above is worth probing further, for such criticism appears faithful to the instrumentalist tradition and reveals some difficulties for its practitioners. The instrumentalist dissenter claims that "we as judges can alter these concepts as we desire to serve useful goals." If we take the dissenter at his word, his criticism has the following implications: The majority's premise that capacity for rights assumes capacity for duties is a true proposition of law; the court has the capacity to make it false by changing the law; and such modification is perfectly proper. Thus, on a literal level, the dissenter must be understood as arguing either that changing the law in order to serve useful goals is *authorized by law* or that the court *should act unlawfully*. Assuming that instrumentalists do not typically call on courts to act unlawfully, we should probably understand them as supposing that the law empowers courts to act as courts of equity. This is an interesting proposition, but it may not be what is really meant; its literal meaning readily can be doubted.

Recall our discussion of the formalistic model of legal justification, which, together with the source-based view of law, led to the idea that law consists of whatever can be read from authorized texts or is literally implied by them. I argued earlier that this cannot be assumed to exhaust "the law," because an adequate account of what the law requires and allows may take us beyond the four corners of its texts. Hence, we can understand the idea of *changing a legal concept* (*e.g.,* to effect equity), which the dissenter prefers, in two ways: as a matter of adjusting our understanding of the law by going beyond a doctrinaire or literal reading of it (which may be inadequate), or as a matter of changing law by neglecting some binding considerations or introducing others without adequate legal basis. If the latter is what the instrumentalist dissenter has in mind, he is calling on the court to act unlawfully. If he has the former notion in mind, however, then he desires not so much a change in the law as a change in our understanding of it.

I doubt that the latter is the appropriate interpretation of the dissenter's opinion; it would be more characteristic of an instrumentalist to maintain that the law on the subject is really indeterminate. In that case, we cannot read the dissenting opinion literally. The dissenter does not believe that the court should "alter these concepts as we desire to serve useful goals," but instead he believes that the law needs to be shaped because it is not yet capable of deciding the case at hand. Because he believes the court is engaged in a legislative activity (which is not just a matter of correcting an inadequate understanding of existing law), the dissenter urges the court to serve useful goals. If that is what the dissenter means to say, then his criticism of the majority opinion is poorly framed, at best.

In sum, if we take the instrumentalist at his word, he is urging the court to ignore existing law and illegally change it. If we take him in some other way suggested by his general position, then we find his comments at best hyperbolic and unilluminating. As I believe that Summers accurately captures the spirit and character of instrumentalist criticisms of formalistic legal practice, I must demur from his appraisal of those criticisms. Very little legal method can be traced to formalistic legal theory. Instrumentalist criticisms of judicial practices seem themselves to suffer from overgeneralization and logical confusion. Furthermore, instrumentalists appear to embrace a naively utilitarian normative theory, and their recommendations concerning judicial legislation are, accordingly, unreliable.

If my original suspicions were sound, formalism is a nontheory, developed by instrumentalists who see themselves as battling theory-laden judicial practice that ignores human values. Instrumentalism is itself half-formed out of radical empiricism, developed on the verge of skepticism toward theory as well as substantive values, including those with which it wishes to be identified. Ambivalence about theory, values, and the law itself runs right through instrumentalism. This makes that body of legal doctrine an accurate reflection of a significant stream of American thought.

4

Moral aspects of legal theory

This paper concerns the so-called separation of law and morals, and its place in legal theory. The subject is suggested by John Austin's famous remark, "The existence of law is one thing; its merit or demerit is another."[1] I shall refer to such a doctrine as the separation thesis, though one of the aims of this paper is to distinguish different ways in which the separation of law and morals can be conceived.

The separation thesis is regarded as a dividing line in legal theory: legal positivists are supposed to accept it and natural lawyers to reject it. Those who accept it seem to regard it as an important truism, neglect of which invites both moral and theoretical confusion.

The meaning of the separation thesis, as suggested by Austin's remark, may seem perfectly clear, and this may explain why the doctrine has received little systematic attention. The most extensive discussion is provided by H. L. A. Hart in his valuable Holmes lecture,[2] which defends the doctrine along with legal positivism. Hart's approach has been widely adopted. However, his formulation of the thesis appears to be falsified by his own arguments, and his discussion suggests other versions of the doctrine, with widely divergent implications.

Critics of positivism have not helped much to clarify the issues. Lon Fuller's reply to Hart,[3] for example, suggests considerable confusion, and Ronald Dworkin's critical discussions of positivism,[4] which seem to have some bearing on the matter, fail to address it clearly.

The separation thesis is ambiguous, and its foundations are unclear. It

"Moral Aspects of Legal Theory," *Midwest Studies in Philosophy* 7 (1982): 223–54. Copyright © 1982 by University of Minnesota Press and reprinted with their permission. Earlier versions of this paper or of parts of it were presented at the University of Miami, the University of California, Riverside, Lycoming College, Cornell University, Oberlin College, and Mansfield State College. I am especially grateful for comments given on these and other occasions by John Bennett, Andrew Houston, Stephen Massey, Dale Oesterle, Gerald Postema, Robert Summers, and William Wilcox.

1   John Austin, *The Province of Jurisprudence Determined* (London, 1954), p. 184.
2   H. L. A. Hart, "Positivism and the Separation of Law and Morals," *Harvard Law Review* 71 (1958): 593–629 (referred to hereafter as Separation).
3   Lon Fuller, "Positivism and Fidelity to Law – A Reply to Professor Hart," *Harvard Law Review* 71 (1958): 630–72.
4   Ronald Dworkin, *Taking Rights Seriously* (Cambridge, Mass., 1978), chaps. 2–3.

turns out to be an unreliable test for jurisprudential allegiances. It lacks any regular relation to both natural law and legal positivism.

I distinguish a Minimal Thesis, which many have endorsed, from two other notions of the separation of law and morals. The Explicit Moral Content Thesis seems closely tied to positivism, but for reasons that are not entirely clear. The Expanded Thesis seeks to represent more faithfully the spirit of the Minimal Thesis.

1. THE MINIMAL SEPARATION THESIS

The claim that law and morals are separate invites confusion. What is meant by "morals," and what sort of "separation" is at issue? Some parts of the answer seem fairly clear. No one doubts that people have moral beliefs, some of which are widely shared, and that these affect and are influenced by the law. Nor does anyone doubt that officials such as judges draw upon moral ideas when interpreting, applying, or extending the law. Such interactions are not at issue.

A distinction introduced by Hart may be useful here, namely that between " 'positive morality,' the morality actually accepted and shared by a given social group," and "the general moral principles used in the criticism of actual social institutions including positive morality," which Hart calls "critical morality."[5] As a first approximation, we could say that the separation in question concerns critical, not positive, morality. The question is not whether law interacts with moral beliefs but whether law inevitably satisfies the moral conditions that it ought to satisfy.

The distinction between positive and critical morality suggests that critical morality consists of moral beliefs that are true, sound, or justified, whether or not they are accepted. But then a formulation of the separation thesis in terms of critical morality might be too narrow, or at least misleading. For some adherents of the separation thesis embrace conventionalistic conceptions of morality. Hart, for example, discusses moral rights and obligations as if they were creatures of social rules that reflect values which are widely shared in one's community.[6] This collapses the distinction between critical and conventional morality for rights and obligations – though only by endorsing conventionalistic truth conditions for certain moral judgments. Hart and other positivists have in any case been concerned with and have engaged in moral criticism of law. This

---

[5] H. L. A. Hart, *Law, Liberty, and Morality* (Stanford, 1963), p. 20.
[6] H. L. A. Hart, *The Concept of Law* (Oxford, 1961), pp. 80–88, 163–80. (This work is referred to hereafter as *Concept.*) Hart's discussions of morality, in *Concept* and other works, leave room for moral judgments that are not bound by conventional moral positions, but his treatment of claims about moral rights and obligations implies that their truth conditions are conventionalistic.

critical attitude does not ensure that there is one unique basis for soundly appraising law, but it does seem to assume that sound moral appraisal of law is possible and thus that moral judgments are not inherently arbitrary.

Some positivists do not have this view of morality and so may be understood to think of the relations between law and morality somewhat differently. Hans Kelsen, for example, seems to hold that law is a matter of objective fact but moral ideas are essentially arbitrary, so that law is independent of morality and can be understood without the use of moral judgment. Others who insist on the separation of law and morals are anxious to ensure that practicing lawyers advise clients reliably, which cannot be done if one assumes that law satisfies moral standards. These theorists do not seem to assume that moral judgments are capable of being sound. Therefore, if one wishes a formulation of the separation thesis that encompasses all these attitudes toward morality, one might hesitate to develop it in terms of critical morality.

Hart may attempt to cover the entire range of theoretical conceptions of morality to be found among those who endorse the separation thesis when he refers to what is at issue as a "distinction" between law and morals.[7] But this term is unhelpful. For law and morals could be distinct – two different things – even if they were connected in ways that positivists have been anxious to deny. Law and morals could be distinct, for example, even if nothing was law unless it was just and all rules that it was morally imperative to have enforced somehow automatically acquired the status of law. For this does not imply that all moral principles are incorporated into law or that all laws are derivable from moral principles. For that matter, law and morals could be distinct even if they were coextensive.

We need an idea stronger than that of a mere distinction to capture the essence of the separation thesis. In reflecting on the range of ways that law may be thought to be connected with (inseparable from) morals, Hart arrives at what appears to be his general formula for the separation thesis, "that there is no necessary connection between law and morals or law as it is and ought to be."[8]

This formula is not unambiguous. What sort of "necessary connection" might be relevant? If law and accepted morality influence each other, one would suppose there can be causally necessary connections between law and moral beliefs. But these seem irrelevant. So it is natural to suppose that the relevant sort of separation is conceptual. The separation

[7] See Separation, p. 594 and *passim*.
[8] Separation, p. 601, n. 25; compare *Concept*, p. 253.

MORAL ASPECTS OF LEGAL THEORY

thesis then becomes the doctrine that there is no conceptually necessary connection between law and morals or between law as it is and law as it ought to be.

But this formula will not do, as Hart himself appears to concede (he provides the argument but does not explicitly draw the relevant conclusion). Hart believes that one can extract a principle of justice from the mere concept of law.[9] He holds that the root idea of justice is expressed by the precept "Treat like cases alike." This requires interpretation, which must vary with the context. Hart contends that when the justice of a law or of a legal system is at issue, standards independent of the law must be invoked to determine whether the law respects those resemblances and differences that justice requires it to respect and prescribes the morally appropriate treatment of them – for (Hart seems to say) law is not necessarily just. But when the law is to be applied to particular cases, and justice in the application of the law is at issue, then, Hart holds, the law itself provides the proper basis for deciding which cases are to be treated alike, which are to be treated differently, and how cases are to be treated. Hart reasons that a system of law necessarily includes at least some general rules and that one who applies general rules is committed to treating like cases alike according to the standards laid down in those rules. Thus Hart claims to find implicit in the concept of law a principle of justice which requires officials to treat cases in the way the law requires. Justice in the application of the law to particular cases requires that officials act within the guidelines that are laid down by law. This applies even when the law is outrageously unjust, though in such cases, of course, the requirements of this principle may be outweighed by conflicting moral considerations. "So there is," Hart says, "in the very notion of law consisting of general rules, something which prevents us from treating it as if it is utterly neutral, without any contact with moral principles."[10]

I believe this argument is unsound: the conclusion is mistaken and the derivation is invalid. I do not believe there is a valid principle of justice that requires universal adherence to the law by officials without further conditions needing to be satisfied. Just as agreements can be so immoral as to prevent their being morally binding, the law can be so unjust as to prevent an official from acquiring even a "prima facie" (nonabsolute, overridable) obligation to be faithful to the law. This is admittedly a controversial claim. It seems clear, however, that Hart's argument is unsuccessful. Even if we assume that each principle of justice specifies some way of "treating like cases alike" and that general rules of law can be understood to specify ways of "treating like cases alike," we cannot val-

---

[9] Separation, pp. 623–24; compare *Concept,* pp. 155–57.   [10] Separation, p. 624.

idly infer that following the law involves respecting any principle of justice, that it involves treating like cases alike in one of the ways that justice requires. Hart's argument suggests that there is an analogy between applying law and acting justly, because he assumes that both can be understood in terms of acting on general rules or principles. But his argument shows no convergence between just action by officials and adherence to the law. And, if I am right about the limits of the putative principle of justice in the application of the law that he endorses, no argument can establish such a connection.[11]

But the immediate point is that, even if Hart's argument were sound and showed that there was at least one conceptually necessary connection between law and critical morality, it should not be taken as falsifying the separation thesis. For Hart's conclusion does not seem to touch the central idea of the thesis. Hart appears to acknowledge this when he observes that a legal system "might apply, with the most pedantic impartiality as between the persons affected, laws which were hideously oppressive, and might deny to a vast rightless slave population the minimum benefits of protection from violence and theft."[12] We can go further. Even if the concept of law were somehow capable of generating all the moral standards by which the law should be appraised, it would not follow that the law, or the officials charged with administering it, satisfied those standards. Some sorts of conceptually necessary connections between law and critical morality provide no threat to the separation of law and morals as positivists and others seem to have understood it. This may explain why Hart does not retract the separation thesis when he discerns a principle of justice in the concept of law and thus a "necessary connection" between law and morals.

But while Hart does not retract the separation thesis, neither does he provide a satisfactory formulation of it. I suggest the following as a starting point for our discussion: Law is subject to moral appraisal and does not automatically satisfy whatever standards may properly be used in its appraisal. I believe that this expresses the minimal idea that defenders of the separation thesis wish to endorse. I shall call it the Minimal Separation Thesis.

The Minimal Thesis (or something very much like it) may be acceptable not only to those who believe in critical morality but also to those who are agnostic on the matter. It may even be acceptable to radical moral skeptics. But if we ignore skeptical doubts about the possibility of there being any standards that may properly be used in the appraisal of

---

[11] I discuss this further in "On Formal Justice," *Cornell Law Review* 58 (1973): 833–61 [reprinted in this volume].

[12] Separation, p. 624; compare *Concept,* p. 202.

the law, we can load our formula more heavily in the opposite direction and say that law is subject to moral appraisal and does not automatically merit good marks. In brief: law is morally fallible.

The Minimal Separation Thesis, so understood, appears to be the basic doctrine that Hart defends (though it may not be the only one to which he is committed), and it is one that most partisans of the separation thesis would, I think, acknowledge as their own. This is shown by the fact that defenders of the separation thesis usually rest their case on the possibility of unjust, immoral, or otherwise bad law such as laws used to enforce chattel slavery or other forms of exploitation and invidious discrimination.

The nature of this argument is not entirely clear. On the one hand, it is sometimes suggested that the separation thesis merely reflects our ordinary ways of speaking about the law, which allow for the possibility of bad laws.[13] It reflects, in other words, what Hart calls the "wider" concept of law that we have, which does not impose moral conditions on what can count as a law, as opposed to a "narrower" concept that would impose such conditions but which we do not in fact have.[14] On the other hand, this argument does not proceed on the basis of some established analysis of the concept of law but seems to be regarded by legal positivists as a constraint on any acceptable analysis – as a condition that must be preserved by any plausible theory about the nature of law. Furthermore, the argument presupposes some consensus in moral judgment, for it does not proceed from some established theory of morality but rather calls our attention to clear, uncontroversial, and real examples of laws that fail to meet minimal moral requirements.

However this line of reasoning can be understood to work, it would seem to have very limited implications. From the premise that there are or can be bad laws, we cannot infer that there are, so to speak, no relevant necessary connections between law and critical morality – that there are no moral conditions on what can count as law. Many legal positivists appear to assume, for example, that the normative content of a given legal system (what the law of a community requires and allows) is equivalent to a set of legal rules. From some real examples of bad laws, one could not infer that all members of such a set are morally fallible. For all we can tell from such an argument, every legal system might incorporate some rules that are guaranteed to be morally defensible. The Minimal Thesis is therefore very weak, and in this respect it may fail to capture everything that is intended by defenders of the separation of law and morals. I shall later suggest an expansion of the Minimal Thesis, but

[13] Separation, pp. 620–21. [14] Concept, pp. 203–307.

meanwhile it will be useful to consider the Minimal Thesis in relation to both natural law and other aspects of legal positivism.

2. NATURAL LAW AND THE MINIMAL THESIS

The first point that needs to be made is that the Minimal Thesis fails to distinguish legal positivism from natural law. Aquinas, for example, quite plainly says, "Laws framed by man are either just or unjust,"[15] and Lon Fuller, one of the most prominent recent critics of legal positivism, never denies that laws can be unjust. Both writers acknowledge that human laws are morally fallible, and this seems to place no strain upon their general theories of law.

It may be worth expanding on this point. Aquinas is noted for his declaration, "Law is nothing else than an ordinance of reason for the common good, promulgated by him who has the care of the community."[16] It might be inferred that Aquinas means that nothing counts as an ordinary law, or as part of an ordinary legal system, unless it satisfies the appropriate moral standards. But to read Aquinas in this way would saddle him unnecessarily with inconsistent doctrines. One might read Aquinas in this way if one assumed, for example, that Aquinas's approach to legal theory is like Austin's, and that his general declaration corresponds to Austin's general analysis of law. Austin defines the genus law so that "positive law" – the category in Austin that corresponds to "laws framed by man" in Aquinas – is a species of that genus. But Aquinas's approach to legal theory is different. His most general characterization of law is meant to suggest the standards by which human conduct ought to be judged, as well as the standards to be used in appraising laws framed by humans. Not all laws framed by humans, but only those that are just, fall under Aquinas's general characterization of law.

And Aquinas's intentions seem clear. A central part of his purpose is to develop a theory about one's moral obligation to obey the law. Laws framed by humans "bind in conscience" when they are just, that is, when they serve the common good, distribute burdens fairly, show no disrespect for God, and do not exceed the lawmaker's authority. If laws framed by humans fail to satisfy these conditions, they are unjust and then they do not automatically "bind in conscience." One is morally bound to obey such a law only when circumstances happen to demand it, in order to

---

[15] Thomas Aquinas, *Summa Theologica*, I–II, Q. 96, Art. 4. The text used here is that in *Basic Writings of Saint Thomas Aquinas*, ed. Anton C. Pegis (New York, 1945), vol. 2. This passage is on p. 794 of that text, which is cited hereafter.

[16] *Ibid.*, p. 747 (Q. 90, Art. 4).

prevent scandal or disturbance.[17] So Aquinas does not deny the reality of unjust human laws. He acknowledges the moral fallibility of law.

Fuller considers himself a natural lawyer because he believes there are moral conditions on what can count as law. Fuller argues that the concept of law implies an "internal morality" which must be satisfied if we are to have a system that qualifies as law. Law is purposive: It is used to regulate behavior by telling people how they are expected to behave. Officials are not faithful to this purpose unless they lay down rules that are capable of being used by people to regulate their own behavior. Thus Fuller argues that the internal morality of law demands that laws be promulgated, clear, consistent, prospective, and otherwise possible to comply with, reasonably interpreted, and scrupulously adhered to by officials. To the extent that these conditions are not satisfied, a system lacks the quality of law and must be referred to by some other name.[18]

Up to a point, Fuller's ideas about the internal morality of law are remarkably like Hart's theory of justice in the application of the law to particular cases. Both writers claim to find moral principles implicit in the concept of law and thus to establish some necessary connections between law and morality. Fuller's argument also seems to fail. It amounts, I think, to the development of some elementary principles of social engineering. He claims that a system that deserves the name law contains rules that are followable, but he fails to show that unfollowable rules are morally deficient or, most important, that the grounds for regarding such rules as morally deficient (as opposed to ineffective guidelines for behavior) can be extracted from the concept of law. Fuller relies on our common assumption that it is unfair to penalize individuals for conduct that they could not help doing or that they had no reason to believe would be punishable, but he gives us no reason to suppose that this conception of fairness is implicit in the concept of law.[19]

In any case, Fuller acknowledges that in other respects laws do not always meet the minimum requirements of morality. While he holds that systems with internal morality tend to have better law, he does not deny that such systems can have bad laws.[20] He too accepts the Minimal Separation Thesis.

---

[17]   *Ibid.*, pp. 794–95 (Q. 96, Art. 4).
[18]   Fuller, "Positivism and Fidelity to Law," pp. 660, 664–65. This view is developed further in Fuller, *The Morality of Law* (New Haven, 1964), chap. 2.
[19]   I discuss this more fully in "The Internal Morality of Law," *Proceedings of the Aristotelian Society* 71 (1970–71): 105–19 [reprinted in this volume].
[20]   Fuller, "Positivism and Fidelity to Law," pp. 636, 645; *The Morality of Law*, chap. 4.

3. ANALYTIC JURISPRUDENCE
AND THE MINIMAL THESIS

Since the Minimal Separation Thesis is not the exclusive property of legal positivism, does it nevertheless have some special relation to positivistic thinking about the law? Is it implicit, for example, in other general doctrines that define legal positivism? If so, we would have reason to conclude that positivism offers a distinctive rationale for this doctrine.

Individual positivists have had specific theories about the nature of law that might warrant their support of the Minimal Separation Thesis. If law is believed to be determined by conditions such as Austin or Hart identified, for example, then one might well be justified in thinking that law is morally fallible. Take Austin as a case in point. Austin claims that something is required by law just when it is coercively commanded by some determinate individual or set of individuals whose coercive commands are generally complied with by the members of a community and who does not generally comply with the coercive commands of any other human being. This imposes no recognizably moral conditions on what can count as law, and Austin clearly intends his theory to allow that laws be either just or unjust.

It seems reasonable to suppose that Austin is right – that such coercive commands might be either just or unjust. But we must be careful here, since this does not follow from the Austinian analysis alone. For all we can tell so far, the conditions that determine when something is required by law might imply conditions that determine when something is good, right, just, or the opposite. We need more than a theory of law to generate the separation thesis. We need some information about the relations between the conditions that are supposed to determine law and the conditions that determine moral value. I shall return to this point a bit later.

Even if we could infer a separation thesis from specific theories of law, such as Austin's, that would not provide us with the answer to our original question, which concerned the relations between legal positivism as a general type of theory and that doctrine. We need to consider what is distinctive of and also common to positivistic thinking about the law.

It is not easy to define legal positivism, to identify its central tenets or assumptions. Hart offers us some help when he surveys several doctrines that have been associated with positivism. He points out that some are not accepted by all positivists. The residue might help us understand what positivism represents.

Hart's survey includes the following five doctrines: (1) the imperative theory of law, or the idea that law is a coercive command; (2) the separation of law and morals; (3) a distinction between the analytic study of legal concepts (which we can call analytic jurisprudence) and other studies of law, such as inquiries concerning the history of law, the relation between law and other social phenomena, and the normative standards to be used in appraising law; (4) formalism, or mechanical jurisprudence, which holds that a given body of law at a given time is capable of providing a unique answer to every legal question that arises and "in which correct legal decisions can be deduced from predetermined legal rules by logical means alone"; (5) moral skepticism, or the idea that "moral judgments cannot be established, as statements of fact can, by rational argument, evidence or proof."[21]

Three of these doctrines cannot be used to define legal positivism. The imperative theory of law, though advanced by Bentham and Austin, is rejected by Hart and other positivists; few positivists have been moral skeptics; and few, if any, positivists endorse mechanical jurisprudence.

The only two doctrines that survive Hart's survey are the separation thesis and the distinction between analytic jurisprudence and other inquiries concerning law. These are accepted by Hart and, apparently, by positivists generally. But these two doctrines seem incapable of defining a school of legal theory. They tell us little about the law or how to go about understanding it. Hart's survey seems to leave the idea of legal positivism with too little content. Is there anything else that we can add?

One point that Hart fails to mention is what might be called the social conception of law. This idea, which seems central to legal positivism, is, very roughly, the notion that law is firmly rooted in social facts. Let us add this to our list and consider its relations to the separation thesis.

First let us consider the relations between the Minimal Separation Thesis and analytic jurisprudence. The latter is concerned with distinctively legal concepts, including the concept of law itself, as well as the nature and essential structure of legal systems. The idea that there can be such an inquiry, distinct from a study of, say, the standards that may be used in appraising law, tells us nothing about the separation of law and morals. And it would seem contrary to the spirit of such an inquiry to assume that law and other legal concepts have no significant connections with moral concepts. For that is precisely what such an inquiry is supposed to determine.

It is sometimes suggested that analytic jurisprudence must be value-neutral, but it is unclear what this should be taken to mean. It might mean that we should not enter upon such an inquiry with the assumption

---

[21] Separation, pp. 600–601, n. 25; compare *Concept,* p. 253.

that law has any special relations to morality. But neither should we assume the contrary. So far as the idea of analytic jurisprudence is concerned, the possibility of conceptual relations between law and morals is an open question.

The idea that analytic jurisprudence should be value-neutral might also be taken to mean that one can engage in the study of legal concepts without considering any substantive moral values. But it is unclear why one should wish to do this, especially if one wishes to determine whether there are any significant connections between law and morality.

Positivists have generally presented their theories of law as if they were trying to describe the concept of law, the essential nature of law, or something else similarly given. If one believes that morality is not similarly "given," one might think it appropriate to proceed by ignoring moral issues in the analytic study of law. But this would be mistaken, in two ways.

First, it would be a mistake to assume that morality, in the relevant sense, is not similarly "given." If there are true as well as false, correct as well as incorrect, sound as well as unsound answers to moral questions, then morality is as much a "given" as anything else that might be investigated. There seems no reason to assume the contrary here, and only a radical moral skeptic should be tempted to do so. Since moral skepticism is not a defining feature of legal positivism or a position endorsed by most positivists, this is not an approach that should be identified with positivistic theory.

Second, it may turn out that moral notions, or notions that are common to both law and morality, are needed for a proper understanding of law. Consider, for example, the idea of a justified judicial decision. This is a problematic notion, which may be given a weak or a strong interpretation. On the weak interpretation, justifying a legal decision is like placing a mere label on past or future conduct. It has no implications concerning how one should behave or should have behaved, beyond, perhaps, what considerations of prudence might determine. One whose past or future conduct has been so labeled may proceed, in good conscience, to ignore such declarations. On the strong interpretation, justifying a legal decision is establishing how someone should behave or should have behaved, in good conscience. On this interpretation, a justified judicial decision is not a morally neutral matter. To justify a decision, in the strong sense, one must appeal to considerations that are capable of determining how people should behave. If one assumes that a judicial decision can be justified only by appeal to law, justification in the strong sense requires that legal considerations be capable of determining how people should behave. They cannot be morally neutral.

74

Dworkin, for example, has such a view of law.[22] He regards law as a system with moral pretensions, since it claims to justify what it does to people as well as the judgments that it makes of their behavior. For this reason, Dworkin seems to hold, legal justification aspires to be justification in the strong sense, and it succeeds only if it provides such justification. This is not just a theory about how decisions ought to work, when viewed from a detached moral point of view, but involves a claim about how to understand the nature of judicial reasoning when it is most successful from a strictly legal point of view. Dworkin argues, for example, that only if we view the law in such a way will we be able to understand the judicial techniques of statutory interpretation and the use of judicial precedents.

Dworkin claims that moral values are implicated in judicial reasoning in two ways. It first assumes the idea of fairness in the sense of treating like cases alike. New cases must be dealt with on the basis of the same general considerations that determined how past cases were treated. Second, in identifying these general considerations one must go beyond the authoritative texts that emerged from past legislative and judicial decisions and be guided by their rationales and by the reasons for a system in which both legislation and judicial precedents have such authority. These underlying principles must fit together into a coherent system and reflect the deep values of the community, but they must also be capable of justifying (in the strong sense) decisions that are made in the name of the law.

This theory is not obviously sound, but neither is it obviously crazy. In order to appraise it, not only must one entertain possible connections between law and morals, but one's inquiry must be informed by an adequate understanding of the relevant moral values. One of the problems to be considered, for example, is the possible role of fairness in motivating judicial decisions. Dworkin appears to believe that considerations of fairness always argue that new cases be dealt with like past cases in all legal contexts. But it is not clear that this is so. If a legal system is not terribly unjust, both substantively and procedurally, then considerations of fairness may require that new cases be treated like past cases. But if the law of a community is sufficiently corrupt and past cases have been dealt with in a sufficiently immoral manner, then I think fairness cannot require that new cases be treated similarly, though the law may require it. One's view of this matter will turn on one's view about fairness, as well as the possibility that the only plausible account of the underlying rationales of past legislative and judicial decisions yields principles that

---

[22] Dworkin, *Taking Rights Seriously,* chap. 4.

are morally indefensible. It might turn out, in other words, that Dworkin does not succeed in showing that law presupposes the relevant moral values, but only that legal systems that satisfy some moral minima do so.[23]

It is worth mentioning that positivists typically suggest modes of thinking about the law that are not far removed from Dworkin's. I have in mind especially the way in which positivists distinguish between moral and legal concepts such as obligation. There is clearly a close relation between the concepts of legal justification and of legal obligation, since judgments of obligation are one of the principal subjects of judicial decisions.

The usual positivistic idea is that legal and moral obligations are conceptually distinct and have independent existence conditions. The necessary and sufficient condition for the existence of a legal obligation is that one be required or forbidden by law to behave in a certain way, and this is assumed to imply no moral conditions. But the typical mode of analysis of legal and moral obligations to be found in positivistic theory puts them on a par as two species of a single genus with parallel implications. If one is under an obligation, moral or legal, then one's behavior may be criticized accordingly. One may be held at fault for failing to live up to a legal obligation just as one may be held at fault in the moral case. Or one may be held to have a reason to behave in the way the law requires in just the same sense in which one may be held to have a reason to behave in the way that morality requires. The two reasons, modes of criticism, or obligations may be given different labels, but on these theories that seems to be the only difference between them.

When positivists think of legal obligations in this way, as strictly parallel to moral obligations, their thinking about the relations between law and morality reflects assumptions like those that underlie Dworkin's the-

[23] Dworkin's view is not entirely clear. In "Hard Cases" he assumes that a legal system (or the "political scheme" determined by the constitution) "is sufficiently just to be taken as settled for reasons of fairness" (*Taking Rights Seriously*, p. 106), but he also assumes that the relevant conditions were satisfied in Nazi Germany and are satisfied in contemporary South Africa (*ibid.*, pp. 326–27). Dworkin and I may differ about the conditions required for an argument from fairness. In any case, Dworkin does not assume that such considerations of fairness, represented by law, exhaust the relevant moral considerations to be taken into account by judges or other officials. They determine what counts as law, but sometimes a judge should not follow the law. [After this passage was written, Dworkin's view was clarified. He acknowledged that law's injustice can extinguish any justification for enforcement; see " 'Natural' Law Revisited," *University of Florida Law Review* 34 (1982): 186–87. The point is reaffirmed in *Law's Empire* (Harvard, 1986), where fairness is displaced by political "integrity," which argues for treating new cases like past cases, suitably interpreted. I examine *Law's Empire* in "Reconstructing Legal Theory," *Philosophy & Public Affairs* 16 (1987): 379–93.]

ory. It appears to be assumed that law, no less than morality, has a kind of legitimate authority to determine how we should behave and how we and our conduct may properly be appraised. I believe this is mistaken, and also that it is an inappropriate position for legal positivists to take. But my objections turn on substantive matters of moral theory and would not show that such an idea about the legitimate authority of law is unintelligible. This may perhaps reinforce the point that, although a theory like Dworkin's can reasonably be doubted, it cannot be discounted at the outset of an inquiry into the nature of law and its relations to morality. Furthermore, such theories cannot properly be appraised without the benefit of insight into moral as well as legal matters.

4. THE SOCIAL CONCEPTION OF LAW AND THE MINIMAL THESIS

Our next question is whether the separation of law and morals can be derived from the social conception of law. Our first task is to decide how the social conception of law is to be understood – the general idea, as distinct from specific theories that link law to specific social conditions.

The general idea is something like this: the existence and content of law is determined by some range of facts about human beings in a social setting – facts about their behavior, history, institutions, beliefs, and attitudes. The relevant range of facts may concern moral convictions, but we are concerned with such matters only so far as they are facts that happen to be relevant to what law is. Joseph Raz has expressed this general idea in the following way:

A jurisprudential theory is acceptable only if its tests for identifying the content of the law and determining its existence depend exclusively on facts of human behaviour capable of being described in value-neutral terms, and applied without resort to moral argument.[24]

Raz calls this the "strong social thesis," which can be seen to have two distinct parts. One is that law is determined by social facts; the other is that law is not determined by moral considerations. Let us take them in that order.

What if anything follows about the separation of law and morals from the idea that law is completely determined by facts about human behavior that are capable of being described in value-neutral terms? To answer this question, we must look at the possible relations between social facts on the one hand and law and morality on the other.

[24] Joseph Raz, *The Authority of Law* (Oxford, 1979), pp. 39–40.

According to the social conception of law described by Raz, law is completely determined by some range of facts. But Raz leaves open the nature of the relation between propositions of law and the relevant factual propositions. If one thinks of a theory about what law is as analyzing the concept of law, this relation is, presumably, conceptual, and the theoretical claims connecting propositions of law with relevant factual propositions will purport to be analytic truths. But one may wish to allow the possibility that a theory about law is not analytic but rather describes in most fundamental terms the basic features of law or of a legal system, so that the most general propositions of such a theory are synthetic, just as the most general propositions of a scientific theory may be classified as synthetic rather than analytic.[25] In either case, however, we may understand this sort of theory as claiming that law is determined by some range of social facts.

The same possible relations might obtain between social facts and moral judgments. If ethical "naturalism" in the narrow sense defined by G. E. Moore were correct, moral judgments would be entailed by factual propositions, which might well include facts about human beings in a social setting. But even if naturalism in this sense is incorrect, and no moral judgments are entailed by factual propositions, naturalism in a wider sense might be correct. Some moral principles would then be true, though they would not be true "by definition," and moral judgments would be determined by certain factual propositions. There is of course a third possibility, namely, that no factual propositions are capable of determining any moral value. This third possibility amounts to the truth of radical moral skepticism.

The social conception of law is compatible with each of these three possibilities, including both forms of ethical naturalism. There might be morality-determining facts as well as law-determining facts. And, so far as we can tell, law-determining facts might amount to or entail morality-determining facts. That is, the social facts that determine the existence and content of the law (if the social conception of the law is right) might be capable of supporting and might even entail moral judgments about the law and about conduct performed under the law. The social conception of law does not exclude this possibility. For this reason, the social conception of law seems to tell us nothing about the moral fallibility of law. For all it tells us, the very facts that determine the existence and content of law might also determine that law is always just or that it is always unjust.

---

[25] One might also wish to leave this matter open, of course, because of doubts about the contrast between analytic and synthetic statements, and especially the application of that distinction to the fundamental principles of a theory.

This conclusion does not depend on the abstractness of the social conception of law. The same results would follow if we considered any specific social conception of law, such as Austin's or Hart's. This is because the issue concerns not just the idea that law is determined by social facts but also the relations between facts and moral value. Since the social conception of law is silent on the relations between facts and moral value, it has no implications concerning the separation of law and morals. Without the benefit of moral theory we can draw no relevant conclusions.

If one believes that the separation of law and morals follows from the social conception of law, this is probably because of considerations like the following. Law is shaped by human actions and decisions and is subject to deliberate control by human beings. For example, we tend to think of law as shaped significantly by legislative and judicial decisions that are made by ordinary mortals. This may seem to lead directly to the separation thesis. Since human conduct is morally fallible, it is natural to suppose that law is likewise fallible.

It is worth mentioning, however, that this line of reasoning can probably be attributed to those natural lawyers who accept the moral fallibility of law. When they think of ordinary law in such terms, they are undoubtedly thinking of law as shaped by human actions and decisions and as subject to deliberate control by human beings. Human beings are fallible, and the law they develop is accordingly fallible too.

But this line of reasoning is too quick. Not everything that is shaped by human actions and decisions and that is subject to deliberate control by human beings is usually regarded as morally fallible in the way that law is. Machines, for example, are created and controlled by human beings, but they are not usually thought of as just or unjust. Nevertheless, we do sometimes think of human creations, such as life-saving inventions and instruments of destruction, in moral terms, at least as good or bad. But when we do, it seems clear that we assume some substantive moral notions, such as the value of human life, welfare, or dignity. What this suggests is that the social conception of law does not by itself entail the separation thesis, but that the argument linking them assumes some substantive moral values. We cannot even begin to understand why and how law is subject to moral appraisal without some substantive conception of what may be taken as relevant from a moral point of view. We prize human dignity, welfare, and fairness, and it is the conviction that these values are not automatically respected by the law that leads one to suppose that law is morally fallible.

I do not mean to suggest that such values are inherently arbitrary or incapable of rational defense. My point is that these values are not implicit in the idea that law is a social phenomenon. So the mere idea of law as social does not provide sufficient basis for inferring that law is morally fallible.

Let us turn now to the second part of Raz's strong social thesis, which claims that law is not determined by moral argument. Raz does not mean that legislation is never motivated by moral considerations, that courts never engage in moral reasoning, or that moral language is never found within the law. His point is that, once the law-determining facts have been taken into account, we have reached the outer boundaries of existing law. So, for example, when courts use moral arguments but are not simply deducing conclusions from moral ideas already placed within the law by legislative or judicial decisions, they must be understood as making new law.

This part of Raz's thesis is independent of the first, the social conception of law. For the thesis takes no stand on moral theory, so it must be compatible with ethical naturalism — the idea that moral value is determined by natural facts (which can presumably be described in value-neutral terms). But ethical naturalism entails that moral argument amounts at bottom to the marshaling of facts. The effect of adding the second part to the strong social thesis is to exclude such facts from the range of facts that are allowed by the thesis to determine law. It means that no facts of basic moral relevance (if there are any) can help determine that something is the law.

So according to the strong social thesis, the class of law-determining facts cannot include any morality-determining facts. This comes very close to implying that law is morally fallible. The intuitive idea at work here is that law has whatever value it has not by virtue of its very nature but rather by virtue of its contingent content (perhaps in relation to the social circumstances). But the strong social thesis does not quite yield the Minimal Separation Thesis. This is because it implies nothing of moral significance and does not even imply that law is subject to moral appraisal. The strong social thesis tells us at most that *if* law is subject to moral appraisal, its morality is an open question.

Even if the strong social thesis provided some foundation for the Minimal Separation Thesis, one would not wish to base the latter on the former. For the latter is much less controversial and more plausible. We can appreciate the character of the strong social thesis by considering the narrowest sort of disagreement that might develop around it.

An example is provided by the Due Process Clause of the U.S. Constitution, which says that no person may be deprived of life, liberty, or property without due process of law. The Constitution does not tell us what constitutes due process of law. If there is a general answer to this question, it can presumably be reached only by moral argument that goes beyond mere deductions from authoritative legal texts. Therefore, Raz must hold that a court faced with the task of initially interpreting this legal provision must go beyond existing law and make new law. Once a court that is empowered to issue authoritative interpretations of the U.S. Constitution interprets this clause, the clause acquires new content that enables future courts to render judicial decisions under the clause without making new law. But the initial interpretation involves judicial legislation.

Now consider Dworkin's understanding of the Due Process Clause.[26] On the most natural interpretation, the clause requires that certain legal procedures be fair. But the Constitution does not explicitly tell us what counts as a fair procedure, and it is arguable that the criteria of fair procedures are not implicit in terms like "due process" or "fair procedure." So when a court is called upon to apply this clause (at least prior to its first authoritative interpretation), it must go beyond the text of the law and its strict logical implications. It does not follow, however, that there is no right answer to the legal question that the court must decide. Suppose there is a right answer to the moral question, what constitutes a fair procedure. That is a substantive problem for moral theory, but one for which there may well be a solution. When the Due Process Clause invokes the concept of a fair procedure without specifying criteria, it seems to assume that there is a right answer to the moral question. If this assumption is correct, a court that is called upon to apply the Due Process Clause must engage in substantive moral argument in order to arrive at an appropriate conception of fairness and apply it to the case at hand. If the court's moral reasoning is sound and it reaches the right answer to the moral question, it will be in a position to reach the right answer to the legal question with which it is faced. In Dworkin's view, this will not involve going beyond the law, for if there is a right answer to the moral question, a court that finds it has simply provided the only right interpretation of the clause. It will have done just what the framers of the Due Process Clause imply can be done and require to be done. On this view, there is no good reason to regard the court as legislating, as making new law. On Raz's view, however, even in this sort of case a court must be understood as making new law, just because it is obliged to go beyond the authoritative text and engage in substantive moral argument. Raz is committed to this conclusion even in those cases where there is a single right answer to the moral question which determines the right answer to the legal question and the court correctly identifies both.

This difference between Raz and Dworkin concerning the character of

---

[26] Dworkin, *Taking Rights Seriously,* pp. 131–40.

court decisions that interpret moral language in the law involves a further difference in their attitude toward subsequent judicial decisions. Since Raz will not recognize a moral argument as helping to interpret the law, but regards it only as adding content to existing law, he cannot appeal to such an argument in criticizing from a strictly legal point of view the actual interpretations that courts place on such legal provisions. Once a court has provided an authoritative interpretation of such a provision, Raz seems committed to placing great weight on that reading of the law. In Dworkin's view, subsequent decisions must take into account past judicial decisions, and so must give some weight to prior interpretations of such language. But since in Dworkin's view there can be a right answer to the moral question which determines the correct interpretation of the clause, any past interpretation of the clause cannot be taken as decisive. Dworkin's reasoning would justify a court's rejecting a prior interpretation of the clause in a way that Raz's reasoning would not. In this way, Raz seems committed to attributing greater legal significance than Dworkin is to certain "facts of human behaviour capable of being described in value-neutral terms."[27]

It seems to me that Dworkin has the better of this argument, at least as it concerns the initial interpretation of undefined moral language in the law. If there is a right answer to the moral question that such language poses, there seems no reason to deny that this answer provides the right interpretation of the law. But if so, courts interpreting such law cannot be understood as making law. They are making law only if they reach the wrong conclusion and their interpretation nevertheless has precedential effect.

So one would not wish to use something like the strong social thesis as a basis for the Minimal Separation Thesis. It should also be mentioned, finally, that Dworkin's view of the matter does not exclude the fallibility of law, and so is at least compatible with the Minimal Separation Thesis, which he otherwise accepts. For Dworkin's argument does not assume that there is always undefined moral language in the law.

5. THE EXPLICIT MORAL CONTENT THESIS

Our findings so far indicate that the separation of law and morals is an axiom rather than a corollary of positivistic thinking. At the same time, the minimal idea that law is subject to moral appraisal and does not automatically merit good marks is not the exclusive property of legal

---

[27] Raz, *The Authority of Law*, p. 40.

positivism. This suggests the question whether positivism endorses some distinctive version of the separation thesis.

Raz's strong social thesis suggests such an idea. Hart suggests a similar idea (and implies it is more widely accepted within the positivistic tradition) when he approvingly describes Bentham's and Austin's version of the separation thesis as follows:

> What both Bentham and Austin were anxious to assert were the following two simple things: first, in the absence of an *expressed* constitutional or legal provision, it could not follow from the mere fact that a rule violated standards of morality that it was not a rule of law; and, conversely, it could not follow from the mere fact that a rule was morally desirable that it was a rule of law.[28]

Hart's wording here implies not that law is morally fallible but rather that law has no moral content or conditions save what has been explicitly laid down by law. I shall call this the Explicit Moral Content Thesis.

The Explicit Moral Content Thesis is different from the Minimal Separation Thesis. The latter does not entail the former: one might hold that law has moral content or that there are moral conditions on what can count as law, though they are not explicitly laid down by law, and still hold that law is morally fallible.

This is what Dworkin, for example, appears to hold. On Dworkin's theory, as we have seen, the content of the law is determined by legally sound judicial decisions that have been or could be made. But past decisions, which are not assumed to be morally infallible, act as moral constraints upon new decisions. The argument from fairness assumes that morally imperfect past decisions can have a proper influence on current ones, though that influence is moderated in two ways. First, it is interpreted in terms of principles that provide the best justification of those decisions, so that the surface language of past decisions (such as the language of statutes), while important, will not always be decisive. Second, some past judicial decisions must be regarded as mistaken from a legal as well as from a moral point of view and therefore as deserving only minimal respect. This theory does not imply that law is morally infallible, though it does imply that there are significant connections between law and morals – connections that have never been laid down explicitly as law. Law is determined, in part, by considerations of fairness. Sound legal decisions must pay due respect to past legislative and judicial decisions, so that the decision it is fair to reach, in light of the actual history of the system, may be different from the decision it would be fair to reach if that history had been different and morally more satisfactory.

As I have already suggested, I do not think this can be part of a sound

---

[28] Separation, p. 599 (emphasis added).

general theory of law, because I do not believe that fairness can play such a role when past legislative and judicial decisions were sufficiently unjust. In that case, whatever argues from a legal point of view that current cases be treated like past cases cannot be fairness. But this objection rests on substantive moral claims, and Dworkin's theory cannot be discounted at the outset. Dworkin's theory thus illustrates that the Minimal Separation Thesis does not entail the Explicit Moral Content Thesis, which would exclude the idea that moral notions like fairness contribute to the content of the law, even though that idea has not been laid down as law in an explicit, authoritative manner.

Hart's suggestion of the Explicit Moral Content Thesis is not misleading. For it is a corollary of a more general Explicit Content Thesis that Hart defends.

Hart argues for the Explicit Content Thesis in his discussion of judicial discretion, or judicial decision making in the absence of sufficient legal guidance.[29] Hart's official purpose in that discussion is to mark out a sensible middle ground between what he regards as the unacceptable extremes in legal theory of formalism, or mechanical jurisprudence, and rule skepticism. Formalism holds that law provides a complete, consistent, mechanical decision procedure, so that sound answers to legal questions can always be deduced from existing law and no room is left for the exercise of judicial discretion, whereas rule skepticism holds that there is always insufficient law prior to a judicial decision, so that judges always exercise judicial discretion. Hart argues, in effect, that formalism is mistaken because there are gaps between laws and that rule skepticism is mistaken because there are laws between the gaps.

Judicial discretion in the relevant sense exists when the law provides insufficient guidance to decide a case, so that no collection of factual findings will enable a court to reach a decision that is uniquely determined by existing law. This might seem to happen when, for example, statutes are poorly drafted. But Hart argues that judicial discretion is an unavoidable feature of law that results primarily and most directly from limitations of language. The terms we use in making law are "open textured": they have a "core" of determinate meaning, represented by cases to which they clearly and uncontroversially apply as well as cases to which they clearly and uncontroversially do not apply, but also a "penumbra" of uncertain meaning, represented by cases to which they neither clearly apply nor clearly do not apply. Hart concludes that laws are "open tex-

---

[29] *Concept,* chap. 7; see also Hart's article, "Philosophy of Law, Problems of," in *The Encyclopedia of Philosophy* (New York, 1967), vol. 7, pp. 268–72.

tured" too, by which he means they have a core of determinate meaning and a penumbra of indeterminate meaning. Hart strongly suggests that laws can be applied syllogistically within the range of their determinate meanings, so that legally sound decisions can be conclusively established. Otherwise, the law is not determinate enough to decide cases and courts have no choice but to make new law as they render decisions. This is the area of unavoidable judicial discretion. It can be reduced by further judicial decisions that add more determinate content to the law, but it can never be completely eliminated. Sometimes the explicit language of the law can be supplemented by the evident aims or purposes of the law in question, and in this way courts may be able to render decisions without exercising judicial discretion, even though the language of the law is somewhat indecisive. But our aims as well as our explicit language are "open textured" too, so that the added appeal to aims or purposes that is evident in the law cannot eliminate judicial discretion entirely.

The importance attached to explicit language in the law is shown by Hart's contrasting treatment of legislation and judicial decisions. Modern legislation provides us with authoritative texts employing language that allows us to infer general rules. Hart accordingly regards the rules created by legislative enactments as determinate just to the extent that the words used have clear meanings and their purposes are helpfully clear. But judicial precedents are regarded differently by Hart, because their language does not similarly allow us to infer general rules for all cases to which they are applied. Precedents that decide cases in relation to specific sets of facts about them can generate rules for a narrow range of cases just like the ones that have been decided. But precedents are also appealed to for guidance in a much wider range of cases, where it is unclear what should be inferred from the prior decisions. Hart treats this as the absence of an "authoritative or uniquely correct formulation" of a rule covering the wider class of cases, and holds that any such use of judicial precedents involves the exercise of judicial discretion.[30]

Similar considerations govern Hart's treatment of moral language in the law. He assumes that terms like "fair rate" and "safe systems of work" have a core of determinate meaning, represented by cases to which such terms uncontroversially apply or do not apply, plus a penumbra of uncertain meaning, represented by cases in which such terms apply only controversially. It should also be mentioned that Hart regards the criteria of existing law as "open textured" too. In a given legal system, a "rule of recognition" determines which other rules have legal standing. The

---

[30] *Concept*, p. 131.

rule of recognition is determined by agreement among officials as to what counts as law, and it is determinate only so far as there is very precise agreement on such matters.

Hart seems to conceive of the law as consisting of rules identified chiefly in linguistic terms. This may seem perfectly natural, in view of the importance generally attached to the language of statutes and decisions. Thus Hart infers that law is gappy because of the "open texture" of language. But this inference is strictly invalid. Suppose it is granted that linguistic expressions are "open textured" or unavoidably somewhat vague. It does not follow that there are determinate facts only where our current linguistic resources enable us straightforwardly to express them. The same applies to the law. Even if we assume that legal formulations are unavoidably somewhat vague, we cannot infer from this alone that the law is indeterminate whenever legal formulations have indeterminate implications. For this ignores the possibility that law has further resources which help to determine how to decide cases when the language of the law is unclear.

Hart ignores, for example, the sort of possibility that Dworkin finds within the law. Dworkin seems to hold that the content of the law is identical not with a set of canonically formulated rules but with what it would be fair for courts to find in cases given relevant past decisions. Arguments from fairness can overcome the indecisiveness of language. Hart's exclusion of such possibilities suggests that he conceives of the law essentially in linguistic terms – as a collection of rules with canonical formulations, which are based either on explicit legislation or on "very general agreement"[31] among officials about the specific import of judicial precedents and other aspects of the law.

The notion of "open texture" suggests a more fundamental assumption about the law. The idea of "open texture" assumes that linguistic terms are applied by reference to a set of criteria, all of which are clearly satisfied in some (core) cases, but which conflict in other (penumbral) cases. Within the core meaning of a rule, it can be applied syllogistically. Within a rule's penumbra, however, it cannot be applied syllogistically, for considerations can be adduced on both sides of the linguistic issue. This suggests another contrast within the law – between cases that can be decided uncontroversially because legal considerations fall overwhelmingly on one side and cases that are controversial because legal considerations can be adduced on both sides of the issue. The more fundamental assumption about the law that may underlie Hart's theory of judicial discretion, then, is this: the law is determinate when, and only

---

[31]   *Ibid.*

when, reasonable disagreement about it is absent. When the identification and implications of a rule of law are uncontroversial, there is no judicial discretion. But when law is controversial, when competent lawyers can develop plausible arguments on both sides of a legal question and a decision cannot be made mechanically but must involve weighing reasons on both sides, then the law must be regarded as indeterminate in the sense that there is scope for judicial discretion. Judges can decide such cases only by adding determinate content to the law, by engaging in "creative judicial activity" that amounts to legislation.[32] Law is determinate just where it is uncontroversial.

A linguistic version of this idea would be the Explicit Content Thesis, that law has no content or conditions save what has been explicitly laid down as law (or is precisely agreed upon by competent officials). A corollary of this view, already expressed in Hart's discussion of moral language in the law, is the Explicit Moral Content Thesis, that law has no moral content or conditions save what has been explicitly laid down by law (or is precisely agreed on by competent officials). This doctrine goes considerably further than the Minimal Separation Thesis, as we have seen.

Our consideration of the strong social thesis gave us no reason to suppose that there cannot be inexplicit moral content in the law. If there is a right answer posed by undefined moral language in the law, for example, then we have no reason to regard judges who interpret such language as exercising judicial discretion.[33]

The Explicit Moral Content Thesis seems, however, to be suggested by a number of legal positivists. Hart offers a linguistic argument for that thesis, but nonlinguistic considerations might well provide the deeper motivation. That is the possibility we must now explore.

6. THE MODEL OF RULES

According to Dworkin, legal positivism holds that law consists of standards, which he calls "rules," that are identifiable by their "pedigree" (or social origins) rather than their "content" (or moral acceptability); that these rules can be identified, interpreted, and applied more or less "me-

---

[32] *Ibid.*
[33] If the Explicit Moral Content Thesis is implausible, then so is the more general Explicit Content Thesis. If the Explicit Content Thesis is tied to the notion that law is determinate insofar as it is capable of providing syllogistic arguments for judicial decisions, it seems vulnerable to Dworkin's criticisms of the model of rules. For part of Dworkin's point is that judicial decisions can be sound from a strictly legal point of view even when they are nondeductive, taking into account considerations on both sides of a legal issue. I discuss a logical version of the Explicit Content Thesis (a "formalistic model" for legal justifications) in "Legal Formalism and Instrumentalism – A Pathological Study," *Cornell Law Review* 66 (June 1981): 949–72 [reprinted in this volume].

chanically" (by syllogistic reasoning); and that in cases which cannot be so decided judges can reach decisions only by exercising "discretion" and making new law. This is what Dworkin calls "the model of rules."[34]

Dworkin argues that these claims are false because the law is not exhausted by "rules" but includes standards that he calls "principles," which are determined in part by their content; these principles cannot be identified, interpreted, or applied mechanically; and principles help decide cases, so that judicial decisions can be fully based on law even when rules have been exhausted (sometimes even when rules must be changed) and decisions can only be justified by nondeductive arguments.

Dworkin's attack on legal positivism appears initially to fail because it is unclear why positivists should be thought committed to the model of rules. Let us suppose that positivists do conceive of the law as determined by what Dworkin calls "pedigree," since this is, roughly speaking, the social conception of law. The model of rules goes much beyond this: it conceives of law as a codelike collection of hard and fast rules that can be identified mechanically and that are capable of deciding cases either mechanically or else not at all. But the notion of pedigree does not seem to entail this conception of law. Positivists recognize legislation, and legislatures are capable of laying down legal standards that cannot be and are not meant to be applied mechanically.

Despite this, if positivists accepted the Explicit Content Thesis, Dworkin's objections would have some point. It may initially appear that they do not do so. Hart, for example, claims that rules are somewhat vague, which suggests that he does not regard law as equivalent to a codelike collection of hard and fast rules. But this is misleading, since Hart regards the law as having determinate content, sufficient to decide cases that arise, only insofar as it resembles such a collection of rules. All the rest is mere penumbra.

Suppose that Hart's view represents the positivistic tradition. The question we then face is, why should positivists conceive of law in this way – as limited to the explicit language of its authoritative texts, supplemented by agreement on some matters among officials?

Dworkin has offered an answer to this question:[35]

The important question is not, however, whether Hart or any other particular legal philosopher is committed to the thesis that the test for law must make law reasonably demonstrable. That thesis is connected to a more general theory of law – in particular to a picture of law's function. This is the theory that law

---

[34] Dworkin, *Taking Rights Seriously*, chaps. 2–3.
[35] In the revised version of Dworkin's "Reply to Critics," published as an Appendix to the Harvard University Press (1978) edition of *Taking Rights Seriously*.

provides a settled, public and dependable set of standards for private and official conduct, standards whose force cannot be called into question by some individual official's conception of policy or morality. This theory of law's function acknowledges, as it must, that no set of public rules can be complete or completely precise. But it therefore insists on a distinction between occasions on which the law, so conceived, does dictate a decision and occasions on which, in the language of positivists, the judge must exercise his discretion to make new law just because the law is silent. This distinction is vital, on this view of law's function, because it is important to acknowledge that when reasonable men can disagree about what the law requires, a judicial decision cannot be a neutral decision of the sort promised in the idea of law. It is more honest to concede that the decision is not, in this case, a decision of law at all.[36]

According to Dworkin, then, the model of rules is tied to legal positivism because it is "a necessary part" of "a political theory about the point or function of law" that is embraced by positivists.[37]

This first claim that Dworkin attributes to positivists is connected to a second claim, which involves the notion of pedigree. According to Dworkin, positivists hold that

The truth of a proposition of law, when it is true, consists in ordinary historical facts about individuals or social behaviour including, perhaps, facts about beliefs and attitudes, but in nothing metaphysically more mysterious.[38]

On this view, what law is can turn on the moral beliefs that people have, but not on the truth of a moral proposition. For that would make law turn on "moral facts," and Dworkin believes that the empiricist leanings of legal positivists make them regard "moral facts" as metaphysically suspect. That is one reason why positivists tend to "reduce" propositions of law or their truth conditions to "ordinary historical facts." This explains why Dworkin believes that his criticisms of the model of rules, with its attendant theory of judicial discretion, are effective against legal positivism in general. But Dworkin's explanation needs careful scrutiny, because it is not obviously valid and imputes to positivists very questionable modes of reasoning.

Consider Dworkin's claim that one of the factors influencing the development of legal positivism is reductionistic empiricism. Dworkin holds that this leads positivists to think of truth conditions for propositions of law in terms of "ordinary historical facts about individuals or social behaviour including, perhaps, facts about beliefs and attitudes." But, he claims, this attitude leads positivists to reject the idea that the truth of a proposition of law might depend on the truth of a moral proposition

[36] *Ibid.*, p. 347. [37] *Ibid.*
[38] *Ibid.*, p. 348.

because as empiricists they tend to regard such "moral facts" as "metaphysically mysterious."

Dworkin may be right that positivism has been strongly influenced by reductionistic empiricism, but his particular way of construing that influence seems falsified by the evidence. Unlike logical positivists, legal positivists (with a few noteworthy exceptions) have generally regarded moral questions as objectively, empirically decidable. This holds not just for the utilitarians, such as Bentham and Austin, but also for those with conventionalistic moral theories such as Hart. These major figures within the positivist tradition lack the reason that Dworkin claims they have to regard "moral facts" as metaphysically suspect.

The empiricism that is generally associated with legal positivism might, however, be relevant in another more general way. A reductionistic empiricist could be expected to regard the law as reducible to observable phenomena. It would be natural for him or her to place great weight on such things as authoritative decisions and the texts that they spawn, and perhaps to regard the substantive content of the law as chiefly determined by the words of those texts. Even so, this is a highly speculative interpretation of the impact of empiricism on the development of legal positivism. It might help to account for Bentham's views, but it is unclear that it applies to positivists generally, including Hart.

In any case, according to Dworkin, the chief factor shaping positivistic theory is not metaphysical but "a political theory about the point or function of the law." This holds "that law provides a settled, public and dependable set of standards whose force cannot be called into question by some individual official's conception of policy or morality." On this theory, Dworkin says, "it is important to acknowledge that when reasonable men can disagree about what the law requires, a judicial decision cannot be a neutral decision of the sort promised in the idea of law" and so should not be considered a decision determined by existing law. When law is controversial, it must be regarded as indeterminate – not merely unclear, but not yet fully formed. Real law is clearly identifiable, and in particular is not subject to moral interpretation.

There is evidence that one or two legal positivists have viewed the law in some such way – not only have they embraced the model of rules, but their ideas seem to have been shaped by some ideas about how law ought to be. There is evidence, for example, that Bentham wished to conceive of law in codelike terms (much like the model of rules) because he thought that law would best serve utilitarian ends if it took such a form.[39] More

---

[39] See Gerald Postema, "The Expositor, the Censor, and the Common Law," *Canadian Journal of Philosophy* 9 (1979): 643–70, and "Bentham and Dworkin on Positivism and Adjudication," *Social Theory and Practice* 5 (1980): 347–76.

recently Joseph Raz endorsed an argument like the one that Dworkin attributes to positivists.[40] But is unclear that other legal positivists have looked at the law in any such way or that they would welcome any such suggestion. Hart, for example, does not seem to use or endorse such an argument, and it is not clear that he could consistently do so.

Dworkin claims not merely that positivists have both a theory of what law is and a theory of how law ought to function but also that their theory about what law is has been shaped by their theory about how law ought to function. There is little evidence of this. Bentham notwithstanding, positivists have generally presented their theories of law as if they were trying to describe the concept of law, the essential nature of law, or something else similarly given. They do not say, "This is the way I conceive of the law because law so conceived is capable of functioning as it ought to function."

Hart, for example, contrasts "wider" and "narrower" concepts of law, where the narrower concept places moral conditions on something's being the law. He believes that the wider concept makes moral criticism of law possible. But Hart does not embrace the wider concept on the ground that law would better serve its purpose if it were that way. He clearly believes that the wider concept is the one we have – that he is faithfully describing our shared concept of law.[41]

One can imagine a positivist reacting to Dworkin's diagnosis as follows: "If we are right and law is (as you put it) 'reasonably demonstrable,' then of course it will have the merit of certainty, as compared with informal standards. And if law were not reasonably demonstrable, then of course it would not have this merit. But you have put the cart before the horse in claiming that our conception of the law is shaped by our prizing clear public rules. Our point is that law can serve this important purpose just because that is, as a matter of fact, part of its nature. To suppose that we are led to this view of law's nature by our desire for law to provide clear public rules is ungenerously to imply that we have indulged in wishful metaphysical thinking."

We should look once more at Raz's strong social thesis, which includes the Explicit Moral Content Thesis. For one of Raz's arguments for his thesis resembles the argument that Dworkin attributes to positivists generally.

Raz first claims that the strong social thesis "reflects and systemizes several interconnected distinctions embedded in our conception of the law."[42] We distinguish, for example, between the legal skills of judges, which are engaged when they apply the law, and their moral character,

[40] Raz, *The Authority of Law*, pp. 50–52, discussed below.
[41] Separation, pp. 620–21; *Concept*, pp. 202–7.
[42] Raz, *The Authority of Law*, p. 52.

which are at work when they develop law. We also make a distinction between settled and unsettled law, the latter but not the former comprising cases in which moral arguments are employed.

I find this argument unpersuasive. It does not provide sufficient reason to reject Dworkin's approach to the interpretation of moral language in the law, as exemplified in the Due Process Clause.

Raz also claims that these distinctions and his thesis "help to identify a basic underlying function of the law: to provide publicly ascertainable standards by which members of the society are held to be bound so that they cannot excuse nonconformity by challenging the justification of the standard."[43] The point of all this is to make possible a system of cooperation, coordination and forbearances, which, Raz says, "is an essential part of the function of law in society."[44]

Raz's second argument is more directly relevant to our immediate concerns. But it turns out that his use of it does not support Dworkin's diagnosis. For Raz does not argue that we should conceive of law in this way because law so conceived performs a desirable function. His first argument tries to show that law in fact has such a character, while the second argument connects that character with a desirable social function.

It may nevertheless be useful to examine Raz's second argument, since it offers a rationale for the Explicit Moral Content Thesis.

His argument goes something like this: The social order is liable to break down if substantive moral arguments used in adjudication are counted as helping to interpret the law, because that would encourage members of the society to break the law in the hope of avoiding the legal consequences by "challenging the justification of the standard."

Let us assume for the sake of argument that a society needs a system of forbearances, cooperation, and coordination and that it is one of law's principal functions to secure this by providing publicly identifiable standards. The question that we face is whether such a system would be weakened if the moral arguments used in adjudication were to count as contributing to the interpretation of the law.

It may seem at first as if Raz's thesis has no practical implications, but only concerns how we describe the results of litigation. If that were right, it would seem implausible to claim any connection between that thesis and the maintenance of social stability. But I think Raz's thesis makes a difference to litigation itself. I shall consider two sorts of cases, one in which Raz and Dworkin might well agree, at least initially, and one in which they might be expected to disagree.

The first sort of case involves the explicit use of undefined moral lan-

---

[43] *Ibid.*   [44] *Ibid.,* p. 51.

guage in the law, as in the Due Process Clause. If there is a right answer to the moral question posed by that clause, Raz would presumably wish a court to reach a decision that is informed by that answer. I say "informed by that answer" because, for reasons already given, Raz and Dworkin may disagree about how much weight later courts should give to an earlier reading of the clause that was based on an unsuccessful moral argument or a defective theory of interpretation. Even given this difference between their views, however, it is difficult to understand why Raz believes the social order is liable to break down if we view the law as Dworkin does. We have no evidence that a social order has broken down or is likely to break down if courts read moral language in the law as Dworkin recommends.

One might believe that moral language would best be excluded from laws so that they might have greater clarity and certainty. But this line of reasoning is irrelevant to our present concerns. Moral terms are found in legislative and judicial language, and the issue here is whether their application involves interpreting or adding to the law.

The main area of disagreement between Raz and Dworkin is suggested by the case of *Riggs v. Palmer*,[45] which was used by Dworkin in his attack on legal positivism. Elmer Palmer murdered his grandfather in order to inherit property under his grandfather's will. The statutes governing wills made no explicit exception for such a case, and it was arguable that Palmer should be confirmed as heir. Other relatives challenged this reading of the law, the New York State Court of Appeals found sufficient reason to consider their appeal, and ultimately ruled in their favor. Although the Court was divided, there was no disagreement about the language and the literal reading of the statutes. Disagreement centered on whether to engage in "equitable construction" in the light of conflicting legal doctrines, such as the common law maxim that no one should be permitted to profit from his own wrong.

Dworkin seems to imply that even in such a case a court can be considered as discovering law, whereas Raz suggests that he would regard the *Riggs* court as having changed the law because it did not follow the literal reading of the statute but was diverted by moral arguments. If Raz does not believe this, his thesis has little practical effect and cannot be thought to make much difference to social stability. So let us assume that Raz believes the *Riggs* court changed the law. This suggests that he would have endorsed the opposite finding, which would have secured the inheritance to the murderer. It is difficult to see how this would promote social stability by reinforcing the relevant forbearances.

---

[45] 115 N.Y. 506, 22 N.E. 188 (1889), discussed in *Taking Rights Seriously,* chap. 2.

Cases will undoubtedly vary, so that following Raz's recommendations might sometimes favor social stability. But Raz has given us no
reason to believe that a concept of law which excludes nonexplicit moral
content systematically promotes social stability.

To return to Dworkin's argument: Why should he believe that a theorist might be led to a conception of law by a political theory about the
proper function of law? Wouldn't this manifest theoretical confusion?

Dworkin sometimes suggests that there is an intimate connection between analytic and normative jurisprudence – between theories about
what law is and theories about what law ought to be – but he has never
made the connection clear. It is true that his "rights thesis," which holds
that "judicial decisions in civil cases . . . characteristically are and should
be generated by principle not policy,"[46] couples a normative with a descriptive claim, and his argument for this thesis seeks to show that moral
notions are needed for a proper understanding of successful judicial decisions. But this result, if achieved, would not mean that descriptive theories are impossible unless coupled with normative claims, or that moral
notions cannot be avoided in any plausible account of judicial decision
making. Dworkin has defended a particular theory; he has not defended
any relevant meta-theoretical claim.

Our examination of the separation thesis does suggest that there may
be some connections between analytic and normative jurisprudence that
legal positivists tend to ignore. We have found, for example, that the
separation thesis, which has helped to shape positivistic legal theory, is
not a morally neutral doctrine but represents a detached, critical attitude
toward the law. But this does not tend to show that legal theory is impossible without a normative foundation.

One might try reasoning as follows. Certain officials play a decisive
role in determining what counts as the law of a community. In systems
like ours these are preeminently judges of the highest courts within their
respective jurisdictions. Judges refer to statutes and cases when deciding
what counts as the law of their jurisdictions, but they do more than that.
They are also required to say what law is when statutes and cases conflict
or are unclear or when no established rule of law seems to exist. To do
this, they must work with a conception of what counts as law – what
considerations are relevant to a legal determination. Indeed, this is required even for them to use statutes and cases in the way that they do.
This amounts to a theory of law – a theory about how law is to be
determined.

This line of reasoning suggests that what counts as law is theory-

---

[46] Dworkin, *Taking Rights Seriously*, p. 84.

dependent. But there are different views of the matter. On one view, when judges are guided by unequivocal statutes and cases they are simply doing what the law plainly requires them to do, and when they go beyond the reach of unequivocal statutes and cases they are going beyond the law. On this way of thinking about the law – suggested, as we have seen, by Hart and others – theory plays no essential role in law. Judges may have theories to help them decide when law fails them, but they do not need theories when the law is clear. On this view, law is not theory-dependent. Furthermore, the argument we have sketched says nothing about the character of the theory that judges use, for example, why it should be considered a normative theory, a theory about how law ought to be, as opposed to a theory about the nature of law. Even if law were theory-dependent in something like the sense suggested, it would not follow that what counts as law is dependent on a conception of what law ought to be.

Dworkin may be understood as arguing that law is theory-dependent because law does not stop when cases are hard. Theory plays an essential role in law because judges do not inevitably make law but rather are capable of finding law when they are obliged to go beyond unequivocal statutes and cases, which they cannot do without a conception of what counts as law. More generally, his argument is that this sort of theory determines what considerations are binding on a judge. A theory of law is a theory of (among other things) judicial duty. The law of a community is represented by the sound judicial decisions that might be made; these decisions presuppose a theory about how judges are required to decide cases; and theories of this kind are subject to appraisal just like theories of any other kind. So on Dworkin's view the law of a community is dependent on a true theory of law – the theory that is capable of generating uniquely sound judicial decisions.

This tells us something about Dworkin's attitude toward theories of law. But it does not tell us why we may not think of such a theory as internal to a legal system, insulated from, say, moral considerations. A possible answer may be suggested as follows. Court decisions succeed in identifying and interpreting law when they are justified. But the idea of a justified judicial decision is a "contested concept." On one view, as we have seen, a decision can be justified only if it provides an adequate basis for the determination of obligations and provides reasons for the behavior of those whose conduct is at issue. Any attempt to defend a theory about justified decisions cannot ignore such claims, so the foundation of any theory of law must involve issues of moral theory. Judicial decisions determine the law, but these decisions must be informed by a theory that can be defended only in the light of substantive political considerations. Positivistic theory regards it as politically desirable that the determina-

tion of law be conducted in a morally neutral manner. Dworkin disagrees. But both approaches presuppose an answer to the question, what
is a justified judicial decision, and this involves moral argument.

This is but the crudest sketch of an argument that seeks to show how
analytic and normative jurisprudence are inseparably connected. It may
help to explain why Dworkin believes it is not unreasonable for positivists to be guided by a political theory when arriving at a theory about
what law is. The development of such an argument and its appraisal must
be postponed for another occasion.*

7. AN EXPANDED SEPARATION THESIS

One reason that is sometimes given for believing that a theory of law
cannot be morally neutral is that law makes legitimate claims to determine how we ought to behave. The very idea of law involves that of
legitimate authority, which automatically creates an obligation to conform or provides one with reason to comply. I shall conclude with a
discussion of this idea in relation to the separation of law and morals.

I believe at least three types of moral considerations help to determine
whether one is under an obligation to obey the law: the moral quality of
the law itself (for example, whether it respects our rights and how it
affects our welfare), the moral history of the law (for example, whether
it is the product of a fair lawmaking procedure), and the moral relations
of the individual to the political system (for example, whether one has
freely undertaken to obey the law). These factors are somewhat independent, and it would seem that they contribute in complex ways to the
determination of whether one is under an obligation to obey the law. For
example, it seems possible for one to be under an obligation to obey the
law, by virtue of an explicit undertaking to do so, even if the law is
morally imperfect both in quality and in history. If the law is not terribly
unjust and the system not terribly unfair, most public officials may be
morally bound to comply with existing law because they have undertaken to do so. But this point should not be overgeneralized. We cannot
assume that this is automatically the position of every individual who
falls under the scope of the laws, or even every public official (since officials can literally be coerced into serving and may not have made any
morally binding commitment to comply with the law). Furthermore, it is
arguable that any binding commitment to comply with law, while com-

* A crucial claim of *Law's Empire* is that theories about the nature of law are motivated
  by theories about the point of having an institution like law. Dworkin grounds this
  claim on a general theory of "constructive" interpretation, which he applies to the
  interpretation of social institutions, such as law.

patible with a range of moral deficiencies in law, is nevertheless limited by some moral minimum that a social system must satisfy if it is to be capable of generating obligations of obedience. Just as the promise to cooperate in a rape is not morally binding, so the promise to obey the law is limited by what one can be morally required to do.

For reasons such as these, I believe it is a mistake to suppose that everyone who falls under the laws of a community is morally bound to obey the law. The existence of such an obligation depends on moral conditions that are not automatically satisfied whenever one is legally required to behave in certain ways. But the considerations that might be marshaled to show this involve substantive issues in morality or moral theory. The idea that there is an automatic obligation to obey the law is wrong but not unintelligible.

Furthermore, the idea that there is an automatic obligation to obey the law is compatible, for reasons already suggested, with the idea that law is morally fallible and is in fact deficient. So the Minimal Separation Thesis does not entail that there is no automatic obligation to obey the law.

It may therefore come as no surprise that legal theorists have a variety of views about the existence of such an obligation, and that the issue does not neatly divide natural lawyers from legal positivists. Some natural lawyers, such as Aquinas, deny that laws made by humans automatically "bind in conscience," whereas other natural lawyers, such as Fuller, seem to say the opposite.[47] The position of legal positivists on this question is less clear. Perhaps surprisingly, however, positivists tend to suggest that law involves a legitimate claim to authority that demands our respect.[48]

Hart, for example, seems to endorse what he calls Bentham's "general recipe for life under the government of laws," namely *"to obey punctually; to censure freely."*[49] Bentham does not credit the idea of a moral obligation any more than that of a moral right, so it might be unfair to suggest that this formula expresses his acceptance of the idea that there

---

[47] Fuller, "Positivism and Fidelity to Law," p. 632.

[48] Fuller shrewdly observes that Hart seems committed to "the ideal of fidelity to law" *(ibid.)* because Hart assumes that officials charged with administering bad law are presented with a moral dilemma. This commits Hart to rejecting the idea that law is an "amoral datum" (assuming that law does not merit respect unless it satisfies some minimal moral conditions). Fuller's failure to defend that point adequately or to identify the relevant conditions has, I think, obscured the significance of his observation.

[49] Separation, p. 597. Hart describes Bentham's "recipe" as "simple," but he does not criticize it, and his repeated insistence that law has "authority," along with his views about moral and legal obligations, strongly suggests that he endorses the idea of an automatic obligation to obey the law (though one that might be overridden by countervailing considerations). Hart does, however, suggest the contrary position too.

is an automatic obligation to obey the law. But Hart recognizes moral obligations, and his approval of Bentham's formula seems to accept the idea that there is such an obligation.

One who believes there is always an obligation to obey the law might claim it is only "prima facie" – not absolute but overridable. But I question whether there is automatically even a "prima facie" obligation to obey the law, regardless of its history, its content, its effect on human beings, and other circumstances.

Someone might argue that life under law is better than social life without it or that for other reasons there is always a presumption in favor of obeying the law. But premises like these would not show that there is always a moral obligation to obey the law. At best they would show that one cannot dismiss the idea without further argument. An argument in favor of a moral obligation does not automatically confirm the existence of that obligation. For the argument may fail.

It is worth noting that legal positivists typically do two connected things that tend to confuse the general issue. On the one hand, they introduce the idea of a "legal obligation," something that is automatically created by legal requirements and prohibitions, regardless of their moral quality and history and independent of the specific relation of the individual to the political system, while on the other hand they present morality in relation to law in such a way that either morality cannot be understood as meriting any respect or law must be thought to merit as much respect as morality.

I have already discussed the first of these points and now wish to concentrate on the second. Austin and Hart, for example, who discuss these matters most systematically, treat moral and legal obligations as fundamentally on a par – as grounding reasons for action and modes of criticism that differ only in the labels "moral" and "legal." The existence conditions for these two categories of obligation are assumed to differ, but the sorts of implications the two kinds of obligations are supposed to have are essentially the same. Furthermore, given their ideas about the conditions under which one is under a moral obligation, such writers seem to imply that law enjoys as much legitimate authority as morality. According to Austin, moral obligations are created by God's commands, and he recognizes that these obligations bind only by coercing.[50] Hart's view is not significantly different, since he takes moral obligations as determined by the values that people generally share within a community, regardless of their merit, so that "in one society," for example, "it may be a wife's duty to throw herself on her husband's funeral pyre, and

---

[50] Austin, *The Province of Jurisprudence Determined*, Lecture I.

in another, suicide may be an offense against common morality."[51] It should be emphasized that Hart employs no distinction here between "critical" and "conventional" morality: Conventional morality does not exhaust moral notions, but it establishes the moral rights and obligations that we can be said to have.

This sort of theory seems simultaneously to inflate law and to disparage morality. If moral truths can be understood to help determine how we ought to behave, someone with these views about law and morality might well believe that law likewise helps to determine, in a similar normative way, how we ought to behave. Law may be credited with as much legitimate authority as morality.

Although these views about law and morality are compatible with the Minimal Separation Thesis – with the idea that law is morally fallible – they do seem to clash with the spirit of this thesis as it is usually understood. It is difficult to understand why someone with such a conception of morality would be concerned, as Hart evidently is, with the moral fallibility of law. In his Holmes lecture, Hart argues that the separation thesis is required to maintain a critical, detached attitude toward law and to sustain our moral sensibilities. The judiciously moralistic spirit of Hart's discussion seems to clash, however, with his conception of morality.

The Minimal Separation Thesis, as we have seen, does not rest upon more fundamental doctrines of positivistic legal theory. Nor is it the special property of legal positivism. Although some radical moral skeptics have endorsed something like the separation thesis, the most plausible foundation for the separation of law and morals appears to be a detached, critical attitude toward law. This attitude turns on moral perceptions rather than morally neutral observations. It may be reasonable therefore to suggest that a natural extension of these attitudes beyond the Minimal Separation Thesis would not take us to the Explicit Moral Content Thesis (a dubious doctrine which seems to have different motivations) but rather to an Expanded Separation Thesis, which would deny that there is any automatic obligation to obey the law.

A first approximation of the Expanded Separation Thesis may be formulated in this way: No moral judgment follows from the fact that something is the law. The intuitive idea, mentioned before, is that the existence of law does not ensure the satisfaction of any moral requirements. But

---

[51] *Concept*, p. 167. In context, this must be taken as expressing Hart's own views and not as merely describing exotic moral convictions. Although Hart's notion of "critical morality" implies that conventional moral attitudes are subject to criticism, he never suggests that any such criticisms affect the truth conditions of statements about moral rights and obligations. This tension is commonly found in conventionalistic theories of obligation.

the suggested formulation is inadequate. For one thing, it does not imply that law is subject to moral appraisal. For another, it might be verified in an irrelevant way, by a successful refutation of ethical naturalism in Moore's narrow sense.

The general idea I wish to express may more accurately be conveyed as follows: The existence and content of law is determined by facts that make law subject to moral appraisal but do not guarantee it any moral value; the basic, most general law-determining facts do not entail or otherwise ensure any morality-determining facts.

This is, I think, the sort of doctrine that most sympathizers of legal positivism have meant to endorse. It captures more satisfactorily and thoroughly than the other versions we have considered the detached, critical attitude toward law which assumes that law does not automatically merit our respect but rather must earn it.

I am not confident that this doctrine is sound, though I am unaware of any good argument against it. I would not claim that this doctrine is an incontrovertible truism, which simply reflects our ordinary ways of speaking. The doctrine rests on moral as well as legal perceptions.

Some differences between the Expanded Separation Thesis and the Explicit Moral Content Thesis are worth mentioning. The Expanded Thesis tries to make the point that something can be law even though it does not meet moral conditions. This is meant as a point about law in general, not about the law of a particular system. For the law of a given system might impose (explicit or inexplicit) moral conditions on what can count as law. The Expanded Thesis maintains that there can be a legal system that lacks such conditions.

The Explicit Moral Content Thesis says nothing about the relations between law and morality in general, save that moral conditions on what counts as law must be explicit. If we view this as an attempt to make the point of the Expanded Separation Thesis, we can see that it fails, for two reasons. First, it is too weak because it does not imply that there can be a legal system that lacks (implicit or explicit) moral conditions on what can count as law. Second, that thesis is too strong because it needlessly rules out moral conditions on what counts as law, just because they are inexplicit. But one can allow for the possibility that law is sometimes determined by inexplicit moral conditions, without implying that there cannot be a legal system without such conditions on what counts as law.

Consider Dworkin's theory, which claims that fairness serves as a tacit condition on what counts as law. It is sometimes observed that Dworkin's argument draws heavily on features of Anglo-American law that may not be shared with other systems of law. So Dworkin's argument cannot be used to show that fairness serves as a tacit condition on what counts as law in any system. But his argument can also be seen as directed against the Explicit Moral Content Thesis, and not against the separation of law and morals. Dworkin does not deny that law is morally fallible, nor does he construct an argument that can be understood to show that there are moral conditions on what counts as law in any system. But he does argue that moral conditions underlie what counts as law in our own system, and this argument, if effective, would refute the Explicit Moral Content Thesis.

It is possible that those who endorse the Explicit Moral Content Thesis have meant all along only to endorse an Expanded Separation Thesis. It seems more likely, however, that legal positivists have endorsed the Explicit Moral Content Thesis, instead of an Expanded Separation Thesis, for definite reasons, namely, their conviction that law is clear and uncontroversial, insofar as it is determinate, coupled with the conviction that law automatically enjoys a kind of legitimate authority and automatically merits some measure of respect, however slight. This is why they emphasize the explicit content of law and flirt with the idea that there is always an obligation to obey the law.

We have found that the minimal idea of the separation of law and morals is not the special property of legal positivism and that if positivists have a distinctive doctrine in this area it is the Explicit Moral Content Thesis. If that is what separates legal positivism from natural law, then positivism is a tradition that betrays the moral concerns of many who have thought it congenial. Their detached, critical attitudes toward law, which allow law whatever respect it truly earns, but no more, are better expressed in other ways.

5

Formal justice and judicial precedent

Despite the encroachment of legislation on matters that used to lie within the province of the common law, considerable scope remains for the judicial practice of following precedent, without challenging the authority of written law. For decisions must still be rendered where legislation has not yet intervened, and interpretations of written law can be accorded precedential force.

Why should courts follow precedents? When past decisions are unobjectionable on their merits, the practice is relatively unproblematic. It might, perhaps, be justified by the usual argument that it makes judicial decisions more predictable. That justification hardly seems, however, to confront the fact that precedents may have been unfortunate, unwise, and unjust. Why should courts show any respect at all to such decisions?

This Article concerns an argument which, if sound, would support a doctrine of precedent with unlimited scope – one that would provide some justification, though not overwhelming justification, for following all precedents, however regrettable they may be. The argument holds that respect for precedent is required by the principle that like cases should be treated alike.

Although that argument is challenged here, no claim is made that a practice of precedent cannot be justified. The larger purpose of this Article is to clear the way for a systematic inquiry into the sound reasons for, as well as the legitimate scope of, such a practice.

The argument to be examined is sketched in section I. Section II takes up the notion of following precedent, to show both that it is not empty but also that it can be understood in more than one way. Section III

"Formal Justice and Judicial Precedent," *Vanderbilt Law Review* 38 (1985): 495–512. Copyright © Vanderbilt Law Review. An earlier version of this paper was published as Lyons, "Formal Justice, Moral Commitment, and Judicial Precedent," 81 *J. Philos.* 580 (1984). Material from that paper is used with permission of *The Journal of Philosophy*. The author would like to express his thanks for comments on the earlier version from Thomas Scanlon and other participants in the American Philosophical Association symposium in which it was presented; from those who commented when it was presented at the University of Utah; and from Sterling Harwood. Research for and writing of this paper were supported in part by a Constitutional Fellowship from the National Endowment for the Humanities.

considers one interpretation of the idea that like cases should be treated alike, as a "formal" principle, which leaves the doctrine of precedent unsupported. Section IV considers another interpretation of the idea, the requirement of moral consistency, which is inadequate to validate the argument, but for different reasons. Section V considers some other grounds for the practice of precedent.

I. THE FORMAL JUSTICE ARGUMENT

The reason most often given for the practice of precedent is that it increases the predictability of judicial decisions. As a consequence, it increases security, minimizes risks that might otherwise discourage useful ventures, and generally avoids frustrating expectations.

One might quibble with this line of reasoning. It is unclear, for example, that expectations that might be frustrated by the failure to follow past decisions would even be formed, unless there already existed a more or less regular practice of following precedent. But quibbles like that do not undermine the other claims made on behalf of predictability. These are plausible claims that I do not wish to challenge. Their implications, however, are limited, considered merely on their own terms.

Arguments like these refer to benefits supposedly brought about by the practice of precedent, and such benefits depend on variable circumstances. Even under the most favorable conditions, following precedent can have disadvantages too, if only for those who lose out in court. So the point of these arguments must be that following precedent does more good than harm, overall.

Clearly, following an unwise or unfortunate precedent can sometimes do more harm than good. The same applies to the general practice, at least within a given jurisdiction over an extended period of time. The possibility cannot be ruled out *a priori*. Such reasons for the practice therefore seem incapable of endorsing it in all circumstances, under all conditions. So far as this sort of argument is concerned, the practice can sometimes lack justification.

To clarify this point, we must distinguish between the limited scope and the limited weight that a principle or doctrine might have. Principles are rarely regarded as "absolute"; it is understood that they can be overridden in some circumstances. Such principles can be said to have limited weight. A principle's scope is its legitimate sphere of application, which is different from, and largely independent of, its weight.

A principle prescribing that judicial precedents be followed might have unlimited scope but limited weight. This is suggested when a case to be decided should be distinguished from a precedent because of overriding differences between the two – when the significance of the differences is not determined by precedents alone. Then the principle would seem to argue for following the precedent because of its similarities to the case to be decided, but it is overridden by whatever considerations argue for different treatment of the case. This gives no reason to conclude that the principle has limited scope, though it must have limited weight.

Consider the role of precedent within the widening sphere of legislation. Where legislation has intervened, it is generally understood to take priority over previous case law. But this is compatible with the idea that the applicable principle of precedent is overridden by the doctrine of legislative supremacy. The point of understanding the principle as applicable within the context of legislation is that it would still be relevant to interpretive decisions. The principle would prescribe that past interpretations of statutes be followed – always, presumably, with the qualification "other things being equal," which represents its limited weight.

This suggests one reason for the importance of the notion that respect for precedent is a matter of treating like cases alike. The principle that like cases should be treated alike is assumed to have unlimited scope. Any reason it provides for the practice of precedent would hold for all situations in which precedents are available.

A second reason for the importance of that argument is that treating like cases alike is often regarded as a requirement, indeed perhaps the central or most fundamental requirement, of justice.[1] When so viewed, the practice of precedent is placed on a moral footing. It implies that the failure to follow precedent is not merely unwise but positively wrong – "other things being equal," that is, unless the failure can be justified by circumstances that permit an injustice to be done.

The standard argument for the practice of precedent, by contrast, has more problematic moral status. While it may be a good thing, by and large, for officials to promote benefits and minimize burdens by making judicial decisions more predictable, it is controversial whether this is always morally permissible, even other things being equal. It may be held, for example, that justice takes priority over this kind of utility, so that benefits should be promoted *only* on the condition that they be distributed fairly. A practice that merely perpetuated social injustice would be morally problematic.

This is particularly important if we suppose that a principle of precedent has unlimited scope – or at least includes among the precedents to be followed those that are morally deficient as well as those that are unproblematic. Regarding the principle that like cases should be treated

---

[1] A good source for this view is H.L.A. Hart, *The Concept of Law* 155–56 (1961).

alike as a principle of justice implies moral grounds for respecting flawed precedents.

The idea that there might be moral grounds for respecting morally deficient aspects of a legal system is not implausible, and it is often embraced. It is not implausible because it would merely represent the hard moral fact that principles often seem to conflict. It is embraced, for example, when it is held that there can be a general moral obligation to obey the law (incumbent more strongly, perhaps, on officials than on private citizens), which applies, at least sometimes, to bad as well as good law.

I shall call the idea that the practice of precedent respects the requirement that like cases be treated alike, *the formal justice argument*, because its premise, for reasons we shall later consider, is usually regarded as "formal."

One finds the formal justice argument suggested in the jurisprudential literature.[2] It is not developed or discussed extensively, perhaps because the inference from premise to conclusion seems so simple and direct that elaboration is unnecessary. The idea seems to be this: The requirement that like cases be treated alike is understood to imply that, once we have dealt with a situation in a certain way, it is incumbent on us, other things being equal, to deal with similar situations in similar ways. From this it may seem a simple short step to a principle of judicial precedent, because the latter may seem just a specific case of the requirement that we follow our past practice generally.

II. FOLLOWING PRECEDENT

One aspect of the formal justice argument needs to be considered first: both the premise and the conclusion incorporate the problematic notion of a "like" or "similar" case. The "cases" referred to by the conclusion are those decided in a court of law, whereas the class of "cases" covered by the premise must be much broader, including, perhaps, any situation in which one might form a judgment and act accordingly. We can limit our attention just now to the narrower class of cases, for that will enable us to focus at once on the idea of following precedent. The problem concerning "similar cases" in the broader sphere is basically the same.

The basic problem is simple. Take any case that is to be decided and any other case that has already been decided. However similar they may be, in respects that may seem important, they will also be different in some respects, and vice versa. Some general facts about one case will be

---

2 See, e.g., M. Golding, *Legal Reasoning* 98 (1984); N. MacCormick, *Legal Reasoning and Legal Theory* 73ff (1978).

general facts about the other, and some general facts about one case will not be general facts about the other. So objective grounds exist both for *and* against regarding *any* past case as "similar" to one that is to be decided.

As a consequence, a principle prescribing that decisions follow those that have already been made in "similar cases" can seem literally impossible to follow. If all the factual aspects of cases were relevant, and any similarity and any difference between cases were sufficient to make them similar and different, respectively, then each past case would both be and not be a precedent for any case to be decided. On that interpretation, the principle would be impossible to follow because it would be, strictly speaking, incoherent.

This conclusion can be avoided only by limiting the range of cases that can be counted as "similar" to, and thus as precedents for, a case to be decided. But, it might be argued, any limitation of that sort would deliberately ignore objective similarities between the case to be decided and those that are excluded from the class of precedents, as well as objective differences between the former and those included in the class of precedents. For this reason, any interpretation of the principle of precedent that avoids incoherence might be considered inherently arbitrary.

Consequently, it might be thought that the very idea of precedent, and along with it that of following precedent, is inherently unclear, so that we need not worry about the logic of the formal justice argument; for its conclusion could make no determinate difference to judicial practice. Courts might speak of "following prior decisions in similar cases," and the like, but any actual use of precedents would be either confused or arbitrary.

A solution to this problem depends on the possibility of a nonarbitrary distinction between similarities among cases that are relevant and those that are irrelevant to the practice of precedent. I argue in this section that a nonarbitrary distinction seems available, though there is more than one way of understanding both the distinction and the doctrine of precedent.

Let us begin with what seems the most natural and straightforward way of understanding the practice of precedent, one that also seems to conform to the intention of the formal justice argument. The premise of that argument is understood to require that we continue generally to deal with cases as we have been doing, and the conclusion is understood to require that we continue specifically to decide legal cases as we have been doing.

The most natural way of understanding this in the judicial realm is in terms of following the legal judgment that is represented by a previous court decision. Suppose that a court has decided a case by regarding some of its factual aspects as grounds for certain legal consequences. Call these the grounding aspects of the case. That case would seem to count as a precedent for another when the latter case has factual aspects that are the same as grounding aspects of the former case. For the purpose of following precedent, these similarities between the two cases are relevant, and no others are relevant – though other aspects of the cases might of course be relevant for other judicial purposes.

This elementary idea enables us to say what it is to follow precedent in a relatively simple situation. Suppose that all the grounding aspects of the precedent are also factual aspects of the case to be decided. The cases might otherwise be very different. To follow that precedent, the court deciding the later case would simply decide the issue in the same way the earlier one was decided.

Before going further, it may be useful to note how this approach to understanding the practice of precedent applies to past decisions that have interpreted written law. Suppose that a given text has been construed by a court. In arriving at its reading, the court may have formed a judgment concerning the determinate relevance of such things as the specific wording of the text, the specific type of text it is, its legal origins, its proposed applications, and so on. To form such a judgment is, in effect, to regard certain factual aspects of a case as grounds for certain legal consequences, where the consequences concern the specific meaning to be attached to the text and its acknowledged legal ramifications. To follow an interpretational precedent amounts to following a court's judgment as to the legal difference such factors make to the reading of a text.

Now I do not mean to suggest that is generally easy to identify and follow a precedent, so understood. The past court's legal judgment may be unclear; it might never have been clear, even to that court. So it may be impossible, in principle as well as in practice, to follow the legal judgments represented by some past decisions, even though the cases might reasonably seem quite similar to the one that is to be decided. But these difficulties give us no reason to suppose that it is never possible faithfully to follow prior decisions in similar cases. A court can have had determinate grounds for its decision, and there can be adequate evidence of it now. This means that a principle of precedent, on this natural reading, can have determinate implications for practice.

The complications should not be underestimated. Precedents are not usually so perfectly "on point." Suppose that some, but not all, of the grounding aspects of a precedent are factual aspects of a case to be decided. On the present conception of the practice, there is in principle a way to follow that precedent if, but only if, the court that decided it regarded that proper subset of grounding aspects as sufficient grounds for certain legal consequences. To follow that precedent, the court deciding the later case would attach those consequences to the relevant factual aspects of it and decide it accordingly. Any other way of deciding the case would not amount to following precedent, on this conception.

As matters become even so slightly more complicated, it is clear that precedents become increasingly difficult to follow. The court that decided the earlier case may have formed no legal judgment concerning the significance of the relevant proper subset of factual conditions; for it might not have needed to do so. Even if it did so, it might not have expressed that judgment clearly. This is just the beginning of the complications.

Perhaps the most serious difficulty for the practice of precedent is the incidence of conflicting precedents – past decisions that provide, in effect, incompatible guidance for a judicial decision. Two similar cases might have been decided differently, so that the precedents conflict most directly, or the case to be decided might have aspects in common with each of two past cases while those cases share no relevant aspects. Either way, while it may be possible to follow each precedent, it will be impossible to follow all precedents.

Because it is impossible to follow all precedents, a reasonable doctrine of precedent would not require courts always to follow all precedents for a given case. But we cannot say, *a priori,* what more specific guidance a reasonable doctrine would provide for such a case. That presumably depends, most importantly, on what grounds there are for following precedents and how those grounds may be implicated when precedents conflict.

While the possibility of conflicting precedents tells us that they *can* not always be followed, other factors are taken as reasons why precedents *should* not always be followed. We have already noted two such reasons: intervening legislation and differences that are taken as justifying differential disposition. Such complications make it difficult to say when, precisely, precedent should be followed, but they do not suggest that the very notion of following precedent is inherently unclear. They indicate rather the need to become clear about possible justifications for the practice.

Before we consider the formal justice argument in that role, we should note that the practice of precedent can be understood quite differently. In either describing or endorsing the practice, one might not conceive of it in terms of faithfully following a past court's legal judgment. One might hold, for example, that the *justifiable* use of past decisions as determinate points of departure for current ones involves construing them in the best light possible. One would seek to determine whether, and if so how, past decisions could have been justified; only such decisions would be assumed to merit subsequent respect. The precedential import of a justifiable past decision would be given by the standards, such as the principles or other values, that provide the best justification for it. A past case would constitute a precedent for a new case when at least some of the standards so identified can be applied to the current case.[3] The notion of justification that is employed in this conception of the practice requires clarification, but I shall defer comment until later. For now it may be noted that, if the criteria of justification can be fixed, then the idea of following precedent has determinate implications for judicial decision under this interpretation too. I do not mean that it would generally be easy or always possible to apply such a conception. Just as courts in some past cases may have failed to form a relevant and clear legal judgment, so courts have rendered decisions that cannot be justified. Such cases could not serve as precedents under the two respective conceptions of the practice.

We might call these two conceptions the historical and the normative, respectively. The normative conception might seem problematical because its use involves recourse to value judgments, which are not required under the historical conception. Any discomfort with that fact must stem from the notion that courts may not legitimately employ value judgments, even when interpreting precedents, rather than from skepticism about value judgments themselves. For one who inquires into the possible justification of such doctrines as judicial precedent must assume that value judgments are differentially defensible – that they are not inherently arbitrary.

It may turn out that the various attempts that have been made to characterize and justify the practice of precedent can be understood as modeled on either or both of these two conceptions, emphasizing either fidelity to the legal judgments that courts have already in fact embraced, or fidelity to past practice only insofar as, and in the respects in which it is, justifiable.

III. FORMAL JUSTICE AS A FRAMEWORK

We turn now to the premise of the formal justice argument and begin with the problem of "similar cases." For reasons already noted, it could be held that the principle requiring that like cases be treated alike is impossible to follow or else can be followed only in an arbitrary manner.

---

[3]   This approach to precedent is discussed in D. Lyons, *Ethics and the Rule of Law* 92–104 (1984).

Until it is supplemented by "criteria of relevant similarities," it "cannot afford any determinate guide to conduct."[4]

The question that we face, then, is whether the principle has any interpretation that would solve this problem and render the argument sound. Two different approaches to its interpretation are in fact available. On the view we shall consider in this section, the words "treat like cases alike" express only the bare "form" of principles of justice and no determinate content. In the next section we will examine a determinate interpretation that has been placed on those words.

We can understand the first approach as follows. Justice requires certain patterns of dealing with situations. That is what the *concept* of justice involves. But this concept is subject to many different interpretations, some of which are incompatible with others. These are specific *conceptions* of justice – different theories of what justice requires and allows.[5] A coherent egalitarian conception of justice, for example, would tell us that all people should be treated alike in certain determinate respects (for it would be impossible to treat everyone alike in all respects). Nonegalitarian conceptions would emphasize that we should "treat different cases differently" – a formula that is usually thought to complement the requirement that like cases be treated alike – but they would also tell us, in effect, which cases are to be treated alike.

One merit of such a view concerning not only justice but also other broad moral concepts is that something very much like it seems needed to account for some important facts about morality. For example, two individuals who do not seem conceptually confused – who seem to have no difficulty manipulating the concept of justice, and who do not seem to be talking at cross purposes – can disagree about what justice fundamentally requires and allows. This appearance would be illusory unless something like the concept-conception distinction were applicable.

The plausibility of the distinction is suggested, moreover, by its applicability to a much wider range of concepts, not all of them normative. Something like it is needed to explain, for example, how scientists can develop increasingly accurate conceptions of a natural phenomenon under a fairly constant concept. The concept of heat does not tell us what heat fundamentally is, but the concept admits of various conceptions. The caloric conception, which regarded heat as a substance with negative mass, gave way for good reason to the current conception – of heat as the kinetic energy of molecules. One such conception can be an improvement over another only if the concept of heat retains a fairly constant reference, independent of the competing conceptions under it.

---

[4] *See* H.L.A. Hart, *supra* note 1, at 155.

[5] *See, e.g.,* J. Rawls, *A Theory of Justice* 5–6 (1971).

The example of heat suggests how the superiority of one conception over another is determined by factors that go beyond concepts alone, such as the objective facts. If there are better and worse conceptions of justice, that will not be determined by the bare concept. But the analogy with heat is not meant to imply that there must be superior and inferior conceptions of justice, no less that the matter must be determined by objective facts. We cannot rule out that possibility, but neither can we rule out the possibility that there are a number of equally valid, though competing, conceptions, none of which is best. That question is left open by the application of the concept-conception distinction. In the original terms, the fact that definite criteria of similarities that are relevant for the purpose of doing justice are required if justice is to have determinate requirements does not imply that such criteria are objectively determined. That question is left open by our recognition of the need for such criteria.

The formal justice argument does not leave such matters open. The argument assumes that some ways of acting *are just* and that others *are unjust,* so it presupposes that there are significant limits on admissible conceptions of justice. But it does not tell us what those limits are, nor on this reading does it identify any general conception of justice. All the argument tells us, in effect, is that whatever those limits may be, they insure that the practice of judicial precedent is a matter of treating like cases alike in a way that justice more generally requires.

To put the matter differently, the formal justice argument presupposes that criteria of relevant similarities among cases to be treated alike are not inherently arbitrary but are discoverable. But, on the present reading, the formal justice argument gives us absolutely no reason to believe what it claims about the practice of precedent. If we regard the premise of the argument as "formal," in this first sense, then the argument as a whole amounts to a framework waiting for substantiation.

What needs to be shown is that there is a reason, grounded upon justice or something else, for following past decisions even when they were brutally inhumane and outrageously unjust. That seems on its face a dubious proposition, and the formal justice argument has not yet been found to give us any reason to believe it to be true.

IV. CONSISTENCY AND CONSERVATIVISM

A formal justice reason may seem to be provided by the second approach to understanding the requirement that like cases be treated alike, which holds that it has determinate, even if minimal and only "formal," implications. On this view the premise is regarded as "formal" not because it amounts to a mere framework without substantive implications, but because it is thought to represent a logical constraint of moral consistency.[6]

Consistency, in this sense, involves the logical compatibility of beliefs or judgments, and not, for example, their truth, wisdom, or justifiability. In the present context, it concerns the logical compatibility of one's moral judgments, such as the way in which one judges acts or other things at different times and in different situations.

It is quite plausible to suppose that logic constrains moral judgment in this way, for one's judgments are not completely independent of one another. They have implications that might be contradicted either directly or indirectly by other judgments. Most important here, one's judgment of specific cases, such as individual acts performed by oneself or others, often reflects general standards. One's judgments are not all ad hoc. This can be true even when one does not consciously deliberate when forming a moral judgment. One can simply have a disposition to appraise certain sorts of situations in certain ways, a disposition that is exemplified in judgments that one makes about specific cases. That would seem indeed to be a psychological platitude.

We can understand this in the following way. Moral judgments, as opposed to mere visceral reactions that can be expressed in words, presuppose some general standards. That is because a judgment is predicated on the idea that relevant facts in the case ground one's judgment of it. But to believe that certain facts are relevant in a certain way in one case is to believe that the same facts are relevant in the same way in other cases, other things being equal. One need not be able to articulate one's standards on demand. The point is that in making a judgment one is committed to the idea that it can be grounded in some way on the facts, and this commits one to the view that such facts are similarly relevant in similar cases, the relevant similarities being determined by the standards that one applies. Thus consistency requires one to "treat like cases alike."

It is important to appreciate that no part of the constraint of moral consistency or such presuppositions of its applicability as we have considered makes use of the notion of a uniquely true, correct, or sound moral judgment. This minimal constraint concerns merely how one's judgments, both specific and general, hang together. And yet this constraint has some determinate implications. It says, in effect, that one must apply the same standards to all cases that one is not honestly prepared to distinguish on principled grounds. That does not tell us what cases to distinguish or more generally what principles to apply. But it does tell us

---

[6]   This is suggested by both Golding and MacCormick. *See supra* note 2.

to be faithful to our own deepest values, whatever they may be, and to judge specific matters accordingly.

There is some point to all of this; for we are not implacably consistent in our judgments. Despite our deepest moral beliefs, there are times when we are inclined to judge some acts or persons either more indulgently or more severely than others, without any grounds that we would acknowledge honestly. One may be too forgiving of a loved one's weakness or of one's own predicament, or one may be exceptionally demanding of oneself or of those to whom one is intimately related. One may judge strangers too harshly or bend over backwards not to do so. The constraint of consistency is meant to counsel against such deviations from one's own general standards.

The result of a violation is not an injustice but that sort of incoherence of which one is guilty whenever one's beliefs or judgments are incompatible. Of course, there may be more to a violation than that, as when one tries to deceive oneself or others into judging in a way one could not honestly endorse.

It is easy to see how this constraint may be thought to require that we go on as before, at least in our judging. Unless we have genuinely modified our moral commitments, consistency requires that we apply them to new cases that arise, whether or not we like the results of doing so.

The requirement that one continue judging as before is parallel to the historical conception of following precedent. If a doctrine of precedent adds anything to the requirement of consistency in judgment, it may seem to be merely the requirement of a closely related kind of consistency – of one's actions with one's honest judgments. For the doctrine of precedent requires not only that one judge, in the narrow sense of forming a judgment, consistently, but also that one act accordingly – consistently with one's judgment. Both elements are of course included in the complex notion of judicial decision.

Thus, the requirement that like cases be treated alike, when understood as expressing the constraint of consistency in judgment, may seem like adequate support for a principle of precedent on the historical model. Consistency requires that we go on as before, and the doctrine of precedent requires the same sort of thing in a specific context, only more so – for it requires also the consistency of action with judgment. If the doctrine of precedent added only that last bit to the requirement of consistency, it might seem like straining a point to criticize the formal justice argument, so construed. But the seemingly tight logic of the argument is in fact an illusion.

There are two significant, nontrivial, apparently unbridgeable gaps within the argument. One concerns the most problematic implications of precedent on the historical model. The other concerns the distinctive social character of the practice of judicial precedent.

Morally the most significant implication of a doctrine of precedent on the historical model is the notion that any departure from the most inhumane, unjust, unconscionable precedent requires justification. This sort of doctrine holds that, if a court has attached legal consequences to certain facts because it regards that as appropriate for legal purposes, then that judgment deserves some measure of respect.

The constraint of moral consistency is parallel to this sort of doctrine only if it has what we may call a conservative bias, as my formulations were meant to suggest it has. But in fact it has no such bias. That is because we are free to change our moral opinions honestly. The constraint of consistency does not mean that we are prohibited from modifying, qualifying, refining, or otherwise revising our moral judgments, including the standards we apply. We are free to reject judgments that we made in the past, if they can no longer be supported by the standards we now accept; indeed, we are bound by the constraint of consistency to do so.

The absence of a conservative bias is not peculiar to this application of the constraint of consistency. It is pervasive. I cannot be convicted of inconsistency just because I change my understanding of some aspect of the observable world about me or its microstructure. Perhaps I should not change my views without good reason. But consistency does not prevent me from acquiring such reason, from either experience or a reappraisal of it.

So the conservative presuppositions of the present version of the formal justice argument have no basis in the demands of consistency. The idea that one should go on as before, without qualification allowing for changes in one's honest views, is not a corollary of the principle that like cases be treated alike, on the present reading. Of course, it may be argued that the notion of treating like cases alike is most properly understood in just such a way, as incorporating a conservative bias. We should be willing to consider such an argument. But we can find no basis for the idea either in the "form" of principles of justice or in the bare requirement of moral consistency. To assume the validity of a conservative bias without some such supporting argument would amount in this context to begging the question at issue, which is whether, and if so why, morally indefensible decisions should be accorded any measure of respect.

This is not to argue against the idea that a defensible doctrine of precedent might have a conservative bias; it is only to deny that such a doc-

114

trine enjoys support from a noncircular version of the formal justice argument. There may still be warrant for a conservative doctrine on the historical model, but that remains to be seen.

Even if we supposed that justice or consistency somehow required such deference to past judgment, regardless of its flaws, there would remain another substantial gap within the formal justice argument. Judicial practices vary, but any doctrine of precedent requires that a court take into account decisions made by other courts – not merely superior courts within the same jurisdiction, for deferring to their judgment involves respect for authority within a hierarchy, and not merely precedent. No doctrine of precedent is limited to prior decisions rendered by the same judge.

But the rational constraint of consistency does not require that we agree – that I bring my judgments into conformity with yours or that you bring yours into line with mine. Neither your nor my judgments can be faulted as incoherent on the ground that we fail to agree. The constraint applies to each individual's judgments and beliefs, not to all beliefs taken collectively.

A doctrine of precedent based on the constraint of consistency thus would concern only the decisions of each judge separately. Even if we assumed that consistency involved a conservative bias, it would require only that a judge follow the paths that she herself has already laid down, not that she take note of signposts erected by others.

There is, finally, the complication that doctrines of precedent apply most directly to the decisions that are rendered by courts, and that courts can have more than one member. It is unclear how a constraint of individual consistency in moral judgment would apply within that context. But even if we personified courts so that the constraint applied directly to them, that still would not make it incumbent on any court to respect decisions rendered by other courts.

More than the mere idea that like cases should be treated alike is required, then, to ground such a doctrine of judicial precedent. It might be suggested, however, that our mistake has been to focus on the historical model, with its conservative bias, when the normative model for the practice of precedent is available. For the normative model, it might be held, accords with the constraint of moral consistency. That is because a normative doctrine of precedent holds that past decisions should be followed only if they can be justified, and just when, other things being equal, the standards that provide the best justifications for such precedents are applicable to the current case to be decided. To accord best with the constraint of moral consistency, we must not understand justification here in narrow legalistic terms, which often would be of little use anyway, but must be prepared to apply standards that are sufficiently independent of the law to be usable in its appraisal.

The trouble with this suggestion is that it does not enable the formal justice argument to do any real work. It seems sound in claiming that a normative practice of precedent would accord with the constraint of moral consistency, because a judge so deciding cases would embrace only standards she could honestly accept and respect only decisions she could justify under those standards. But this is not to say that such a practice is required by the constraint of consistency, which is what must be true if the formal justice argument, so construed, is to make any difference here. For that to be the case, any alternative judicial practice must violate the constraint of moral consistency either directly or indirectly. But this means either that any alternative judicial practice is in itself incoherent, or else that it could not be justified within a self-consistent set of values. We have absolutely no reason to reach that conclusion. True enough, we have insufficient reason to believe that a justifiable practice of precedent would include a conservative bias, for we need positive reason to believe that a justifiable practice would respect unjustifiable decisions. But that possibility is, as we have noted, no stranger than the idea that one might have to act when principles conflict. We have no *a priori* reason to suppose that a judicial practice of precedent with some conservative bias is itself incoherent and cannot be justified, therefore we have no reason to suppose that only a normative practice of precedent is justifiable. A normative doctrine of precedent would not seem to violate the constraint of moral consistency, but it seems so far to receive no special support from it either.

V. BEYOND THE FORMAL JUSTICE ARGUMENT

A fresh start seems needed, but only a few brief comments can be offered here. We might ask, for example, whether a conservative bias can be justified. Why should a practice of precedent be expected to show any measure of respect to bad as well as good decisions?

The usual rationale for the practice, that it makes decisions more predictable, provides, as we have seen, something of an answer, but its justificatory force remains unclear. The points we have already made might be reinforced as follows. Not every frustrated expectation would seem to merit our concern. Not every instance, for example, is a matter of unfair surprise. This holds even within the legislative realm. The grandson who murdered in anticipation of inheriting under his grandfather's will, which seemed assured by the language of the relevant statute, no doubt suffered some frustration when he was denied those gains by the New York Court of Appeals,[7] but it would be implausible to characterize such surprise as unfair. This suggests that not every expectation encouraged by a judicial decision has an equal claim to our concern, and that we should be suspicious of rationales for the practice of precedent that fail to discriminate accordingly. The perpetuation of an unjust precedent is, in effect, the commission of an injustice to yet another party, whereas the failure to perpetuate an unjust precedent may visit no unfair disadvantage on the party who otherwise would have won.

One might object that all expectations encouraged by judicial decisions deserve judicial consideration because the decisions on which they are based embody a commitment to decide subsequent cases in the same way. One might go further: the judicial commitment to follow the same rule thereafter can account for the distinction between ordinary and "legitimate" expectations. Expectations that have been thus encouraged by courts are made legitimate in that way, and legitimate expectations are precisely those we have an obligation to respect.

The point is well taken, but still it must be qualified. Our basic question is whether any practice of precedent – a practice that would involve just the sort of commitment in question – can be justified, and if so whether it would involve a commitment to respect all past decisions, regardless of their merits, other things being equal. The argument that expectations established by such a commitment have a valid claim to judicial concern gives us no reason to believe that such commitments should be made. Furthermore, there may be limits to the binding force of such commitments, whether we like it or not. Just as agreements can be void *ab initio* in the eyes of the law, I would argue that the same applies to some commitments from a moral point of view.[8] We cannot assume, therefore, that judicial commitments to follow precedents have proper application when the precedential decisions themselves were unjustly decided.

If a conservative bias is to be defended in a practice of precedent, the most promising line of argument may be this. Suppose that a practice of precedent can be justified, initially within limits suggested by the occasional need for judicial rule-making. Two considerations, perhaps among others, would seem to argue for a judicial policy of respecting precedents generally, rather than one that calls for an attempt to differentiate the desirable from the undesirable precedents. It may be argued, first, that within a system like ours, with a doctrine of judicial deference to legislation emerging from a popularly elected legislature, it is appropriate for

---

[7] Riggs v. Palmer, 115 N.Y. 506, 22 N.E. 188 (1889).
[8] *See* D. Lyons, *supra* note 3, at 84–85.

courts to minimize apparent changes in the law they are charged with administering. It may also be argued, second, that a policy encouraging courts to pick and choose among precedents, in order to ensure that only acceptable ones be followed, is at worst counterproductive and at best ineffective. Such arguments require, however, considerable elaboration and substantiation, which is precisely the sort of effort it is my overriding purpose to encourage.*

---

* Justification for what is here called "a conservative bias" in a practice of precedent has been offered by R. Dworkin in " 'Natural' Law Revisited," 34 *U. Fla. L. Rev.* 165 (1982), and *Law's Empire* (1986), and by M. A. Eisenberg in *The Nature of the Common Law* (1988). Dworkin's approach is discussed in the last essay in this volume. (Discussion of Eisenberg must await another occasion.)

6

Derivability, defensibility, and the justification of judicial decisions

Philosophers of law generally appear to assume that there is a very close connection between a judicial decision's being *required by law* and its being *justified*. In this paper I shall try to show that this assumption is mistaken.

Legal theory recently has focused on the problem of "hard cases," in which there is reason to doubt that the law requires a particular decision, to the exclusion of alternative possible decisions. The relevant question is not whether the law requires that a judge render some decision or other, thus deciding those cases, but whether the law that can truly be said to exist before a decision is rendered requires one particular decision. Discussions of this issue often seem to assume that this is equivalent to the question, whether a particular decision is uniquely justifiable.

Less attention has been paid to what we may call "easy cases," in which it seems clear that the law requires a particular decision. What is said about them, however, does appear to assume that a particular decision's being required by law is equivalent to its being justified.

Those who believe that there is a significant connection between a judicial decision's being required by law and its being justified would no doubt agree, upon reflection, that the connection is not one of equivalence. Some qualification of the view under discussion would seem to be required by considerations such as the following. First, someone who believes that no particular decision is required by law in a hard case need not hold that no decision can then be justified. It may be possible for a court to justify a particular decision, to the exclusion of the alternative decisions, even when no decision is required by law. In that event, any

"Derivability, Defensibility, and the Justification of Judicial Decisions," *The Monist* 68 (1985): 325–46. Copyright © 1985, The Monist, La Salle, Ill. 61301. This paper develops an argument that I sketched in "Justification and Easy Cases," presented to the Eleventh World Congress on Philosophy of Law and Social Philosophy in Helsinki. Versions have also been presented at Syracuse University, the University of Massachusetts at Amherst, Hobart and William Smith Colleges, the University of Minnesota at Morris, the University of Calgary, Wayne State University, and the University of Michigan at Ann Arbor. I am grateful for the many helpful comments I received on those occasions. The argument was originally sketched in "Justification and Judicial Responsibility," *California Law Review* 72 (March 1984): 301–22.

justification must turn on doctrines that come from outside the law. If so, however, we should not assume that a judicial decision can be justified *only when* it is required by law. In other words, we must allow that a judicial decision's being required by law is *not*, in general, a *necessary* condition of its being justified.

Second, and perhaps more controversially, it seems possible for a judicial decision to be justified, *all things considered*, even when it is contrary to a decision that is required by law. This can happen when the injustice that would be done by following the law provides sufficient reason for a judge not to follow it and to render a different decision. If we wish to leave room for this possibility, then we must allow that a judicial decision's being required by law is *not* always a *sufficient* condition of its being justified, all things considered.

I mentioned these two complications not in order to discredit the assumption that is commonly made about the justification of judicial decisions, but rather to make it as plausible as possible. The point is to render any objections to the assumption that much more significant. If the assumption is mistaken even when it is suitably qualified, then this would imply that any stronger, less modest version of the assumption is likewise mistaken.

We are now in a position to formulate the assumption that I wish to discuss. What seems to be assumed is that a judicial decision's being required by law provides at least some measure of justification for it. In other words, a judicial decision is at least "prima facie" justified if it is required by law. I shall call this view *the doctrine of legalistic justification,* and I shall often refer to it simply as "the doctrine."

Why is the doctrine worth criticizing? First, if it is mistaken, the fact has some morally significant implications for the justification of judicial decisions. It would also imply that a judge can be placed in a difficult moral predicament, even in easy cases.

Second, I believe that the doctrine has a bearing on the so-called "positivist" position that is usually labelled "the separation of law and morals."[1] This holds, in part, that specific laws and legal systems can fail to satisfy minimal moral requirements, as a consequence of which there may be no obligation to obey the law. But "the separation of law and morals" is usually understood to go further – to say, for example, that there is "no necessary connection between law as it is and law as it ought to be," or, more generally, between legal and moral appraisals (or, most extremely, between legal and moral ideas). I believe that something like this

---

[1] I discuss this doctrine further in "Moral Aspects of Legal Theory," *Midwest Studies in Philosophy* VII (1982): 223–54 [reprinted in this volume].

is correct. But it is a noteworthy and surprising fact that some of those who explicitly endorse "the separation of law and morals" also appear to embrace the doctrine of legalistic justification. Now, it is not entirely clear how best to understand "the separation of law and morals," but, however it is best understood, it would seem to clash with the doctrine of legalistic justification. The result is that positivistic writings often appear to encompass inconsistencies – or, at the very least, to be strained by internal tensions. This tends to blur the contrast between opposing jurisprudential schools of thought and to confuse the issues. I hope to dispel some of that confusion.

I

My discussion of the doctrine will concentrate on easy cases. For that is where any problems for the doctrine can be seen most clearly, with fewest distractions. Furthermore, easy cases deserve closer attention than they have been given. Indeed, it turns out not so easy to explain what is meant by the distinction between hard and easy cases. So I shall begin with a few observations about the distinction, mainly in order to insure that difficulties with it do not affect the arguments to follow.

There is no standard way of drawing the distinction between hard and easy cases, and some ways of drawing it beg the currently disputed question, whether hard cases are (sometimes, always, or never) decidable on the basis of existing law. This happens, for example, when the term "hard case" is understood to mean "case that is not decidable on the basis of existing law." I shall offer a provisional sketch of the distinction which has the merit of leaving this question open.

Let us begin with hard cases, so as to get an idea of what may be thought to distinguish them from easy cases. In complex systems of law such as those with which we are most familiar, the problem is rarely, if ever, that the law provides absolutely no guidance for a decision, but rather that plausible and perhaps quite reasonable arguments are available on both sides of the legal question. Suppose, for example, that a court must decide a case that falls within an area of disputed, unclear, or unsettled law. It is not that there are no relevant statutes, constitutional provisions, or judicial precedents, but rather that these require further interpretation before they can be used to decide the case, and that any interpretation that makes it possible to decide the case one way rather than another must compete with an alternative interpretation that would decide it differently. Neither interpretation is untenable; arguments supporting the competing interpretations have a reasonable basis in law. So reasonable disagreement by competent judges and lawyers concerning

121

how to understand and apply the law is possible. Such disagreement can persist even after a court has rendered its decision – even after a decision has been rendered by a court that has the "final say" in such matters.

We can understand this situation in the following way. In such a case, given the presumed or established facts, no decision is *logically required* by established legal doctrines. That is because conflicting legal considerations cannot be eliminated. Arguments may well be possible concerning the relative importance of the competing considerations, but it remains impossible to *deduce* a dispositive proposition of law from a combination of the given facts and established legal doctrines without ignoring some relevant legal considerations.

We can use this as the basis for one way of distinguishing hard from easy cases. We might say that an *easy* case is one that can be decided by applying established legal rules or other legal standards within *logically conclusive* arguments, without ignoring any relevant legal considerations. A *hard* case would then be one that cannot be so decided.

The appropriateness of drawing the distinction in this way is suggested by the fact that some theorists appear to have inferred, from the conditions that are here used to define hard cases, the conclusion that those cases are legally undecidable, that is, that no particular decision is then required by law. The operative assumption appears to be that a particular decision is *required by law* if and only if a corresponding dispositive proposition of law is *logically required* (entailed) by the relevant and applicable established legal doctrines.[2]

This way of drawing the distinction leaves open the question, whether hard cases are (sometimes, always, or never) legally decidable. We can see this in the following way. The question, whether there is a uniquely required decision in a hard case, is equivalent to the question, whether some dispositive proposition of law is *true*. And it seems, on general theoretical grounds, an open question, whether such a proposition of law *can be* true, even when it cannot be deduced from a combination of the given facts and established legal doctrines (and even when there can continue to be reasonable disagreement about whether the proposition of law is true). For consider the alternative answers to this question. An affirmative answer involves the idea that legal propositions are in this important respect just like most propositions outside the law. Most propositions about existing states of affairs outside the law can be supported, if at all, only by nondeductive, logically *in*conclusive arguments, which often must take into account conflicting considerations. From the fact

---

[2] See my "Legal Formalism and Instrumentalism – A Pathological Study," *Cornell Law Review* 66 (June 1981): 949–72 [reprinted in this volume].

that we cannot conclusively establish a proposition about the natural world by deducing it from observed facts and established doctrines, for example, it cannot safely be inferred that there is no such state of affairs. (I say it cannot "safely" be inferred, in order to acknowledge that there is, in effect, philosophical disagreement about this matter, which applies to the following point.) *Truth,* in general, does not presuppose the availability of *proof.*

Perhaps the law is like that; but then, perhaps, it is not. We would not be justified in merely assuming that propositions of law are in this respect different from propositions outside the law. But there are grounds for believing that law is different from other aspects of the natural world. The law that exists within a given jurisdiction has been determined, to a great degree at least, by more or less conscious, deliberate human decisions (legislative decisions, for example). This makes it possible to argue with some plausibility that the law is no more determinate than the decisions that determine it. So it may be argued that there is nothing to the law, in relevant respects, beyond established legal doctrines, which themselves can be somewhat indeterminate. If that were so, then for legal propositions truth might presuppose the availability of proof. If these issues can be considered open, then the way I have sketched the distinction between hard and easy cases leaves open the question whether hard cases are (sometimes, always, or never) legally decidable.

But my sketch of the distinction must be taken as provisional. The contrast between hard and easy cases may be more complex than I have suggested, and it may be only a matter of degree. For example, decisions in all cases may presuppose some fundamental doctrines that themselves require interpretation. One such doctrine is "legislative supremacy," which can be understood in alternative ways (with more or less emphasis on "the letter of the law," "legislative intentions," and "legislative purposes," as well as on consistency among established legal doctrines taken all together). A case that seems, on the surface, unambiguously decidable on the basis of a relevant statute may turn out, on further inspection, to be more complex, and thus not as "easy" as it first appeared. For it can make a great deal of difference if the case is decided on the basis of the statute's "plain meaning" rather than its arguable intention or purpose. It can also make a difference if the doctrine of legislative supremacy is understood so as to allow or even require courts to take into account established principles of the common law (which themselves may be somewhat unclear) as well as other arguably relevant considerations.

But I think the sketch will do for present purposes. Perhaps there are no easy cases, as described. We can then view the argument that I shall present as concerning the *degree* to which legal considerations that argue

123

for a particular decision provide *some measure* of justification for such a decision. My argument may then be taken as attempting to show that legal considerations do not themselves provide any measure of justification for judicial decisions.

I shall deal with the doctrine of legalistic justification in the following way. In the next section, I will consider some promising approaches to the justification of judicial decisions in hard cases. This will suggest the character of the conditions that make it plausible to think of judicial decisions as justifiable. Then I will turn, in section III, to easy cases. I will use an example to bring out the problematic character that judicial decisions can have even when they are assumed to be required by law. Here I will present my main argument against the doctrine. In section IV I will consider a possible objection to my argument based on the idea that I have misconstrued it. I will consider an alternative interpretation of the doctrine that renders it a truism concerning "legal" justification. Finally, in section V, I will consider the idea that there is a pervasive judicial obligation of fidelity to law.

II

Until recently, legal philosophers had no clearly developed theories of adjudication for hard cases. This can be understood as a consequence of two interacting factors: the nature of "analytical" jurisprudence and the assumption that hard cases cannot be decided on the basis of existing law. Given the latter assumption, if decisions are to be justified, they must be justified on the basis of a *normative* theory, which tells judges how they *should* reach decisions when legal guidance has been exhausted. Such decisions would then be seen as making law. But analytical jurisprudence has traditionally seen its job as that of faithfully describing and understanding law as it is, not as that of providing normative guidance based on extralegal principles. Existing law could only set limits on legally possible alternative decisions.

How, then, is a court to justify a particular decision, to the exclusion of the alternatives, in a case that is legally undecidable? Here is one very natural suggestion that might be made. Not just any arbitrary decision can be justified. By the same token, not just anything that might be offered as a reason for deciding a case one way rather than another is capable of truly justifying a decision. When it is taken for granted that the law does not require any particular decision, then it seems most plausible to suppose that a decision could be justified only by showing that it represents a fair way of settling the legal dispute or is on other grounds morally defensible.

124

In such a case, for example, it may be held that one particular decision would best serve the cause of "economic efficiency." Such reasoning may well play a central role within a justifying argument, but I believe it would not be sufficient. What needs to be shown is that the legal dispute arises in a context in which it is *fair* to decide matters on economic grounds, and perhaps also (if this is not already implicit) that there are no overriding moral objections to deciding the case in such a manner.

The appeal to economic efficiency is to be taken only as an illustration (of some interest because of the current popularity of "economic analysis" in law). It does not much matter, for present purposes, what sorts of considerations may be regarded as relevant or that they may vary with the context and the nature of the case. What does seem important is this: when considerations such as fairness play a decisive or at least a regulative role in deciding a case, then it seems plausible to regard the decision as capable of being justified. This applies, at least, when the decision cannot be made on legal grounds.

To illustrate this point further, I will consider briefly some new theories of adjudication for hard cases. I should emphasize that I shall not consider all proposals that have been made; I shall not even try to capture the significant complexities of proposals on which I shall draw. I shall only sketch a general approach which promises to provide something that might plausibly be considered a theory of *justification*.

A promising approach begins with the idea that fairness requires that like cases be treated alike. This is regarded by many legal philosophers as the root idea of "the rule of law," and thus it has a natural role in adjudication. Now, in hard cases, there is no simple way of applying this requirement; but there may be a complex way of satisfying it — or at least of coming as close as possible to satisfying it. For, as we have noted, the problem that usually arises is not a dearth of law but rather unclear, disputed, or unsettled law. Relevant statutes, constitutional provisions, and judicial precedents may require interpretation, and interpretations that can be used to decide a hard case are controversial. The promising approach to hard cases proposes a way of interpreting past legislative and judicial decisions that permits us to satisfy (or to come as close as possible to satisfying) the requirement that like cases be treated alike and, by virtue of that fact, to justify a decision.

Here is how it works. We begin with the idea that we are seeking decisions that can be justified. This imposes a constraint on possible interpretations of past legislative and judicial decisions: we must understand them on the basis of considerations that are capable of justifying them. In the case of statutes, for example, we must understand them (so far as that is possible) as reasonable means to reasonable ends. In the

125

case of judicial precedents, we must interpret them in the light of judicial arguments that are available to justify them. These interpretations will be constrained further by our understanding of legislative and judicial history, at least so far as such information is available. But that history is often ambiguous and then a determination must still be made concerning the best interpretation of such statutes and precedents. In these ways, we can appeal (at least sometimes) to past legislative and judicial decisions for guidance in deciding a hard case, even when those past decisions are superficially unclear, by identifying general aims or standards that are capable of justifying them and that enable us to interpret them so that their persisting legal consequences shall be most conducive to those aims or most faithful to those standards. This approach suggests that we can satisfy the requirement of fairness, that like cases be treated alike, and justify a decision in a novel case accordingly, when we are able to decide the case on the basis of the *very same* considerations that can be held to underlie, by justifying, relevant legislative and judicial decisions.

For present purposes, it does not matter that such an approach to adjudication in hard cases is difficult and may not yield determinate results in all cases. It is difficult to identify and properly balance the constraints of institutional history and justifying considerations; and some past legislative and judicial decisions may turn out to be unjustifiable. What seems important about this approach is that it makes essential use of moral considerations, such as fairness. It is precisely the role of such elements that seems to qualify it as a theory of justification.

III

We turn now to easy cases. It will be useful to illustrate the points I wish to make by reference to a real case. I shall use the case of *Daniels and Daniels v. R. White & Sons and Tarbard*[3] because it is analyzed by Neil MacCormick to illustrate what he calls "deductive justification" in law.[4] It also has certain features that will be relevant for my argument.

The case is this. Mr. Daniels bought a bottle of R. White's lemonade from Mrs. Tarbard at her pub. He took the bottle home and shared the contents with his wife. Because the lemonade contained carbolic acid, Mr. and Mrs. Daniels both became ill. They subsequently sued the manufacturer of the lemonade, R. White & Sons, as well as the owner of the pub, Mrs. Tarbard, from whom the lemonade was purchased. Their suit was only partly successful. Because the Daniels did not prove that the

---

3   (1938) 4 All E.R. 258.
4   Neil MacCormick, *Legal Reasoning and Legal Theory* (Oxford: Clarendon Press, 1978), ch. II.

manufacturer had failed to exercise "reasonable care" (a point it probably would have been quite difficult to prove), the court found in favor of the manufacturer, so the Daniels lost that part of their claim for damages. But it found for Mr. Daniels against Mrs. Tarbard, because she sold him goods that were (by definition, given the facts of the case) "not of merchantable quality" under the Sale of Goods Act then in force.

MacCormick treats this as a case in which the decision was required by the law of the jurisdiction at the time. His analysis of the court's reasoning implies that it culminated in a dispositive proposition of law that was derivable by logically rigorous argument from established rules, given the established facts. So the *Daniels* decision represents what we would count under our provisional distinction as an easy case.

My argument does not assume that this was an easy case in the sense that the decision was conclusively required by law; indeed, it does not even assume that the decision was required by law, conclusively or otherwise. What makes this case a suitable example is that it seems as if the decision was required by law although there are grounds for doubting that the decision was justified. Even if all such cases are somewhat hard, because of their morally problematic character, my argument will still be relevant, for it will apply to those legal considerations that argue for the decision that was rendered.

MacCormick treats the decision in the *Daniels* case as justified precisely because he believes it was required by law. This very strongly suggests the doctrine of legalistic justification. But one of the very great merits of MacCormick's discussion is its explicit reference to background "presuppositions" of the claim that such a decision is justified.[5] Because MacCormick is not committed to the claim that such presuppositions are always true, it would not be fair to say that he is committed to the doctrine of legalistic justification. But it is noteworthy that MacCormick does not consider the possibility that the presuppositions may be false or what effect that might have on the claim that such a decision is justified. That is the point I wish to consider.

I want to discuss the justifiability of the *Daniels* decision, using it only as an example. I do not wish to claim that the decision was unjustifiable. I wish to bring out what may be involved in regarding it as justified and by so doing to challenge the doctrine of legalistic justification. My strategy will be to argue that any plausible account of the background presuppositions must allow for the possibility that they are false, in which case justification may be impossible.

Let us focus on the part of the decision that made Mrs. Tarbard liable

---

[5]   Ibid., ch. III.

to Mr. Daniels for damages. Mrs. Tarbard sold merchandise that she had adequate reason to believe was perfectly all right. She could not reasonably be regarded as having acted negligently. She was nevertheless required to pay damages under a rule that imposed "strict" civil liability. The judge himself remarked, when rendering his decision, that it was "rather hard on Mrs. Tarbard, who is a perfectly innocent person in the matter."[6] Given all that, it seems reasonable for us to wonder how the decision against Mrs. Tarbard could have been justified.

We might begin by saying that the decision against Mrs. Tarbard seems morally regrettable. I put the point this way so as to leave open the possibility that the decision could be justified. It is arguable, for example, that rules imposing strict civil liability are sometimes justifiable, and I do not wish to foreclose that possibility here – or, for that matter, some other ground of justification for the decision. Its justifiability may depend, for example, on whether Mrs. Tarbard had legal recourse against the manufacturer of the lemonade, which might have enabled her to recover her loss by transferring it to the party that appears more clearly responsible (if anyone could be held responsible) for the injuries that were suffered by Mr. and Mrs. Daniels.

However we should ultimately view this particular decision, I think its features help us to see that we may reason about the justifiability of judicial decisions that are required by law in the following way. A decision might be justifiable directly, on its merits, as a fair or otherwise morally defensible way of settling a legal dispute, given the facts of the case. This may be true even when there are significant moral objections to a decision, provided that those objections are outweighed by considerations on the other side. But even if a decision cannot be justified directly, on its merits, it may be justifiable indirectly, on the basis of factors that are extrinsic to the case. For example, the decision may be required by established legal doctrines for which there may be adequate justification. It is a platitude that justifiable rules can sometimes have morally regrettable applications, and we should allow for the possibility. Even if a decision cannot be justified directly, it may be justifiable by reference to the merits of the rules that require it. Of course, these possible grounds of justification are not mutually exclusive; rather, they can be mutually reinforcing.

But we cannot leave matters there, for we cannot assume that established rules of law are always justifiable on their merits. A strict liability rule, like the one that was decisive against Mrs. Tarbard, may not be justifiable. In general, a rule that is decisive in determining a judicial decision may be unjust or in other respects morally indefensible. In that

---

[6] Quoted in ibid., p. 21.

event, a decision that is required by the rule cannot be justified on the ground that it was required by a justifiable rule.

Even so, it may still be possible to justify such a decision. For there may be justification for following the rules of the legal system generally, even when relevant rules cannot be justified on their merits. This possibility is, in effect, entertained by MacCormick. He asks, "Why ought we to treat every decision in accordance with a rule valid by our criteria of validity as being sufficiently justified?"[7] This is taken to be equivalent to the question, "What is presupposed in our regarding a decision that is required by the (rules of) law as justified?" MacCormick answers the question that he poses by observing that both officials and citizens "can and do have reasons for accepting" the "criteria of validity" for rules in the system;[8] – for accepting, that is, the established legal tests for the existence of rules within the system. Examples of such reasons, as given by MacCormick, are:

'it is good that judicial decisions be predictable and contribute to certainty of law, which they are and do when they apply known rules identified in accordance with commonly shared and understood criteria of recognition'; 'it is good that judges stay within their assigned place in the constitutional order, applying established law rather than making new law'; 'it is good that law-making be entrusted to the elected representatives of the people, not usurped by non-elected and non-removable judges'; 'the existing and accepted constitutional order is a fair and just system, and accordingly the criteria of recognition of laws which it institutes are fair and just criteria which ought to be observed'; and so on.

The second last of these is peculiarly appropriate to a more or less democratic political system, and to that extent mingles legal with overtly political values; the last involves an overtly political judgment about the justice of the system, yet it is precisely the kind of judgment which for many honest men and women must underpin their acceptance of a legal system all and whole.[9]

For present purposes, considerations like these must be understood to work in the following way. In a given case, it may happen that neither the specific decision that is required by law nor the rules that require it are justifiable on their merits. Even so, the specific application of those rules may be justifiable indirectly, on grounds relating to the quality of the system as a whole.

This reasoning is analogous to arguments in support of the claim that there is a general obligation to obey the law, so that one should generally obey the law, even when specific laws are morally deficient. Such an argument cites factors relating to the quality of the legal system as a whole, or one's relation to it or to other members of the community. The claim

7 Ibid., p. 63. 8 Ibid.
9 Ibid., pp. 63f.

that there is such an obligation is most plausible when it is moderate, that is, when the obligation is not held to be "absolute" but only "prima facie." This means that there may still be adequate reason for disobeying the law in some cases. The general point of the argument is to show that positive justification is required for disobedience to law.

The argument suggested by MacCormick would seem to have analogous features. It is recognized that there may be moral objections to specific decisions as well as to the laws requiring those decisions, so that it may not be possible to justify the decisions either directly, on their merits, or on the merits of the laws that require those decisions. In order to overcome at least some of the moral objections to specific decisions that are required by law, appeal is made to desirable qualities of the system as a whole or of official respect for existing law. The conclusion of such an argument is that judicial decisions that are required by law are justified.

As in the parallel case, such a claim is most plausible when it is moderate, that is, when the alleged justification for specific decisions that are required by law is regarded as only "prima facie." This allows for the possibility that there might be (in some special cases, and despite the arguments for respecting the legal system as a whole) overriding reasons to regard a decision that is required by law as unjustifiable, all things considered. To distinguish this sort of claim from the claim that there is a general obligation to obey the law, I shall express the conclusion of the argument that is suggested by MacCormick by saying that *the law merits our respect*. My point is that this may be false.

I am prepared to grant that such reasoning as MacCormick suggests may sometimes be sound. But what does this amount to? It is assumed that both specific laws and their applications to specific cases can be morally objectionable, so that positive grounds are *needed* to establish that such decisions are justifiable. To grant that such a claim may sometimes be sound is to grant that there *may* be adequate reason for believing that the law of a particular jurisdiction merits respect so that decisions that are required by law can be justified even when a particular law and the decisions it requires cannot be justified on their merits. My argument does not assume the contrary. But, in granting all of this, one is not assuming that law *always* merits such respect. That would be implausible.

My claim, then, is this. All plausible arguments which purport to show that laws should be followed, even when they or their specific applications are morally objectionable, or which purport to show that judicial decisions that are required by law can be justified, even when neither they nor the specific laws that require them can be justified on their merits –

all plausible arguments to that effect have the following feature: they *cannot* show that the law *automatically* merits such respect. For they assume the contrary. Rather, such arguments seek to show that certain conditions, under which law merits respect, are in fact satisfied, though they are not necessarily satisfied. Relative to the existence of a legal system, the satisfaction of the relevant conditions is always a contingent (and, I venture to say, a problematic) matter.

It does not much matter, for present purposes, what the relevant conditions are. There may be several independent sets of such conditions, the satisfaction of any of which implies that judicial decisions are justified (at least "prima facie") when they are required by law. Let us call any such set *R-conditions*. My argument is that R-conditions are not necessarily satisfied; moreover, they are not always satisfied. It all depends. A system may be fair and just, democratic and humane, for example, but not all systems are like that. The same applies to any other plausible set of R-conditions. A system may be unfair and unjust, undemocratic and oppressive, exploitative and inhumane. Under such circumstances, there may well be no sound argument to the effect that the law (of such a system) merits our respect. There may be inadequate grounds for holding that judicial decisions are justified (even "prima facie") because they are required by law.

This does not mean (and I am not claiming) that no decisions that are required by law can then be justified. It may still be the case that some decisions or the laws that require them are justifiable on their merits. To put the point simply, just as there can be bad laws and regrettable decisions in a generally meritorious legal system, there can also be good laws and fair decisions that are required by law under a generally bad system. But, when no set of R-conditions is satisfied, then some decisions that are required by law will not be justifiable, not even "prima facie." These will be the decisions that cannot be justified on their merits or on the merits of the laws that require them. When a system is generally bad, there must be some such cases, and there probably will be many.

To summarize this argument. Judicial decisions may be justified directly, on their merits, on the merits of the laws that require them, or on the merits of the legal system as a whole. It sometimes happens, however, that decisions which are required by law cannot be justified on such grounds. But this is just to say that the doctrine of legalistic justification is false.

Before considering what I take to be potentially more serious objections to the foregoing argument, I would like to take up one type of objection that could be based on familiar considerations mentioned by MacCormick. It might be claimed that there are *always* some advantages

131

to be gotten from officials' following the law, even under a generally bad system. One may hold, for example (as MacCormick suggests), that officials' following the law always promotes certainty and predictability, which translates into some real advantages for at least some individuals. And it might be argued, further, that this provides a basis for regarding judicial decisions which are required by law as justified, at least "prima facie."

I do not believe that such considerations provide a plausible basis for the claim that judicial decisions that are required by law are always at least "prima facie" justified. In the first place, there is also reason to suppose that disadvantages to some result from officials' following the law, and in some cases we can be sure that they outweigh the advantages. This will often be the case within a generally bad system. In a specific case under a generally bad system, the predictable disadvantages may well outweigh the advantages, thus eliminating this presumption in favor of following the law.

Furthermore, what needs to be shown is that such advantages add up to a plausible set of R-conditions. Under a system that is generally bad – unjust and unfair, undemocratic and oppressive, exploitative and inhumane – the relevant advantages flowing from factors like certainty and predictability are likely to be conferred primarily on those who profit from injustice. This makes it unlikely that such advantages could justify (even "prima facie") those decisions that are required by law that involve injustice to those who systematically suffer injustice under the system.

So, on grounds of justice as well as a realistic accounting of advantages and disadvantages, I do not think that this sort of objection can hope to save the doctrine of legalistic justification. Let us turn, then, to more formidable objections.

IV

It might be argued that I have misconstrued the doctrine of legalistic justification because I have imposed on it expectations of *moral* justification when it must be understood in terms of *legal* justification. When properly interpreted (this objection would go), the doctrine is unaffected by my argument because the conditions of legal justification are automatically satisfied whenever a decision is required by law. For that is precisely what legal justification amounts to.

If the doctrine is understood in the way suggested, then it is invulnerable to criticism. For it then becomes an empty tautology which asserts, in effect, that decisions which are required by law are required by law. And it is certainly true that I have understood the doctrine differently.

132

Is the doctrine then a harmless truism? I think not. That is because "legal justification" is usually assumed to have implications that transform the platitude into an untenable doctrine. The problem is this. Legal justification, in the sense stipulated, is often taken as a "weak" kind of justification, which legal decisions can enjoy even when they fall short of full-fledged "moral" justification. But this is a mistake: legal and moral justification are not related in that way when "legal justification" is *guaranteed* for any decision that is required by law. To explain this, I need to distinguish two uses of the concept of justification. My claim is that these uses are not only distinct but independent.

Consider the idea of justifying a theorem within Euclidean geometry. To justify a theorem is to derive it from given axioms. But a theorem so justified is not shown to be true of physical space. A proposition of geometry may be *derivable within a given system* without being *defensible* in any other respect.

It is possible to construct any number of arbitrary systems within which propositions are derivable. But if we are interested in more than mere derivability, then we must take care how we construct a system. If derivability is supposed to represent something more, then the premises from which a proposition is derivable cannot themselves be arbitrary. If the theorems of a geometric system are supposed to be true of physical space, for example, then the axioms of that system must themselves be true of physical space.

The analogy with legal systems, while imperfect, is I think instructive. It is imperfect because dispositive propositions of law, which determine how the law requires that a case be decided, are not derivable from general legal propositions alone, but only given relevant facts. If for present purposes the relevant facts can be assumed, however, the analogy is unproblematic. If some cases are decidable by reference to existing law, that is because corresponding dispositive propositions of law are derivable within the system; that is, they are derivable from a combination of more general legal propositions and statements showing their applicability to those cases. But to show this is not to show that the corresponding judicial decisions are defensible in any other respect.

In what other respect might a judicial decision be, or fail to be, defensible? To answer this question, we must consider why we are generally concerned about the justifiability of judicial decisions. If we conceived of judicial decisions as, say, part of a complex, esoteric game that is played by officials, a game that involves determining the implications of a complex set of arbitrary premises, then we might not worry about anything other than the derivability of the corresponding legal propositions. We would then be satisfied to use only the notion of "legal justification."

133

Sometimes, we are immediately concerned with the derivability of a proposition of law, when we wish to determine whether a particular decision is required by law. But this does not nearly exhaust our interest in the justifiability of judicial decisions, especially once it is determined that a particular decision is required by law.

Judicial decisions do not merely seek to identify derivable propositions of law. They also have a significant impact on important interests of those who come before the courts, including some who appear involuntarily. This is not merely an accidental or incidental aspect of the judicial process, and the justification of judicial decisions must presumably take this aspect of them into account.

The judicial process obtains against a certain background, which includes the assumption that acts intended to deprive a person of liberty, other valued goods, or even life itself *require* justification. This accounts for our primary interest in the justification of judicial decisions. Judicial decisions typically determine that specific individuals shall be treated in ways that require justification. Here, justification concerns not merely a proposition of law, but also what an official, acting with the force of the state behind her, determines shall be done to other people. In deciding whether such an act is justified, we must take into account factors that go beyond the derivability of a proposition from legal standards. We must concern ourselves with whether such an act is defensible.

This approach to justification was reflected in our discussion of the *Daniels* case. For we assumed that the decision rendered was required by law. When we asked how such a decision could be justified, we were not questioning the derivability of the dispositive proposition of law within the legal system. We were concerned about its defensibility. And our reasoning about the possibility of justifying such a decision acknowledged that the law requiring it might be arbitrary in a relevant sense: both specific laws requiring that decision and the legal system as a whole might fail to satisfy minimal moral requirements, in which case the decision might not be justifiable at all. In other words, derivability does not entail any measure of defensibility.

If all this is granted, I do not mind the suggestion that I have imposed on the doctrine expectations of "moral" justification. We expect judicial decisions to be defensible, in one way or another. This does not mean, however, that they must be derivable directly from moral principles. It does mean that judicial decisions are expected to be defensible either on their merits or else on the merits of the law that requires them. And this is not guaranteed merely by the fact that judicial decisions are required by law.

This is important because the notion of "legal justification," when understood as derivability within a system of law, is sometimes characterized, as I have said, as a kind of "weak justification," and is then treated as if it necessarily contributes to a generic sort of defensibility, of which "moral" justification is merely another species. This amounts to regarding a decision that is "legally justified" as "prima facie" justified. Then the doctrine of legalistic justification is converted from a harmless platitude into a mistaken doctrine. For it becomes inflated into the idea that the mere derivability of a dispositive proposition of law automatically provides some measure of justification for the corresponding judicial decision. My argument was intended to expose this as a mistake.

The mistake is not made in isolation. There is a noticeable tendency among legal philosophers to treat "law" and "morals" as coordinate normative systems in some such way. There is a parallel tendency among moral philosophers to treat "institutional" and "moral" requirements as analogously coordinate. The result is to regard legal and institutional requirements as on a par with "moral" requirements. That involves just the same kind of mistake.

Consider the case of legal requirements. It is first assumed that we can refer to legal requirements on conduct as "obligations." Then it is observed that if one fails to perform as an obligation requires, one's conduct is (at least "prima facie") wrong. But this way of treating legal requirements assumes, in effect, that legal requirements are a species of the genus obligation, of which "moral" obligations are merely another species. The consequences of regarding law and morals in this way come out most clearly in discussions concerning possible justifications for disobedience to law. Legal philosophers generally recognize that there may be justification for not following the law. They sometimes acknowledge this by saying that the law is not the sole or final determinant of how one should behave: The law is always relevant, but one must also consider what morality independently requires. Thus, a failure to obey the law is not automatically wrong; it is only prima facie wrong.

This may appear, on the surface, to be a moderate and even an enlightened doctrine. But it involves a crucial invalid assumption, namely, that justification is always *required* for disobedience to law.

To see the problem here, consider the more or less equivalent notion that there is a general obligation to obey the law. If there *is* such an obligation, then the failure to follow the law *is* (at least "prima facie") wrong. In using "wrong" here, I am assuming, in effect, that there are *sound* standards for behavior, violation of which is (at least "prima facie") wrong. We may call these standards "moral," if we like, so long as we do not confuse them with merely customary or idiosyncratic standards that may be arbitrary and indefensible. Merely arbitrary standards

135

could not be the basis for sound criticism of behavior. The idea that there is a general obligation to obey the law, like the idea that justification is required for disobedience to law, assumes that there are relevant sound standards for behavior.

If there are some sound standards for behavior, then one of them might amount to an obligation to obey the law. Such a standard implies that disobedience to law is (at least "prima facie") wrong and requires justification. But similar implications do not flow from the mere existence of legal standards, when no assumptions are made about their justifiability or the merits of the larger system of law. From the mere fact that there is a legal requirement, we can infer that contrary behavior is "legally wrong," or in other words unlawful, but we cannot infer that contrary behavior is (even "prima facie") wrong in the sense that assumes sound standards for behavior. If the legal requirement is unjustifiable and the legal system as a whole is not meritorious, then no justification is required for disobedience to law.

So "legal" and "moral" obligations can be regarded as coordinate when, but only when, "moral" justification is taken to be relative to standards that are merely customary, idiosyncratic, or otherwise arbitrary. That is not the sort of justification we have been concerned with here. That is not what defensibility amounts to. Our concern about the justifiability of judicial decisions assumes that there are sound standards for judging what people do to one another. These are the standards we invoke when we require that judicial decisions be defensible. The mere derivability of a dispositive proposition of law within a given system does not entail any measure of defensibility for the corresponding judicial decision, because the decision, the laws that require it, and the system as a whole do not necessarily satisfy such standards. That is part of what is meant by "the separation of law and morals."

V

The argument of the preceding section implies an important point: derivability and defensibility in this context concern different objects. Derivability is a property of legal *propositions* relative to a given system of law, whereas defensibility is attached to judicial *acts* within a given legal context.

This suggests that we should focus more sharply on the judicial act, as well as another objection to my argument. One might claim that I have looked for grounds of justification in the wrong place. What needs to be justified is not *what* is done, but the *doing* of it. It may be argued that *rendering* decisions that are required by law is justified, because the officials who do so are under an obligation of fidelity to the law that they are charged with administering. They are obligated to apply the law as they find it.

This line of argument is promising because it invokes a consideration that is not merely legal. The judicial obligation of fidelity to law concerns the moral responsibility of officials such as judges. Furthermore, it is reasonably understood as both more demanding and more extensive than a general obligation to obey the law that might be incumbent on any ordinary citizen. It is more demanding because an official who seeks or consents to serve in a position of public trust has made a commitment, a voluntary undertaking, to follow the law, and such a commitment must be added to whatever ground there is for a general obligation to obey the law that may be shared by other members of the community. Because it is more stringent, it is plausible to regard its implications as more extensive. A judge may be under an obligation to render decisions that are required by law *even when those decisions could not themselves be justified*. At the same time, however, it is plausible to suppose that such an obligation, while strong, might be overridden in very special cases. But this moderating qualification is compatible with the idea that the obligation provides some measure of justification for rendering decisions that are required by law.

It is important to emphasize that this argument does not support the original doctrine of legalistic justification. It does not tend to show that the substantive decisions *themselves* are justifiable, but rather that a judge can be justified in *rendering* decisions that cannot themselves be justified either directly or indirectly. It is relevant to the moral predicament of a judge; but it cannot provide much comfort to those who are unjustly treated by decisions that are required by law.

With that qualification understood, let us ask whether the appeal to a judicial obligation of fidelity to law can be relied upon to show what is now claimed, that judges are always justified in *rendering* decisions that are required by law. I do not think it can. My reasoning turns on two aspects of the judicial obligation of fidelity to law: the conditions of its acquisition and limitations on its scope. These factors are independent; each separately reveals the inadequacy of the present claim.

The first can be explained as follows. For reasons already suggested, the obligation must not be confused with a merely legal requirement. It does not depend, for example, on a ritualistic performance which may be required by law, such as an oath to uphold the law. It would seem to rest, rather, on a general understanding that an official such as a judge occupies a position of public trust. By the same token, however, we cannot assume that someone who occupies a judicial (or other official) position is under an obligation of fidelity to law. For such an obligation depends on conditions that may not be satisfied. As in the case of promises and other undertakings, agreeing to serve on the bench has the normal moral consequences if, but only if, it is not secured by coercion.

Consider the following sort of case. A corrupt regime wishes to exploit the name of a respected jurist, but she is unwilling to serve in that capacity. So it takes her family and other innocent persons prisoner and plausibly threatens to torture them unless she agrees to serve. If she agrees, we cannot regard her as having voluntarily undertaken to follow the law that they provide for her to administer. So, from the fact that a person occupies an official position, it does not follow that she is under an obligation of fidelity to law.

This argument assumes that there is a morally significant difference between occupying an institutional position and having an obligation to perform as the institutional rules require, such that the former does not entail the latter. This assumption is tenable if we distinguish between merely institutional requirements and genuine obligations in the way suggested earlier. Once that distinction is made, it is an open question whether someone who occupies a position within an institution, such as a judge, is under an obligation to respect its requirements. My example illustrates that point.

The foregoing argument is sufficient to undermine the general claim that judges are always justified in rendering decisions that are required by law. That claim assumes that the judicial obligation of fidelity to law entails (at least "prima facie") justification for following the law. If the obligation cannot be assumed, then neither can the dependent justification.

Though the foregoing argument is sufficient, it can be reinforced, I believe, by noticing limitations on the scope of judicial obligations. Like some other obligations, these are somewhat open-ended. What the judicial obligation of fidelity to law requires one to do, for example, depends significantly on the law that a judge is charged with administering. But there are limits to what one can become obligated to do even under an open-ended obligation.

Consider the following case. Suppose that a subordinate official assumes an open-ended obligation to follow the orders of his superiors, and suppose that he is ordered by them to take and share with them bribes. We might assume that these are illegal orders. In that case, the obligation to follow orders of one's superiors would simply not apply. This is analogous to the case of a judge who refuses to apply a statute that has not been properly enacted and so lacks legal force.

Now consider the case of a volunteer soldier who is understood to be under an open-ended obligation to obey the orders of his superior officers. Suppose that he is ordered by an officer to murder some innocent civilians. We cannot so readily assume that the laws regulating a soldier's military duties make an exception for such orders. It may be the soldier's institutional duty to obey all the orders of his superior officers. But I do not believe that such an order comes under the scope of his *moral* obligation to obey the orders of his superior officers. This is analogous to the case of a judge who is required by law to render a decision implementing an official policy of genocide. I see no reason to suppose that the judicial obligation of fidelity to law covers such a case.

My claim requires clarification. I am not arguing that open-ended obligations are *extinguished* in some such cases. The soldier and the judge may continue to be under an obligation to follow orders and follow the law, respectively, in subsequent cases that fall unproblematically under the scope of the open-ended obligation. Nor am I arguing that the open-ended obligation is merely *overridden,* as might happen when there is a conflict of obligations. My claim (which I recognize is not uncontroversial) is that open-ended obligations have limited applications. This is based on the assumption that one cannot acquire an obligation to do certain things, such as to commit acts of genocide or rape. Once the distinction is drawn between merely institutional and genuine moral obligations, I see no good reason to deny this.[10]

[10] These limitations on officials' moral obligation of fidelity to law are analogous to limitations on another argument for official adherence to existing law. It is sometimes suggested that fairness requires (at least "prima facie") that officials adhere to the laws that they are charged with administering, because fairness requires that like cases be treated alike, and in that context the law must be understood to determine what cases are alike and their appropriate treatment. The notion that fairness requires treating like cases alike is, of course, an empty doctrine and provides no practical guidance unless it is supplemented by criteria of similarities (as well as criteria of appropriate treatment for such cases) which are required when one wishes to treat cases fairly. The argument currently under consideration assumes that either (a) the mere existence of legal prescriptions or (b) the mere historical fact that officials have regularly treated cases in a legally prescribed manner, is sufficient to trigger a sound argument from fairness, such that deviation from (a) existing law or (b) uniform legal practice by officials, without more, constitutes at least a "prima facie" kind of unfairness. But (a) it is a gratuitous assumption (the falsity of which is suggested by the argument in the text) that the mere existence of legal prescriptions, even when they do not satisfy minimal moral conditions, determines for the purposes of fairness which cases must be considered similar and their appropriate treatment. (b) Suppose that the law of a particular jurisdiction tells officials to discriminate invidiously against blacks, according them less respect than is accorded whites as well as fewer benefits, resources, and opportunities. Suppose, further, that these racist prescriptions have regularly been followed by officials in that jurisdiction. Why should we suppose that any sort of fairness requires, even "prima facie," that such discriminatory treatment continue, just because it has regularly been practiced? An argument from fairness cannot be generated unless past practice satisfies some minimal moral conditions. If past practice has been sufficiently immoral, fairness cannot require its continuation,

I should also add that I do not mean to ignore the moral predicament of the soldier and the judge. The soldier's predicament is especially difficult, for he might have to pay with his life for refusing to follow his officer's order. The clear threat of such a consequence might *excuse* him for executing the order, but this is not the same as the notion that his obligation to obey provides him with even a "prima facie" justification for carrying it out. A judge is less likely to be faced with so difficult a choice; she might be able to refuse, with relative impunity, to follow the outrageous law. In that case, a judge might have no excuse, no less a "prima facie" justification, for committing innocent people to the gas chambers.

These examples are extreme; unfortunately, they are far from unimaginable. They also help to bring out a problem concerning emphasis on the judicial obligation of fidelity to law (beyond the fact that it will not save the revised doctrine of legalistic justification). The shift of focus, from *what* is done to the *doing* of it, might encourage us to neglect factors that should be regarded as central. One sometimes has the impression that reflective jurists and philosophers wish to emphasize the stringency of judicial obligation because they are concerned about the possible effect on judicial practice of the suggestion that judges might sometimes be justified in not following the law. That concern is understandable. But it should not close our minds to the fact that what happens to people under the law is of primary importance.

not even "prima facie." I discuss this further in "On Formal Justice," *Cornell Law Review* 58 (1973): 883–961 [reprinted in this volume], in *Ethics and the Rule of Law* (New York: Cambridge University Press, 1984), pp. 78–86, in "Formal Justice, Moral Commitment, and Judicial Precedent," *Journal of Philosophy* 81 (1984): 580–587, and in "Formal Justice and Judicial Precedent," *Vanderbilt Law Review* 38 (1985): 495–512 [reprinted in this volume].

7

Constitutional interpretation and original meaning

I. CONSTITUTIONAL ORIGINALISM

By "originalism" I mean the familiar approach to constitutional adjudication that accords binding authority to the text of the Constitution or the intentions of its adopters. At least since *Marbury*, in which Chief Justice Marshall emphasized the significance of our Constitution's being a written document, originalism in one form or another has been a major theme in the American constitutional tradition.[1]

Indeed, originalism can seem to be the only plausible approach to judicial review. One might reason as follows: "A court cannot decide whether an official decision conforms to the Constitution without applying its rules. The Constitution was written down to fix its content, and its rules remain unchanged until it is amended. Courts have not been authorized to change the rules. So courts deciding cases under the Constitution should follow the rules there laid down. By what right would courts decide constitutional cases on any other grounds?"

That challenge is conveyed by writings on judicial review that are regarded as originalist. But it is misleading. Most of the positions that are condemned by contemporary originalists accept the authority of the Constitution.[2] Although originalists present the issue as fidelity to the Constitution, it primarily concerns, I shall argue, how the Constitution is to be interpreted.

"Constitutional Interpretation and Original Meaning," *Social Philosophy & Policy* 4 (1986): 75–101. This is a revised version of a paper presented on March 14, 1986, to the conference on philosophy and law sponsored by the Social Philosophy and Policy Center and held at the University of Michigan Law School. Earlier drafts of all or part were presented at the State of Washington Annual Judicial Conference, the University of Utah, the University of Saskatchewan, and the Cornell Law School. I am grateful for comments offered on those occasions as well as comments from Gary Simson, Sterling Harwood, and the editors of *Social Philosophy & Policy*. Research for this paper was supported in part by a Constitutional Fellowship from the National Endowment for the Humanities and a summer research stipend from the Cornell Law School, for which I am also grateful.

[1] Brest, "The Misconceived Quest for the Original Understanding," 60 *B.U. L. Rev.* 204 (1980).

[2] At the same time, it seems that most if not all theorists hold that constitutional cases may sometimes be decided by rules that cannot be attributed to the Constitution. We shall touch on "nonoriginalism" in section III.

A distinctively originalist mode of interpretation assumes that the doctrinal content of the Constitution was completely determined when it was adopted and that constitutional doctrines can be identified by a value-free factual study of the text or of "original intent." It is part of my purpose to show that this type of theory is not only less plausible than its severest critics have suggested,[3] but that significant alternatives to it are available (sections II and III).

An approach to judicial review includes not only a theory of interpretation, which tells us how to understand the Constitution, but also a theory of adjudication, which tells us how to apply the Constitution so interpreted – how it should be used in constitutional cases. Originalist theory is not usually analyzed in this way, but we shall find that the distinction is needed when considering contemporary originalism.

One would expect a distinctively originalist approach to adjudication to hold that constitutional cases should be decided on the basis of doctrines in the "original" Constitution (that is, the Constitution interpreted in an originalist way), and on no other basis whatsoever. I shall show that contemporary theorists who present themselves as strict originalists accept rules for judicial review that cannot be found in or otherwise attributed to the "original" Constitution (sections IV–VI).

A third point I wish to make is that doctrines drawn from general philosophy – ideas about meaning and morals, for example – play a significant role in contemporary originalist theorizing. This point is important because these philosophical notions are dubious and controversial. It must be emphasized, however, that some of the same philosophical ideas have wide currency in legal theory generally.

Although originalism has relatively few defenders, its most prominent champions are highly placed within the federal government. These include Robert H. Bork,[4] Judge on the United States Court of Appeals for the District of Columbia Circuit, Edwin Meese III,[5] Attorney General of the United States, and William H. Rehnquist,[6] Associate Justice of the United States Supreme Court. It is important for us to recognize the quality of the constitutional theories that are embraced by these responsible officials.

This paper is, then, a critique of constitutional originalism. We need a

---

[3] See, *e.g.*, John Ely, *Democracy and Distrust*, ch. 2 (1980); Brest, "The Misconceived Quest"; Dworkin, "The Forum of Principle," 56 *N.Y. U. L. Rev.* 469–500 (1981); and Schauer, "An Essay on Constitutional Language," 29 *UCLA L. Rev.* 797 (1982). MacCallum, "Legislative Intent," 75 *Yale L.J.* 754 (1966) applies here too.

[4] Bork, "Neutral Principles and Some First Amendment Problems," 47 *Indiana L.J.* 1 (1971).

[5] Meese, "Construing the Constitution," 19 *U.C. Davis L. Rev.* 22 (1985).

[6] Rehnquist, "The Notion of a Living Constitution," 54 *Texas L. Rev.* 693 (1976).

better theory. Although I shall not offer one here, I shall suggest some requirements for an adequate theory of constitutional adjudication.

II. ORIGINAL INTENT

Paul Brest's definition of "originalism" mentions two variants — "textualism" and "intentionalism."[7] The difference between them is significant. This section deals with constitutional intentionalism, especially its need for justification and the difficulties of finding any.

An originalist mode of interpretation holds that the doctrinal content of the Constitution was fixed when (or by the time that) the Constitution was adopted,[8] and that constitutional doctrines can be identified by a value-free factual inquiry. An intentionalist version of originalism holds that we must understand the Constitution in terms of the "intentions" of its framers, adopters, or ratifiers,[9] such as the specific applications that they had in mind, those they would have been prepared to accept, or their larger purposes.[10]

Champions of "original intent" seem to regard that approach to constitutional interpretation as so obviously correct that it requires no justification; for none seems to be offered. So it will be useful to begin by noting some aspects of intentionalism that imply its need for justification.

Reference to "original intent" is inherently ambiguous. The following questions indicate some (but not all) of that ambiguity. Whose intentions count? The intentions of, for example, one who drafts a text or one who votes for it? Which intentions count? To establish as authoritative some

---

7 Brest also draws a distinction between "strict" and "moderate" originalism, which I take up below.

8 On this view, the meaning of an amendment would presumably be fixed when (or by the time) it was ratified, and its incorporation into the Constitution would presumably modify (and in that sense fix anew) the doctrinal content of the Constitution as a whole.

9 I shall occasionally use "author" to refer to such an exclusive subclass of the population.

10 This covers both species of intentionalism in Brest's typology. "Strict intentionalism requires the interpreter to determine how the adopters would have applied a provision to a given situation, and to apply it accordingly" (Brest, "The Misconceived Quest," p. 222). This permits "intentions" to include general principles, as most original intent theorists appear to accept. "A moderate intentionalist applies a provision *consistent with* the adopters' intent at a relatively high level of generality, consistent with what is sometimes called 'the purpose of the provision'" (*ibid.*, p. 223). The words I have emphasized suggest the view that "intentions" are relatively concrete or specific whereas "purposes" are relatively abstract or general, so that an appeal to original intent, strictly speaking, should be limited to the former. Brest does not defend this view, which does not square with his definition of "strict intentionalism" and is not required by the concept of intent. On the relevance of abstract intentions, see Dworkin, "The Forum of Principle."

143

particular text, or some text understood in a certain way, or to serve some identifiable larger purposes? Reference to original intent is problematic in other ways too. While two or more individuals can share an intention, it is by no means clear how (or whether it is always possible) to aggregate the relevant attitudes of the members of a group so as to determine their collective intentions.[11]

The answer that one gives to such questions should affect originalist interpretation, so the selection of any particular criterion of original intent as the basis for interpreting the Constitution requires specific justification. In the absence of a satisfactory rationale, we should regard any particular criterion of original intent as theoretically arbitrary. Sad to say, original intent theorists generally ignore these fundamental problems, despite their having systematically been surveyed in law reviews for at least two decades.[12]

But the differences among the various versions of originalist intentionalism do not chiefly concern us now. The point I would like to emphasize is that *any* intentionalist approach requires substantial justification. Intentionalism is a special theory of constitutional interpretation, not a platitude.

Early in our constitutional career, the Supreme Court refused to apply the Bill of Rights to the several states, holding that the first ten amendments restricted only the federal government, although their language does not explicitly limit most of those amendments in that way.[13] In so deciding, the Court made some reference to the intentions of "the framers." Although the Court's grounds for its decision went far beyond original intent, its reference to framers' intent might suggest that the Court followed that criterion of constitutional meaning instead of the apparent meaning of the authoritative text. If that were so, the Court would have followed a special theory of constitutional interpretation, and one that requires substantial justification.

In general, we recognize that we do not always mean what we say or write; *we* may mean something different from the meaning *of the lan-*

---

[11] The most plausible criterion in such cases – which are, of course, most directly relevant here – would refer to the meaning of a text that has been adopted as authoritative. But that criterion would subordinate intentionalism to textualism and would make authors' intent a derivative rather than a basic determinant of meaning. I am here considering intentionalism as a basic general theory of constitutional interpretations. I am not considering, for example, the idea that considerations of original intent may for one reason or another properly play a secondary, subordinate, or supplementary role in constitutional interpretation.

[12] See Ely, *Democracy and Distrust;* Brest, "The Misconceived Quest"; Dworkin, "The Forum of Principle"; Schauer, "An Essay on Constitutional Language"; and MacCallum, "Legislative Intent."

[13] Barron v. The Mayor and City Council of Baltimore, 7 Pet. 243, 8 L. Ed. 672 (1833).

guage that we use. This is reflected in our reading of legal instruments such as wills and contracts. It has also been observed, by advocates as well as critics of intentionalism, that the surest guide to authors' intent is the authoritative constitutional text itself. This is possible only because the text is understood to carry a meaning that stands on its own – that is independent of its authors' intentions.[14]

It follows that intentionalism is a special theory of constitutional interpretation, not a platitude. Either it derives from a failure to appreciate the distinction between the meaning of a text and what its authors meant to convey; or else it presupposes some reason for holding that the meaning of the constitutional text, unlike that of texts generally, is a matter of authors' intent. So intentionalism is either confused or else requires substantial justification.

What might justify intentionalist constitutional interpretation? Originalists might appeal to (1) the idea (not limited to law) that interpretation should generally be governed by authors' intentions; (2) a specifically legal canon of construction; or (3) some theory of political morality that implies that we are under an obligation to respect the intentions of the framers, adopters, or ratifiers.

(1) *Intentionalism as a general approach to interpretation.* The notion that textual interpretation seeks generally to determine authors' intentions is plausible when our primary concern is what some individual had in mind, as in the case of personal communications, studies of literary figures and, in law, wills and contracts. The question is whether our proper concern when interpreting an authoritative public text such as a constitution is to determine what its authors had in mind. The suggestion seems to me implausible.

I do not wish to deny that, just as a poem can be a political statement, law can be read as literature. But law's distinctive functions are significantly different from those of literature and personal communications. Law tells us what we must or must not do, threatening punishment for disobedience. It places the coercive power of the state behind some individuals' decisions. It quite literally regulates death and taxes, war and peace, debts and compensation, imprisonment, conscription and confiscation, and innumerable other matters of direct, vital interest to individuals, communities, and often all humanity. That is the explicit, normal business of the law, including the U.S. Constitution.

An important feature of law's normal business is that it requires justification. The same applies, of course, to judicial decisions, including those

---

[14] This point does not presuppose a general theory of text meaning. The argument of section III would seem to imply, however, that the meaning of a text is not determined solely by linguistic conventions.

145

that turn upon legal interpretation. They require justification, too. The justification of judicial decisions, like the justification of the normal business of the law generally, cannot be understood in narrowly legalistic terms. Adequate justification concerns not merely whether something is required or allowed by law but, also, whether what the law does is what I have elsewhere called "defensible."[15] All of this suggests that the need for justification may properly regulate matters of legal and specifically constitutional interpretation and, thus, that these matters turn on political morality.

(2) *Intentionalism as a theory of legal interpretation.* Could intentionalism be based on a general canon of construction for legal instruments? The possibility is suggested by the fact that statutory construction is said to seek out "legislative intent." But there are several difficulties here. Insofar as constitutional intentionalism relies upon a canon of construction that derives from precedent or common law, there will be some difficulty incorporating such a theory of interpretation into originalism, as I shall explain later.

Another problem is this. Conventions regulate the identification of "legislative intent," such as the authority given to official reports from legislative committees. Such conventions have only problematic application to the U.S. Constitution. The existence of such conventions suggests something else that seems important, namely, that the search for "legislative intent" is not a purely factual inquiry about a consensus that obtained at a particular historical moment. This is suggested also by the fact that statutory construction characteristically seeks to interpret legislation in as favorable a light as possible; for example, as a reasonable and legislatively legitimate means to a reasonable and legislatively legitimate end. Such a normative bias can be explained by the fact that statutory construction seeks to provide, if possible, a grounding for judicial decisions that are justified. If what counts as "legislative intent" is in fact shaped by normative considerations, it could not serve as a model for "original intent," for those who endorse the latter as the criterion of constitutional meaning regard it as a plain matter of historical fact, accessible to a value-free inquiry.

Originalists assume that the Constitution is a morally adequate basis for judicial decisions (as well as for our political arrangements generally). The normative bias within interpretation to which I refer requires that we interpret the Constitution in such a way that it is, if possible, capable of performing that function.

---

[15] See my "Derivability, Defensibility, and the Justification of Judicial Decisions," 68 *The Monist* 325 (1985) [reprinted in this volume].

If statutory construction is no help to constitutional intentionalism, what about the interpretation of other legal instruments, such as wills and contracts? The first point made about "legislative intent" applies here, too: insofar as constitutional intentionalism relies upon a canon of construction that derives from precedent or common law, there will be some difficulty incorporating such a theory of interpretation into originalism.

It might nonetheless be thought that an intentionalist interpretation of contracts[16] could serve as a model for constitutional intentionalism. That is because political rhetoric often refers to the Constitution as the upshot of a "social contract." Now, the idea of a "social contract" is invoked to argue for obedience to law, however objectionable on other grounds it might be, so long as it does not violate constitutional restrictions. This means that a "social contract" basis for intentionalism is dependent on a theory of political morality. To accept intentionalism on this basis, we must establish the legitimacy of a "social contract" argument and its valid application to this case.

(3) *Intentionalism as a theorem of political morality.* Our discussion suggests that we should seek a rationale for constitutional intentionalism in the political morality of constitutional creation and application, that is, in principles that explain why the Constitution is worthy of respect and morally binding. Two ideas are provided by political rhetoric. One, already noted, refers to a "social contract." Another, asserted within as well as outside the Constitution, holds that it comes from "the people."

The latter idea is promising because contemporary originalists, like most constitutional theorists, emphasize the predominantly "democratic" character of our constitutional arrangements. Representative government nicely complements popular sovereignty. Political rhetoric suggests that "the people" knowingly and freely agreed to respect government so long as it conforms to the Constitution, and that "the people" are accordingly bound by that agreement. But this does not yet yield the constitutional theory of original intent, which requires that the Constitution be understood in terms of the "intentions" of a special subclass of "the people," namely, the Framers, adopters, or ratifiers, as opposed to (say) the understanding that one might have of the Constitution based on text meaning.

The present line of reasoning requires us to suppose, then, (a) that "the people" *contracted to accept the intentions of the authors,* by reference

---

16 Insofar as such interpretation is, in fact, intentionalist. It seems relevant that contractual interpretation is not purely a matter of actual intent, but is also regulated by legal norms.

to which the Constitution must therefore be understood, and (b) that *this* makes the Constitution binding on us now. The theory seems fatally flawed.

(a) In the first place, only a small minority of the people of that time and place were permitted to participate in the original adoption process. We lack precise figures, but it should suffice for present purposes to observe that the process excluded not only many adult white males (and, of course, children) but also women, chattel slaves, and Native Americans. It could not have included more than a small fraction of the total population, and willing contractors would have amounted to a smaller fraction still.

In the second place, it is doubtful whether any such contractors would have been morally competent to create obligations to respect political arrangements that continued chattel slavery, second-class citizenship for women, and the subjugation of Native Americans. At the very least, those subject to such arrangements could not be bound by a constitution simply because it was agreeable to others.

(b) In the third place, it is unclear how contracts made by members of earlier generations can bind succeeding generations. This is not to suggest that law can bind only those who have given their consent. But the mere fact that some people some time in the past have accepted a political arrangement cannot by itself automatically bind others. More is required than that to show that later generations are bound.

But the rhetoric of popular sovereignty is nonetheless illuminating. It suggests a commitment to popular government, however narrowly that was at first conceived.[17] Furthermore, the Constitution is a piece of public, not private law. Our proper concern in interpreting it is not to implement the understanding of parties to a limited, private agreement or the personal wishes of a testator, but to establish the basis for political arrangements and justified judicial decisions that legitimately concern the community as a whole. Whatever else is needed for a theory of constitutional adjudication, the legitimate interest of the entire population strongly suggests that the primary criterion of constitutional meaning should be popular understanding, the basic index of which must be text meaning.

Consider the alternative. Interpretation in terms of the intentions of constitutional framers or ratifiers would seem to assume a conception of law like that of the classical legal positivists Bentham and Austin, according to which an exclusive subgroup of the population makes law for

---

[17]   The idea of popular sovereignty was reflected in constitutional *rhetoric* from early on. It became increasingly reflected in the constitutional *system* as time passed, as major changes occurred in the Republic, including of course major constitutional amendments.

others to follow.[18] That is objectionable because of our interest in justi-fication. Interpretation based on anything like that conception of the law will present formidable obstacles to justifying the Constitution, justifying compliance with morally deficient laws so long as they conform to the Constitution, and justifying judicial decisions that those laws require.

The upshot is that constitutional intentionalism is profoundly prob-lematic. There is no obvious linguistic or moral basis for interpreting the Constitution by reference to the intentions of an exclusive political group, as opposed to the meaning of the text. When these considerations are combined with other substantial objections to intentionalism, the theory seems unpromising indeed.

III. ALTERNATIVES TO INTENTIONALISM

In this section, I argue that intentionalism does not win out by default, despite its deficiencies. According to Brest's typology, the originalist al-ternative to intentionalism is textualism, which comes in two varieties. "A strict textualist purports to construe words and phrases very nar-rowly and precisely."[19] Brest appears to argue that this is untenable both as textual interpretation and as originalism: "An originalist would hold that, because interpretation is designed to capture the original under-standing, the text must be understood in the contexts of the society that adopted it."[20] This means that textualism must be "moderate" to be plausible. "A moderate textualist takes account of the open-textured quality of language and reads the language of provisions in their social and lin-guistic contexts."[21]

In other words, Brest judges the only legitimate originalist alternative to intentionalism[22] to be a reading of constitutional language as "open textured."[23] Unfortunately, Brest does not explain what he takes this to mean. But his reference to the spurious precision of "strict" textualism suggests that we might understand "moderate textualism" by reference to Hart's use of "open-textured" when he introduced that technical term into legal theory.[24]

---

[18] This aspect of that theory is discussed by H.L.A. Hart, *The Concept of Law* 41–43 (1961).

[19] Brest, "The Misconceived Quest," p. 204.   [20] *ibid.*, p. 208.

[21] *ibid.*, p. 223.

[22] Actually, Brest seems to believe that moderate *textualism* amounts to the only plau-sible originalist alternative to "strict" *intentionalism*, as he says that "moderate tex-tualism and intentionalism closely resemble each other in methodology and results." *ibid.*

[23] *ibid.*, pp. 205, 223.   [24] Hart, *The Concept of Law*, pp. 121–132.

Following the received wisdom of the time, Hart held that all terms in "natural" languages (which include the language of the law) are "open-textured." An "open-textured" word has a core of determinate meaning, encompassing fact situations to which it uncontroversially applies, and a "penumbra" encompassing fact situations to which the term neither clearly applies nor clearly does not apply. The idea of "open texture" assumes that the meaning of a word is indeterminate whenever there are reasons both for and against applying the word. This aspect of the theory of "open texture" provides a theoretical rationale for a view that is widely accepted by legal theorists, namely, that legal language has indeterminate meaning insofar as its proper application is unclear.

On this understanding, to characterize constitutional language as "open-textured" is to imply that the doctrines given by that language are incompletely formed. Provisions that many theorists seem to believe fit this description to an extreme degree include the so-called "vague clauses" guaranteeing "free speech," "due process," "just compensation," "equal protection," and the like. On the "open texture" model, these provisions are seen as having tiny cores of clear (and therefore determinate) meaning and relatively wide unclear (and therefore indeterminate) penumbras.

This is a politically significant idea. For it implies that, insofar as the judicial process of "interpreting" the Constitution makes its proper application clearer, the process really *changes* the Constitution by making its meaning more determinate. The clearer doctrines resulting from such "interpretations" could not then be attributed to the "original" Constitution. That is the view of constitutional language that Brest seems to regard as the ("moderate") originalist alternative to "strict" textualism.

Given this conception of the alternatives, we can better understand why originalists regard as most significant the dividing line between "strict" and "moderate" originalism. That is because moderate originalism appears to collapse into nonoriginalism.

Originalism regards the authority of the "original" Constitution as axiomatic, whereas nonoriginalism holds that adherence to the Constitution requires justification and that principles of political morality that are capable of providing such justification might also justify deviation from it.[25] To clarify this difference, we can distinguish two categories of doctrines that might be used in constitutional cases. Those that can and those that cannot truly be attributed to the Constitution may be called "constitutional" and "extra-constitutional," respectively. Nonoriginalism is prepared to consider using extra-constitutional doctrines in constitu-

---

[25] Compare Brest, "The Misconceived Quest," p. 225. For a work that might be considered "nonoriginalist," see M.J. Perry, *The Constitution, The Courts, and Human Rights* (1982).

tional cases, whereas a distinctively originalist theory of adjudication would presumably reject any such use of them.

"Moderate" originalism regards unclear constitutional language as "open-textured," or inherently somewhat vague. It also accepts the judicial practice of deciding cases under unclear aspects of the Constitution, but it seems to regard the constitutional "interpretations" that are used as creating, and the resulting decisions as applying, doctrines that are extra-constitutional – judicial amendments to the "original" Constitution. On this view, "moderate" originalism's approach to deciding cases under unclear aspects of the Constitution *is equivalent to nonoriginalism.* Such decisions would be condemned by a "strict" originalist who holds that, as courts have no authority to amend the Constitution, they should refrain from doing so.[26]

It must be emphasized that the line of reasoning sketched in the last few paragraphs assumes that "moderate" textualism regards the Constitution as indeterminate insofar as its proper application is unclear. But we need not assume this; we need not accept the dubious assumption that the meaning of a text is indeterminate whenever it is unclear, or whenever interpretation of it would be controversial, so that the discovery of text meaning is impossible precisely when it is needed.

Instead of discussing these issues in the abstract, it will be useful to consider an approach which agrees that such language in the "original" Constitution does *not* provide *complete* doctrines of just compensation, free speech, and the like. This approach nevertheless provides grounds for attributing the doctrines resulting from sound interpretations to the Constitution. This will provide us with all that we require for present purposes, namely, an alternative to "strict" intentionalism that might justifiably assign meaning to the Constitution and enable courts to decide cases on constitutional grounds.

It has been suggested[27] that the so-called "vague clauses" incorporate "contested concepts." It is the nature of such a concept to admit of competing "conceptions" and thus routinely to *require* interpretation. Contested concepts do not have built-in criteria of application; they are more abstract than that. As a result, different people can use the same (contested) concept while accepting and employing different standards for its application. It would seem, for example, that general normative concepts, such as "right" and "wrong," "good" and "bad," "right" and "obligation," as well as more specific normative concepts, such as particular virtues and vices, are "contested" in this way. When people agree

---

[26] We shall consider the originalist approach to this issue in section V.
[27] R. Dworkin, *Taking Rights Seriously* 132–137 (1977). This suggestion is independent of other aspects of Dworkin's legal theory.

about the "facts" but disagree in their evaluations, their disagreement concerns the principles that determine the proper application of those concepts to particular cases.

The notion of a "contested concept" is explicitly used, for example, in Rawls's theory of social justice, the relevant part of which can be explained as follows. Imagine that you and I disagree about the substantive requirements of social justice. We then differ as to how the concept of justice applies; we differ, that is, about the principles of justice. This is possible if the concept of justice admits of different interpretations, or competing conceptions. That seems to be the case.

Rawls maintains that the mere concept of justice determines no detailed, substantive criteria of justice, only the skeletal requirement that there be no "arbitrary distinctions" between persons but, rather, "a proper balance between competing claims."[28] The task of a theory of justice is to show (not merely to claim) the superiority of one conception (one principle or set of principles) over competing conceptions as an interpretation of this requirement. The possibility of a uniquely correct interpretation of a provision incorporating the contested concept of justice, then, depends on the superior justifiability of a particular conception of justice.

Now consider a constitutional example. Past judicial interpretations aside,[29] a court applying the just compensation clause would not necessarily decide a case as the original authors would have done, nor would it automatically follow a more popular consensus of the time (even if either were possible). Instead, a court would understand the Constitution to mean precisely what it says and thus to require *just compensation*. A court would need to defend a particular conception of just compensation (that is, it would need to defend principles of justice appropriate to compensation) against the most plausible alternatives. It would then apply that conception to decide the case at bar.

Someone might be skeptical about the possibility of justifying such an interpretation. Someone might believe it is impossible to provide a rational defense of, say, principles of just compensation and might therefore claim that a court adopting this approach would inevitably impose its own arbitrary conception of just compensation instead of the conception embraced by the authors of the Constitution or by a broader "original" consensus. (It should be emphasized that, on this view, an "origi-

---

[28] J. Rawls, *A Theory Of Justice* 5, 10 (1971).

[29] If a court works under a doctrine of precedent, then the criterion of a justifiable interpretation cannot simply be fidelity to the "original" Constitution. In that case, past judicial interpretations can presumably affect the content of a justifiable interpretation, even when those past interpretations were mistaken. I ignore that complication here.

nal" conception of just compensation is completely arbitrary and indefensible.). Someone might hold, in other words, that all such principles are inherently arbitrary, so that courts cannot possibly do what is required to implement this approach to the interpretation of "vague" constitutional language.[30] I shall not offer a general critique of such skepticism,[31] but I shall suggest below why it is reasonable to believe that there can be a best conception among competing conceptions of some contested concepts. I shall later show how philosophical skepticism about values is, in this context, incoherent.[32]

Contested concepts do not seem confined to morality and law. Their properties are at any rate similar to those of concepts referring to natural substances or phenomena, such as water and heat. On a plausible understanding of the development of science, for example, the caloric and kinetic theories of heat are (or at one time were) competing conceptions of the concept heat. This is suggested by the fact that "heat" refers to a physical phenomenon that is but partially and imperfectly identified by any prescientific verbal definition of the word, and that something very much like the idea of a contested concept is required to explain how there can be two theories of heat, that is, two different conceptions of the single concept heat.

If, as most people would agree, "heat" refers to a determinate physical phenomenon, there can be, in principle, a best theory of heat. This implies that there can be a best conception of a contested concept, at least in some cases. This suggests, in turn, that contested concepts in the Constitution might have best interpretations.

The kinetic theory of heat has displaced the caloric conception and is currently our best conception of heat. As this example implies, we may be justified in using *our* best conception even if it is not in fact *the* best. Similarly, just as our best conception of heat is liable to change, so we may expect change from time to time in our best conception of, say, just compensation. This involves no moral relativism.

Now if the idea that the Constitution includes contested concepts is correct, then to apply the Constitution in terms of their best interpreta-

[30] We should distinguish such philosophical skepticism about values from concern about the difficulty a court might have trying to identify the best conception of a contested political concept (even when the alternatives are severely limited in number) and from an appreciation of the fact that any attempt to identify the best conception is likely to be controversial. We may also assume that reasonable judges can differ in their interpretations. It should be emphasized, however, that approaches to judicial review that seek to avoid controversial interpretations of the Constitution cannot be assumed to be justifiable by reference to the "original" Constitution. That is precisely one of the points at issue here.
[31] I address some aspects of this issue in *Ethics and the Rule of Law*, ch 1 (1984).
[32] Section VI.

tion is, in effect, to apply doctrines whose application is called for by the original Constitution. But, just as interpretation of the concept heat requires more than mere reflection, any interpretation of this type inevitably draws on resources that are neither implicit in the text nor purely linguistic. It makes essential use of political argument, though at a relatively general or abstract level. So this alternative approach implies that a sound interpretation – one faithful to the meaning of the text – can include substantive doctrines that are not derivable from the text (even supplemented by its original social and linguistic context) but that are identifiable only by reasoning about political principles in the context of the federal system.

It is important to emphasize that this approach to constitutional interpretation, where applicable, requires that an interpreter go outside the "four corners" of the text, its strict linguistic implications, and the relatively specific intentions of its authors,[33] for interpretations and arguments supporting them. But, as this is done because it is understood to be required by the very nature of contested concepts found within the Constitution, both the strategy of argument and its results can claim fidelity to the Constitution. For this reason, the interpretive approach just sketched might reasonably be regarded as "originalist."

As usually understood, however, "originalism" assumes that constitutional doctrines must be identified by a value-free factual study of the text or of original intent and that doctrines that are not implicit in the "original" text or "understanding" cannot truly be attributed to the Constitution. It accordingly rejects without a hearing the possibility of attributing to the Constitution interpretations of those contested concepts that are in the Constitution. That possibility gives reason to withhold assent from the more familiar originalist theories.

IV. ORIGINALIST ADJUDICATION

The Fourteenth Amendment says that no state "shall deny to any person within its jurisdiction the equal protection of the laws." The meaning of this provision is unclear. If (as some suggest) the provision does not have any determinate meaning, how should courts deal with cases under it? The Constitution does not tell us what we should then do.

As I have suggested, a comprehensive theory of judicial review can be understood as having two parts. A theory of interpretation purports to determine constitutional meaning. If well grounded, such a theory should

---

[33] Interpretation by reference to "original intent" also, of course, draws upon information outside the "four corners" of the text.

be welcome when the text is unclear. Furthermore, anyone who holds the text to be misleading needs a good theory to justify such a claim.

But theories about judicial review go beyond straightforward interpretation; they include theories of adjudication, which purport to determine how the Constitution should be applied.[34] Such a theory is required if cases are decided when the meaning of the Constitution is undetermined, or to justify departure from the Constitution's implications.

To illustrate the latter possibility, consider Thayer's famous deferential doctrine.[35] Thayer argued that federal legislation should never be nullified by federal courts unless it cannot reasonably be doubted that the legislation violates the Constitution. He held that this judicial policy was needed to promote respect for federal law and to protect the courts from legislative interference.[36] Thayer did not assume that the Constitution has no determinate meaning when there is reasonable disagreement about its meaning. On the contrary, he insisted that the judiciary should not apply its best interpretation of the Constitution but should defer whenever it is possible to regard the legislature's actions as constitutional.

[W]hen the ultimate question is . . . whether certain acts of another department, officer, or individual are legal or permissible, . . . *the ultimate question is not what is the true meaning of the constitution, but whether legislation is sustainable or not.*[37]

Thayer recommends, in effect, that the courts should sometimes refrain from enforcing the Constitution, even when they have a good, justifiable, and perhaps sound idea of what it means. That amounts to a special theory of adjudication (and, incidentally, one that seems decidedly extra-constitutional).

The distinctively originalist approach to adjudicating constitutional cases would seem to hold that they should be decided exclusively by doctrines that can be found in the "original" Constitution, that is, interpreted in an originalist way. There is a problem here. It is by no means clear that originalist theory can be found within the "original" Constitution. If originalism itself includes extra-constitutional doctrines, then insofar as a court applied and was guided by this theory of adjudication, it would decide cases in a nonoriginalist way!

---

[34] A theory of adjudication would seem to presuppose an independently determined interpretation of the Constitution, to fix whatever is (or is not) to be applied.

[35] Thayer, "The Origin and Scope of the American Doctrine of Constitutional Law," 7 *Harv. L. Rev.* 129 (1893).

[36] These are Thayer's chief arguments for judicial deference. Although he nods in the direction of democratic sentiments, he expresses little respect for the virtue, sense, or competence of legislators, but he fears their collective power.

[37] Thayer, "Origin," p. 150 (emphasis in the original).

It may accordingly seem reasonable to revise the originalist theory of adjudication so that originalism does not prohibit its own application. It would be modified to say that a doctrine may be applied within judicial review if, but only if, the doctrine either is attributable to the Constitution (in the sense required by an appropriate originalist theory of interpretation) or else is a doctrine of originalism itself.

That problem seemed easily solved. But it may suggest how difficult it is to embrace originalism unqualifiedly. Take another example. Raoul Berger's attack upon judicial decisions that fail to respect "framers' intent" leads him to suggest that courts should repudiate all decisions that cannot be grounded upon the Constitution so construed, regardless of "undesirable consequences."[38] But Berger hastily retreats from this proposal, saying:

It would, however, be utterly unrealistic and probably impossible to undo the past in the face of the expectations that the segregation decisions, for example, have aroused in our black citizenry – expectations confirmed by every decent instinct. That is more than the courts should undertake and more, I believe, than the American people would desire.[39]

Berger's retreat appears unprincipled. At best, he invokes an undefined and undefended extra-constitutional principle of constitutional adjudication, which clashes with his originalist pretensions.

Henry Monaghan appears sensitive to Berger's problem. He too says that the school desegregation decisions should not be undone. Unlike Berger, however, Monaghan suggests a judicial principle that would permit leaving those decisions undisturbed, even though he questions their constitutional warrant. His solution is to advocate a doctrine of judicial precedent.[40]

The question now is whether a doctrine of judicial precedent can be attributed to the "original" Constitution. Monaghan appears not to think so. But he believes that such a doctrine can be justified because it serves "the long-run values of stability and predictability for ordering our most fundamental affairs."[41]

[38] R. Berger, *Government By Judiciary* 412 (1977).
[39] *ibid.*, pp. 412–413.
[40] Monaghan, "Our Perfect Constitution," 56 *N.Y.U. L. Rev.* 387–391 (1981); and "Taking Supreme Court Decisions Seriously," 39 *Maryland L. Rev.* 1–12 (1979). We are presumably concerned here with precedents on the same court level, as distinct from precedents that are binding due to the hierarchical structure of a layered court system.
[41] Monaghan, "Our Perfect Constitution," p . 389; compare "Taking Supreme Court Decisions Seriously," p. 7. Lawyers seem to favor consequentialist arguments for precedent over the notion that precedent is grounded upon the fairness of treating like cases alike. For a discussion of this alternative, see Lyons, "Formal Justice and Judicial Precedent," 38 *Vanderbilt L. Rev.* 495 (1985) [reprinted in this volume].

CONSTITUTIONAL INTERPRETATION

Monaghan does not seem to appreciate the awkwardness of his position. In offering a justification for a doctrine of precedent based on its desirable consequences, he commits himself to holding that judicial review may be regulated by *any* principles whose use would serve the same "long-run values." That would permit the use in judicial review of an indeterminate class of useful extra-constitutional principles.[42]

One might, alternatively, suggest that a doctrine of precedent was in fact provided by the "original" Constitution. For the Constitution was grafted on a system whose common law heritage includes, of course, a doctrine requiring courts to respect judicial precedent.[43] The trouble with this way of reasoning, from an originalist perspective, is that it would render the Constitution much less limited doctrinally than originalists tend to view it. It would imply that the Constitution contains a multitude of common law principles.

Monaghan's predicament suggests the instability of originalism. If an originalist believes that there is justification for respecting a judicial principle that is no more controversial than precedent, he not only runs the risk of agreeing that constitutional cases may properly be decided by doctrines that cannot be attributed to the Constitution; he may become committed to accepting a relatively indeterminate theory of judicial review, incorporating all the principles of constitutional adjudication that can be justified by the criteria that are needed to justify a doctrine of precedent.

This point is generalizable. Contemporary originalists are often preoccupied with "restraining" the federal judiciary in constitutional cases and tend to embrace theories of adjudication that are designed in part to limit judicial nullification of decisions made by elected officials. The relevant judicial principles require justification. If such principles cannot be found in the "original" Constitution, they require justification by reference to some principles of political morality. The considerations that are adduced or required to justify such doctrines are capable of justifying an

---

42 Perhaps Monaghan would like to limit the use of consequentialist argument in some unexplained way. It will be difficult to show, however, that such limitations are not ad hoc. Indeed, Monaghan's consequentialist strategy of argument threatens to get completely out of hand. For his argument commits him to approving all principles whose use would serve *any* values that are as desirable as "stability and predictability." It may also be noted that insofar as originalist doctrine, such as strict intentionalism, appeals to past judicial practice, its originalist credentials must be as problematic as those of a doctrine of precedent.

43 Monaghan distinguishes the doctrine of precedent that is needed for constitutional cases from "common law analogies" because of differences in details, and he may infer from these differences that the constitutional doctrine could not be based on common law traditions; "Taking Supreme Court Decisions Seriously," p. 12. But that reasoning is dubious.

indefinite class of other doctrines that are relevant to constitutional adjudication. To endorse an extra-constitutional principle is to commit oneself to endorsing any other principle that is justifiable on the same grounds that justify the one endorsed. Such an approach to constitutional adjudication is hardly consistent with the spirit of originalism.

V. DEMOCRATIC SENSIBILITIES

Constitutional theorizing nowadays puts an emphasis upon "democracy" that we have so far neglected. It arises in contexts like the following. Intentionalists believe that our knowledge of constitutional meaning extends only so far as our knowledge of original intent. What remains unclear can be assigned no determinate meaning. If it is assumed that the "interpretation" and application of unclear aspects of the Constitution involve extra-constitutional doctrines, it would be natural for originalists to prefer that courts refrain from deciding such cases.

One who wishes to justify such a policy of "judicial restraint" might suggest that the defendant should win whenever law is unclear and therefore indeterminate, because then the burden of proof cannot effectively be shouldered by a plaintiff or appellant.[44] This reasoning seems warranted by the notion that courts should decide cases by reference to existing law. Not requiring extra-constitutional doctrines, it seems compatible with originalism.

But extensive use of the burden-of-proof rule would be problematic in our system. Suppose, for example, that district courts in different circuits, believing they had adequate constitutional grounds for doing so, decided similar cases, but did so differently. Suppose, further, that their decisions involved aspects of the Constitution that their respective circuit courts regarded as indeterminate because unclear. If the circuit courts invoked the burden-of-proof rule, the result would in effect establish conflicting constitutional doctrines in different circuits. The federal courts would seem to require some extra-constitutional doctrine to extricate us from that predicament.

The alternative basis for a policy of "judicial restraint" is an argument from "democracy," which concludes that nonelected judges should not nullify decisions made by "electorally accountable" officials. The reasoning may be understood as follows. Insofar as political arrangements are subject to popular control through elections, they are regarded by many constitutional theorists as respecting democratic values. In addition, our system involves a division of political power under which popularly elected

---

[44] See, *e.g.,* Van Alstyne, "Interpreting This Constitution: The Unhelpful Contributions of Special Theories of Judicial Review," 35 *U. Fla. L. Rev.* 229 (1983).

legislatures are authorized to make law and the judiciary is conventionally understood as authorized to interpret and apply, but not to make law.

One who assumes that unclear law is indeterminate will also believe that judges must "legislate" whenever they decide "hard cases." This practice is tolerable, or even desirable, when kept to a minimum; judges are elected, and, most importantly, elected legislatures are able, if they wish, to modify the results by means of subsequent legislation. This would normally be the case except when courts must rule on limits to the legislature's authority.

From that perspective, judicial review by the federal courts of decisions made by elected officials is most problematic. In the first place, federal judges are not elected, but are appointed with indefinite tenure. Popular control is more limited over the federal judiciary than over elected officials (or, more generally, over those who are considered "electorally accountable" – those who, for example, are appointed but serve at the pleasure of elected officials). In the second place, such review concerns the constitutionality of nonjudicial decisions. Decisions made by electorally accountable officials are liable to be nullified by nonelected federal judges, and electorally accountable officials will be unable to override those judicial decisions. It is accordingly held by many constitutional theorists that such judicial review severely strains democratic principles.

These same democratic sensibilities are most seriously offended when judicial review is thought to be combined with "judicial legislation." Therefore, when constitutional cases turn upon the testing of nonjudicial decisions against unclear constitutional provisions, legal theorists tend to suppose that any substantive decision involves judicial revision of the Constitution itself. On the basis of such reasoning, contemporary originalists sometimes hold that decisions made by officials who are answerable to the electorate should not be nullified by nonelected judges unless it is clear that those decisions violate the Constitution.[45]

Some constitutional theorists are thought to lack such scruples. They are accused of claiming that courts may take it upon themselves to change the supreme law of the land. An example of such thinking is discussed by Justice Rehnquist, who quotes from a brief filed in federal court on behalf of state prisoners as follows:

We are asking a great deal of the Court because other branches of government have abdicated their responsibility. . . . Prisoners are like other 'discrete and insular' minorities for whom the Court must spread its protective umbrella because

---

[45] This assumes, of course, that judicial review can be justified despite the argument from democracy. We shall return to that point presently.

no other branch of government will do so. . . . This Court, as the voice and conscience of contemporary society, as the measure of the modern conception of human dignity, must declare that the [named prison] and all it represents offends the Constitution of the United States and will not be tolerated.[46]

Rehnquist understands this to imply that "nonelected members of the federal judiciary may address themselves to a social problem simply because other branches of government have failed or refused to do so."[47] Federal judges would then have "a roving commission to second-guess Congress, state legislatures, and state and federal administrative officers concerning what is best for the country."[48] Rehnquist accordingly describes such a view as "a formula for an end run around popular government, genuinely corrosive of the fundamental values of our democratic society."[49]

Rehnquist's rhetoric is fired by "democratic" flames, so let us look more closely at this argument from democracy. It challenges the legitimacy of judicial review. If we were to formulate the argument rigorously, its conclusion would amount to the following proposition:

Judicial review of a non-judicial decision violates democratic principles to the extent that the reviewing judiciary is less directly accountable to a popular electorate than is the non-judicial decision maker.

To reach this conclusion, a premise like the following is needed:

Democratic principles imply that the more directly accountable an official decision maker is to a popular electorate, the greater the priority that should be given her official decisions.

This claim is dubious. It assumes that democratic standards apply directly to the several branches of a political structure, although the several branches are supposed to complement each other so as to yield a structure that is democratic overall. On the contrary, just as various amendments to the Constitution can be understood as promoting the system's respect for democratic values, rather than compromising that commitment, judicial review may be instrumental in securing that respect.

The sort of premise that seems to be needed by the standard argument against judicial review invokes "democracy" in a problematic way. It seems to invoke a theory of the Constitution. But no attempt is made to explain what relation such a view must have to the Constitution if the former is to qualify as a theory of the latter, no less how a particular theory might be defended. This is especially important because it is un-

[46] Rehnquist, "The Notion of a Living Constitution," 54 *Texas L. Rev.* 695 (1976).
[47] *ibid.* [48] *ibid.*, p. 698.
[49] *ibid.*, p. 706.

certain whether any view can both qualify as a theory of the Constitution, to be used in constitutional interpretation, and be reconciled with "strict" originalism.

More generally, the premise of the standard argument from democracy fails to reflect any appreciation of the values that might explain the importance of accountability to a popular electorate. It is implausible to suppose that "electoral accountability" is a fundamental value. That it is not is suggested, for example, by the qualifications that one would reasonably place on electoral accountability before it could serve in such a role; for example, that elections be free and fair. This strongly suggests that electoral accountability derives its importance from some more fundamental value, such as the right to participate in shaping the rules that may be enforced against oneself or, perhaps, political equality. These values and their relation to electoral accountability require clarification. Until we understand the basic values at stake, we can hardly determine the relation between judicial review and a commitment to democracy. And yet the literature on judicial review is silent on such matters.

Now, a federal judge might find it awkward to endorse the argument from democracy. For it suggests that the constitutional system is "democratic" in such a way as to make judicial review illegitimate. One who endorses such an argument might find it difficult to function honestly in the federal judiciary, where judicial review is firmly established.

It turns out, however, that the argument from democracy is used not to block judicial review but, rather, to establish a presumption against it. It is thought to counsel "restraint." This is illustrated by Rehnquist's response to the argument from democracy. He does not reject judicial review. He endorses it on the ground that the constitutional arrangements including judicial review are given by "the people."[50] Unfortunately, Rehnquist's version of this claim is no more plausible than the one we considered in section II. A specious argument receives a glib reply.

It should be observed, finally, that Rehnquist charges those he criticizes as favoring "the substitution of some other set of values for those which may be derived from the language and intent of the framers."[51] As this formulation suggests, his argument really turns on how the Constitution is to be understood. The quoted brief claimed, after all, that courts have a special responsibility to protect "discrete and insular minorities." This is a proposition with which some constitutional scholars agree.[52] They hold this responsibility to be based on the Constitution, not created by judicial fiat. Rehnquist disagrees with this interpretation and treats its proponents as if they recommend infidelity to the Constitution.

[50] ibid., p. 696.   [51] ibid., p. 695.
[52] See, e.g., Ely, Democracy and Distrust.

161

VI. THE WAGES OF SKEPTICISM

An initially more promising argument regarding judicial review is presented by Professor (now Judge) Bork, who begins by rejecting the crude argument from democracy and by describing our constitutional system as "Madisonian":

> A Madisonian system is not completely democratic, if by "democratic" we mean completely majoritarian. It assumes that in wide areas of life majorities are entitled to rule for no better reason than they are majorities. We need not pause here to examine the philosophical underpinnings of that assumption since it is a "given" in our society.[53]

Bork refrains from reflecting on the values that are at stake. This may be deliberate, for reasons that will emerge presently. But it is unfortunate because Bork, too, appears to offer us a theory of the Constitution.

Bork claims that "the Madisonian model" has two "premises." One is "majoritarian," the other "counter-majoritarian."

> The model . . . assumes there are some areas of life a majority should not control. There are some things a majority should not do to us no matter how democratically it decides to do them.[54]

To reconcile these "premises," we charge the Supreme Court to "define both majority and minority freedom through the interpretation of the Constitution."[55] Thus Bork accepts the legitimacy of judicial review. But, he says,

> the Court's power is legitimate only if it has, and can demonstrate in reasoned opinions that it has, a valid theory, derived from the Constitution, of the respective spheres of majority and minority freedom. If it does not have such a theory but merely imposes its own value choices, or worse if it pretends to have a theory but actually follows its own predilections, the Court violates the postulates of the Madisonian model that alone justifies its power.[56]

This passage suggests Bork's concern that the Court not impose its own "value choices."

He explains that concern in the course of an argument that appears more promising than Rehnquist's because it deals with the issues at a more fundamental level. Bork's argument may be summarized as follows:

1. Judicial decisions *should be* "principled."
2. Judicial decisions either *make* or *implement* "value choices."

---

[53] Bork, "Neutral Principles," pp. 2–3.   [54] *ibid.*, p. 3.
[55] *ibid.*   [56] *ibid.*

3. Judicial decisions that *implement* "value choices" *can* be "principled."
4. There is *no* "principled" way to *make* a "value choice."
5. Judicial decisions *should implement,* rather than make, "value choices."
6. Law creation, such as legislation or the framing of a constitution, involves *making* "value choices."
7. "Courts [reviewing legislation] must accept any value choice the legislature makes unless it clearly runs contrary to a choice made in the framing of the Constitution."[57]

This argument is originalist in spirit, if not entirely in content. An originalist theory of interpretation is suggested by the notion that certain "value choices" were made by the framers and are now available to be implemented by the courts. This corresponds to the idea that constitutional doctrines are fixed when the document is framed. An originalist theory of adjudication is suggested too, as Bork comes near to claiming that only those doctrines embodying the "framers' value choices" should be applied by the Court.

Note that the last step in the argument appears to presuppose a non-originalist principle:

Whenever the Constitution is unclear, the Court should defer to the legislature.

What basis could there be for such a doctrine of "restraint"? Bork has no grounds for suggesting, for example, that the practice of judicial review should be confined because it suffers under a cloud of illegitimacy. For, as we have seen, he has rejected the dubious argument from democracy, endorsed the practice of judicial review, and assigned it an indispensable constitutional function.

Here is one possible explanation of that last step in Bork's reasoning. As we have observed, many legal theorists embrace assumptions about meaning which lead them to believe that law is indeterminate when it is unclear. As we shall presently see, Bork explicitly endorses an even more radical type of philosophical skepticism – about value judgments generally. It would therefore not be out of keeping for Bork to indulge in the semantical skepticism that leaps from "unclear" to "indeterminate." This would lead him to reason that, when (a) the Constitution does not *clearly* contain a doctrine that is violated by a piece of legislation, then (b) the Constitution contains *no* such doctrine, (c) the legislation does not vio-

---

[57] *ibid.,* pp. 10–11.

late the Constitution, and (d) the legislation should accordingly be accepted by the Court.[58]

But the most serious difficulty with Bork's reasoning derives from his value skepticism. To see this, we might begin by asking what is meant by a "value choice." This expression is so commonplace in constitutional theory that we may need to remind ourselves that it is an artifact of theory. Compare the expression with "value judgment." "Value choice" omits any reference to judgment, and so encourages the suggestion of arbitrariness and discourages any contrary suggestion of rational defensibility. The difference fits nicely into Bork's strategy of argument, which explicitly invokes a general philosophical doctrine of skepticism about the rational defensibility of value judgments.

As we have seen, Bork defines the central problem of "Madisonian democracy" as the need to strike a balance between "majority and minority freedom."[59] It is precisely in this context that he says, for example:

Every clash between a minority claiming freedom and a majority claiming power to regulate involves a choice between gratifications of the two groups. When the Constitution has not spoken, the Court will be able to find no scale, other than its own value preferences, upon which to weigh the respective claims to pleasure.[60]

Bork has two examples. One is *Griswold,* which he views as a judicial choice between two "claims to pleasure" and their respective "gratifications." Another is "a hypothetical suit by an electric company and one of its customers to void a smoke pollution ordinance as unconstitutional. The cases are identical."[61]

To make Bork's position perfectly clear, we should consider a different example. Prior to the Fourteenth Amendment, Bork would presumably respond to a suit seeking invalidation of a law banning Jews and Catholics from certain occupations, as follows:

There is no way of deciding these matters other than by reference to some system of moral or ethical values that has no objective or intrinsic validity of its own and about which men can and do differ. Where the Constitution does not embody the moral or ethical choice, the judge has no basis other than his own values upon which to set aside the community judgment embodied in the statute.[62]

My point is not that a refusal to invalidate the statute would have been unfaithful to the law, for the contrary interpretation is, unfortunately, plausible. My point is that Bork's express reason for a judicial policy of

[58] This assumes the use of a burden-of-proof rule discussed in section V.
[59] Bork, "Neutral Principles," p. 3.   [60] *ibid.,* p. 9.
[61] *ibid.*   [62] *ibid.,* p. 10.

"restraint" is that all opposing positions, including the rejection of big-otry, are rationally indefensible, so that, lacking constitutional warrant, a judicial decision favoring one would be "unprincipled" *just because* any "preference" for one side or the other *could not be* "principled." Value "choices" are required to adjudicate between any two opposing views, because moral and political positions are in Bork's view equivalent to preferences. The judicial vindication of a morally motivated claim is likewise equivalent, in his eyes, to favoring one person's gratification over another's. But:

There is no principled way to decide that one man's gratifications are more de-serving of respect than another's or that one form of gratification is more worthy than another.[63]

Such "value choices" might be made by judges or derived from the Con-stitution. If made by judges, Bork maintains, the judicial decisions in which they are embodied are "unprincipled," because value judgments are in general "unprincipled."

Where constitutional materials do not clearly specify the value to be preferred, there is no principled way to prefer any claimed human value to any other.[64]

But if the "value choices" are derived from the Constitution, then the judicial decisions implementing them are "principled."

It is important to emphasize that in these passages Bork is *not* simply asserting the standard originalist claim that judges reviewing legislation should not impose their own values, but should apply doctrines derived from the Constitution. For that is what he is trying to prove. He is argu-ing, in effect, that *when the Constitution is unclear and interpretation of it may seem to require moral reasoning,* judges should defer to the legis-lature. His philosophical skepticism is deployed to show that judges should make no value judgments when deciding constitutional cases.

That is relevant to an earlier argument of this paper. The alternative to "strict" originalism that was sketched in section III requires that courts applying "vague clauses" of the Constitution interpret "contested con-

---

[63]   *ibid.* Bork's note explains: "The impossibility is related to that of making interper-sonal comparisons of utilities." He apparently assumes that if there is any morally defensible criterion for making decisions (including those adjudicating interpersonal conflicts of interest), it is that they should maximize (in Bork's terms) "gratifica-tions." The alleged impossibility to which he refers would make that criterion im-possible to satisfy. Normative welfare economics avoids the problem by giving up the maximizing requirement and replacing it with a conception of economic effi-ciency, such as Pareto's, that requires no interpersonal comparisons of utility. Bork's note suggests that he is unaware of or refuses to consider either economic or deon-tological alternatives to classical utilitarianism.

[64]   *ibid.,* p. 8.

cepts," which requires reasoning about moral or political principles. Bork's view that judges should not make "value choices" seems to mean that courts should not engage in any such reasoning. Bork reasons: judicial review should be neutral, principled, and nonarbitrary; it is impossible to make value judgments that are neutral, principled, or nonarbitrary, so judges should not incorporate value judgments into their constitutional decisions.

Bork's value skepticism is assumed and applied without justification.[65] Needless to say, value skepticism cannot be found within the Constitution. Indeed, the two are clearly incompatible. Thus Bork invokes an *anti*-constitutional doctrine to significant effect.

It is worth noting that Bork's skepticism renders his overall position incoherent. Consider his claim that judges *should* decide constitutional cases in a certain way – that (as he seems to argue) they are *under an obligation* to do so. Bork writes as if he is providing a rational defense for that sort of conclusion about the responsible, legitimate use of judicial power. He appears to believe that his reasoning excludes contrary conceptions of judicial obligation. In his terminology, however, to embrace such a doctrine is to make a "value choice," which according to his value skepticism is irremediably "unprincipled," or rationally indefensible.

The result is a dilemma for Bork. If it is possible to provide good reasons (as Bork purports to do) for his conception of the legitimate (justified, responsible) exercise of judicial power – reasons designed to show that his conception is superior to contrary conceptions – then "value choices" can be principled. On the one hand, the success of any argument for the attribution of an obligation to judges would refute his value skepticism and undermine his argument that value judgments have no legitimate place in constitutional adjudication. On the other hand, his wholesale value skepticism excludes the possibility that any conception of the legitimate exercise of judicial power might be rationally defensible; so his skepticism undermines his own argument for and resulting judgment about responsible adjudication.

Consider now Bork's notion that judges must rely upon the value judgments that are embedded in the Constitution if their decisions are to be "principled." Bork assumes that decisions involving the exercise of judicial review can be "principled" insofar as they are grounded upon constitutional doctrines. This apparently means that the decisions can be justified relative to, or conditional upon, those doctrines.

[65] But see note 63.

166

But conditional justification is only as good as its condition. Recall that one piece of Bork's argument goes as follows:

Law-creation, such as legislation or the framing of a constitution, involves making "value choices."

Another piece says:

There is no principled way to make a "value choice."

Put together, these pieces yield the conclusion that the "value choices" embodied in the Constitution and the corresponding doctrines are themselves "unprincipled" or, in other words, unjustifiable. But if the doctrines on which the justification of judicial decisions depends are themselves unjustifiable, then the same applies to those decisions.

This means that Bork is faced with another dilemma. On the one hand, if "value choices" are unjustifiable, then so are the "value choices" reflected in the Constitution, and the same applies to all that rely on them for justification. On the other hand, if some value judgments can be justified (such as the idea that the Constitution merits respect), then Bork's general value skepticism is unsound, and his main argument collapses.

Bork might seem to avoid this particular incoherence when he remarks that his value skepticism "is not applicable to legislation. Legislation requires value choice and cannot be principled in the sense under discussion."[66] Bork might seem to suggest that there is another sense of "principled" in which the "value choices" embodied in legislation (and thus the legislation itself) can be "principled." Bork might mean, for example, that, rationally defensible or not, legislation by popularly elected officials is *permissible* under both democratic principles and our constitutional system. He might also wish to infer from this that those subject to such laws are under an obligation to respect them.

But this interpretation would not enable Bork to avoid the dilemma. Either he accepts the idea that democratic standards *justify* political arrangements that satisfy them, or he rejects it, presumably because of his value skepticism. If he rejects the idea, then, there is no apparent sense within Bork's skeptical system in which legislation or indeed our constitutional system can be justifiable; there is no apparent sense in which the Constitution can *truly* be said to merit respect, in which judges can *truly* be said to be under an obligation to respect it. If Bork believes that any of these value judgments can *truly* be justified, then he must forsake his objection based on value skepticism to the exercise of moral judgment within judicial review.

---

[66] Bork, "Neutral Principles," p. 8.

VII. CONCLUSION

Originalism seems to derive its initial plausibility from a simplified conception of how written constitutions work. Interpretation in terms of original intent promises a stable, uncontroversial version of the Constitution. But intentionalism faces overwhelming difficulties and appears to lack compensating justification, either in political or linguistic terms. Seeing no promising alternatives, opponents of strict originalism have accepted the need for extra-constitutional doctrines in constitutional adjudication. Originalists appear to reject such heterodoxy, but they unselfconsciously embrace a variety of extra-constitutional doctrines. Their theorizing about the Constitution tends toward the superficially descriptive and has yet to face the substantive value commitments implicit even in ritualistic appeals to democracy. Just as the Constitution cannot be value-free, so our understanding of it must be informed by reflection on the principles it serves.

8

A preface to constitutional theory

We have a plethora of theories about judicial review, including theories about theories, but their foundations require stricter scrutiny. This Essay presents some aspects of the problem through an examination of two important and familiar ideas about judicial review.

The controversy over "noninterpretive" review concerns the propriety of courts' deciding constitutional cases by using extraconstitutional norms. But the theoretical framework has not been well developed and appears to raise the wrong questions about judicial review. Thayer's doctrine of extreme judicial deference to the legislature has received much attention, but his reasoning has been given less careful notice. Thayer's rule rests largely on doctrines of doubtful constitutional standing.

The purpose of this Essay is not so much to answer questions as to raise them — to enlarge the agenda of constitutional theory.

I. INTERPRETIVE REVIEW

Constitutional scholarship has recently employed a distinction between "interpretive" and "noninterpretive" review, which concerns the range of norms used by courts in deciding constitutional cases. As the term suggests, "interpretive review" is based on interpretation of the Constitution; "noninterpretive review" is not so limited, but uses other grounds as well. Thus the normative theory that is labelled "interpretivism" accepts only interpretive review, whereas "noninterpretivism" approves of noninterpretive review in some cases.

These differences concern the core responsibilities of courts engaged in judicial review. They are not limited, for example, to crisis conditions, when courts might be thought to have special reason for departing from their normal role. They apply primarily to review by the federal judiciary

"A Preface to Constitutional Theory," *Northern Kentucky Law Review* 15 (1988): 159-77. This is a descendant of a paper presented to the Constitutional Bicentennial Symposium at the Salmon P. Chase College of Law, Northern Kentucky University, September 19, 1987. Material from the version presented has been deleted in order to minimize overlap with my previously published papers, and new material has been added. I am grateful to participants in the NKU symposium, especially John Garvey, Tom Gerety, and Michael Perry, for comments on and challenging questions about the original version.

169

of decisions made by other branches of the federal government. The role of those courts relative to decisions made by state governments is often treated differently.

The distinction was introduced by Grey in the following terms:

> In reviewing laws for constitutionality, should our judges confine themselves to determining whether those laws conflict with norms derived from the written Constitution? Or may they also enforce principles of liberty and justice when the normative content of those principles is not to be found within the four corners of our founding document?[1]

How useful is the distinction? According to Grey, the "chief virtue" of "the pure interpretive model" is that

> when a court strikes down a popular statute or practice as unconstitutional, it may always reply to the resulting public outcry: "We didn't do it – you did." The people have chosen the principle that the statute or practice violated, have designated it as fundamental, and have written it down in the text of the Constitution for the judges to interpret and apply.[2]

That seems false. Rarely could a court *truly* defend an unpopular decision by saying to a protesting population "We didn't do it – you did." Only small minorities of the population have been permitted to participate in the processes leading to ratification of the Constitution and most of its amendments. Most members of those privileged minorities are no longer alive when the provisions are enforced. Such a defense would rest on fictions.

But let us consider the theoretical framework on its merits. Grey argues that, when engaged in judicial review, "the courts do appropriately apply values not articulated in the constitutional text."[3] He might appear to win that argument too easily. For his initial definition of the distinction seems to limit interpretive review to norms that are *explicitly* given ("articulated") in the constitutional text. That would make the "interpretivist" a straw man.

Scholars accept that constitutional norms need not be stated in the document, but can be attributable to the Constitution on the basis of sound interpretative argument. Relatively uncontroversial examples include checks and balances, the separation of powers, and representative government. While it seems plausible to hold that some such norms are "derived from the written Constitution," they are not treated as if they have been fully "articulated in the constitutional text." They themselves require interpretation.

---

[1] Grey, "Do We Have An Unwritten Constitution?" 27 *Stan. L. Rev.* 703 (1975).
[2] *Id.* at 705.   [3] *Id.*

Grey's initial definition of interpretive review is misleading, but its narrowness is relieved by his acknowledgment that "sophisticated" interpretivism "certainly contemplates that the courts may look through the sometimes opaque text to the purposes behind it in determining constitutional norms. Normative inferences may be drawn from silences and omissions, from structures and relationships, as well as from explicit commands."[4] There is also evidence that Grey accepts "Framers' intent" as a criterion of constitutional meaning.[5] He appears to regard the intentions of the Framers as implicit codicils to the constitutional text. This might expand its "normative content" considerably.

Constitutional lawyers seem to agree that Framers' intent helps determine constitutional meaning. This is, however, a blind spot of constitutional theory. The criterion of Framers' intent desperately requires clarification and justification. Its fundamental difficulties have largely been ignored.[6]

Its difficulties notwithstanding, if Framers' intent is assumed to be a determinant of constitutional meaning, then that affects the interpretive-noninterpretive distinction. Interpretation, and therefore interpretive review, is then taken to encompass norms that can be inferred from the text of the Constitution *or* from the intentions of its Framers. Noninterpretive review includes norms with no such connections to the Constitution.

To understand the distinction better, we have to consider Grey's application of it. He appears mainly concerned with defending decisions based on "those large conceptions of governmental structure and individual rights that are at best referred to, and whose content is scarcely at all specified, in the written Constitution."[7] These are especially important and interesting norms, but it is misleading to regard their use as noninterpretive review.

Consider the fifth amendment's requirement of "just compensation"

4   *Id.* at 706 n.9. Grey goes on, however, to say: "What distinguishes the exponent of the pure interpretive model is his insistence that the only norms used in constitutional adjudication must be those inferable from the text." The entire passage makes sense only if we suppose that "the purposes behind" an "opaque text" can be "inferable from the text." That may be true in some cases.

5   *See, e.g., id.* at 710.

6   The central problems do not concern mere practical difficulties in applying the criterion, such as limited evidence, but its inherent ambiguity and arbitrariness. *See, e.g.,* Dworkin, "The Forum of Principle," 56 *N.Y.U.L. Rev.* 469 (1981), and Lyons, "Constitutional Interpretation and Original Meaning," 4 *Soc. Phil. & Pol'y* 75 (1986) [reprinted in this volume]. It may be too early to say that these criticisms of the criterion have been ignored, for they have appeared only recently. Nevertheless, some of the central difficulties were in effect indicated by MacCallum, "Legislative Intent," 75 *Yale L.J.* 754 (1966).

7   *Id.* at 708.

171

for private property that is taken for public use.[8] As the Constitution explicitly requires compensatory justice but provides no criteria of just compensation, it is most natural to understand the clause as requiring compensation that is truly just. If it does, then the Constitution presupposes that there is a real distinction between just and unjust compensation, one that people can employ.

On this reading, compensatory justice is a constitutional norm. But it is only named; its content is not given. What are we to say, then, about the appropriate criteria of compensatory justice and their use by courts? The question is forced on us by Grey's framework, which is intended to put such provisions in proper perspective. Should the criteria of compensatory justice be classified as *extra*constitutional norms and their use regarded as *non*interpretive because they are given neither by the constitutional text nor by Framers' intent? That would be misleading, because appropriate criteria are needed by courts in applying the *constitutional* norm of compensatory justice. That fact provides a powerful reason for regarding the identification of appropriate criteria as an element of constitutional *interpretation*.

Courts cannot identify appropriate criteria of compensatory justice without answering this question: "What does justice require by way of compensation when private property is taken for public use?"[9] A justified answer would seem to require a systematic inquiry into the principles of compensatory justice. Criteria that are appropriate for constitutional purposes might depend not only on abstract justice but also on social conditions, historical traditions, established economic practice, and prior constitutional interpretation. It is commonplace for courts to make such judgments.

Constitutional scholarship often describes such a process as judges *imposing* their own values on the nation. This assumes either that there cannot be justified answers to moral questions or else that judges are incapable of honest inquiry. But either form of skepticism is incompatible with our subject, the rational appraisal of normative theories about judicial review.

We are properly skeptical about criteria that are proposed without clear justification. There can also be room for doubting the results of an inquiry. But I see no reason to deny that courts might sometimes have adequate reason to regard certain criteria of compensatory justice as appropriate. A court's deciding a case on that basis could not be regarded as unfaithful to the Constitution. Quite the contrary.

---

[8] The occasion for compensation (public takings of private property) will be assumed hereafter.

[9] A sound answer might differentiate among takings.

Working out such aspects of the Constitution surely counts as interpretation. The interpretive-noninterpretive distinction obscures this point and directs us to the wrong questions. We need a better understanding of constitutional interpretation. We need to explore the variety of ways in which a norm can legitimately be attributed to the Constitution.

To suggest otherwise is to invite misguided criticism. When constitutional interpretation is so narrowly understood, the idea of noninterpretive review does not distinguish between norms that lack any connection with the Constitution and norms that are firmly anchored in it, though they require interpretation. Then critics can fail to appreciate the distinction.[10] Plausible objections to the former can mistakenly appear to discredit the latter as well.

Let us now consider briefly another prominent account of the distinction between interpretive and noninterpretive review. According to Ely, interpretivism holds

that judges deciding constitutional issues should confine themselves to enforcing norms that are stated or clearly implicit in the written Constitution [whereas noninterpretivism maintains] that courts should go beyond that set of references and enforce norms that cannot be discovered within the four corners of the document.[11]

Ely attacks this "clause-bound"[12] interpretivism, using arguments like those already suggested. It treats "constitutional clauses as self-contained units"[13] and does not envisage interpretive claims based on several provisions or the Constitution as a whole. "On candid analysis," he says, "the Constitution turns out to contain provisions instructing us to look beyond their four corners."[14] He finds these instructions in "provisions that are difficult to read responsibly as anything other than quite broad invitations to import into the constitutional decision process considerations that will not be found in the language of the amendment or the debates that led up to it."[15] Unlike Grey, Ely does not endorse noninterpretive review. But he avoids it only by renouncing his own definitions.

Interpretive and noninterpretive review are defined by both Grey and Ely so as to encompass the possible varieties of judicial review. Ely's attack on noninterpretivism is directed, however, against theories that do not exhaust the possible varieties of that type. He attacks what one might call *purely* noninterpretive review, which seeks "the principal stuff of constitutional judgment in one's rendition of society's fundamental val-

---

[10] See, e.g., Monaghan, "Our Perfect Constitution," 56 N.Y.U.L. Rev. 353 (1981).
[11] J. Ely, *Democracy And Distrust* 1 (1980).   [12] *Id.* at 11.
[13] *Id.* at 88, note *.   [14] *Id.* at 38.
[15] *Id.* at 14.

ues."[16] This leaves unscathed those versions of noninterpretivism that base judicial review on interpretations of "the document's broader themes," including Ely's theory. Ely defends a "participation-oriented, representation-reinforcing approach to judicial review."[17] According to his own definitions, that theory recommends noninterpretive review. In nevertheless calling his theory "the ultimate interpretivism,"[18] Ely acknowledges that the interpretive-noninterpretive distinction incorporates an inadequate conception of interpretation.

Ely's analytic framework is misleading,[19] and his method of interpretation is impressionistic. He claims, for example, that the Constitution overwhelmingly endorses representative democracy and that its unclear elements should be interpreted so as to promote that value. He recognizes that aspects of the Constitution cannot be encompassed by this interpretation, but he fails to explain the impact of the recalcitrant evidence on his interpretative claims or its consequences for judicial review. Should we regard the Constitution as committed also to principles that are independent of representative democracy? If so, how are unclear aspects of the Constitution to be understood when the two sets of principles conflict? Alternatively, should the Constitution be regarded as committed to some more complex set of principles, which coherently account for all of its provisions? Ely rejects the narrow conception of interpretation that is assumed by the standard idea of interpretive review, but he never clarifies his own conception of interpretation, and so neglects these issues.

In sum, the interpretive-noninterpretive distinction has been unhelpful. It begs the central question of judicial review, namely, the character of interpretative claims and the range of sound supporting arguments.

There is a genuine problem about whether and, if so, when and how extraconstitutional norms may properly be used within judicial review. But that problem can hardly be addressed before we achieve an understanding of interpretative claims that are based on what Ely calls "the broader themes" of the Constitution.[20]

---

[16] *Id.* at 88 note *.   [17] *Id.* at 87.
[18] *Id.* at 88.
[19] I discuss this point in Lyons, "Substance, Process, and Outcome in Constitutional Theory," 72 *Cornell L. Rev.* 745 (1987).
[20] Another problem is to clarify the subject of interpretation. The standard formulations quite naturally imply that it is a document. (A rare exception is Llewellyn, "The Constitution as an Institution," 34 *Colum. L. Rev.* 1 [1934].) But interpretative arguments routinely consider not only "Framers' intent" but also the requirements of institutions that accord with the structural norms of the Constitution (*see, e.g.,* C. Black, *Structure And Relationship In Constitutional Law* [1969], which is frequently cited but whose intriguing theoretical claims about interpretation have never been carefully analyzed or clearly explained) and interpretative judicial precedent. Grey defends "noninterpretivism" by relying heavily on established lines of prece-

II. THAYER'S RULE

According to Thayer's famous "rule of administration" for judicial review, federal courts should nullify federal legislation only when one cannot reasonably doubt that it is unconstitutional.[21]

This extreme doctrine of judicial deference does not seem to be motivated by skepticism about the constitutional basis for judicial review. Thayer appears to believe that judicial review is justified on the ground that Congress has "only a delegated and limited authority under the [Constitution, and] that these restraints, in order to be operative, must be regarded as so much law; and, as being law, that they must be interpreted and applied by the court."[22] Thayer emphasizes that judicial review concerns the constitutional boundaries of legislative authority rather than the wisdom of the legislature's exercise of its authority and that, as a judicial power, it may be exercised only within the context of litigation in which constitutional questions arise.[23]

Against that background, one might expect Thayer to reason that courts should approach the task of reviewing legislation for its constitutionality by seeking a well grounded understanding of the relationship between the Constitution and the legislation under review. This would require a court to base its decision on interpretations of legislative authority and its limits under the Constitution as well as of the challenged statute.

Thayer does, in fact, insist upon that straightforward approach to judicial review, but only when federal courts review legislative enactments by state governments. In those cases, Thayer says, courts should be guided

dent. Like judicial review itself, Ely's own theory starts from an interpretative precedent and relies on precedents throughout. Dworkin maintains that constitutional interpretation concerns not just the constitutional document but "our constitutional structure and practice." *See* R. Dworkin, *Law's Empire* 360 (1986).

21 Thayer, "The Origin and Scope of the American Doctrine of Constitutional Law," 7 *Harv. L. Rev.* 129 (1893) (hereinafter Thayer, "Origin"). The rule is formulated in a variety of ways, but the variations make no difference here. As explained below, the rule applies to relations between the judiciary and the legislature at the federal level.

22 *Id.* at 138; *see also id.* at 129–130 (on the supremacy clause).

23 Thayer contrasts the limited range of cases in which the courts are authorized to "review" legislation for constitutionality with the unlimited scope for review by the legislature. He claims that the legislature cannot act without making such a judgment, and that its judgment may be final, as many of its acts cannot be reviewed by courts. He reasons that, by placing limits on the scope of judicial review, the system implies that the legislature is primarily to be relied upon to review legislation for constitutionality, and that the legislative judgment is entitled to respect. *Id.* at 134–136. This "may help us to understand why the extent of [the judiciary's] control, when they do have the opportunity, should be narrow." *Id.* at 137. But the same might be said about state legislatures and legislation, so Thayer's reasoning does not seem to square with the different treatments he accords federal and state legislation.

175

by "nothing less than" the "just and true interpretation"[24] of the federal Constitution. But Thayer insists that the same does not hold when courts review federal legislation; courts should approach those cases very differently.[25]

Thayer observes, in effect, that two questions must be distinguished. One is whether legislation comports with the Constitution. Another is how courts should deal with challenges to the constitutionality of legislation. These might be assumed to run together. Indeed, there would seem to be a very strong presumption that an answer to the former question (Is this statute constitutional?) determines the appropriate answer to the latter (Should this statute be upheld as constitutional?). But Thayer holds, in effect, that federal courts should not be guided by any such presumption in dealing with federal legislation. In those cases, courts should not be guided by their best interpretation of the statutes and the Constitution. They should not ask whether the legislation *is* constitutional, but whether the courts should sustain it as constitutional. Courts should answer that question by determining whether someone might reasonably believe that the legislation is constitutional. If so, the constitutional challenge should be denied and the legislation upheld. If not – if "it is not open to rational question"[26] whether the act is unconstitutional – then, but only then, should the courts nullify it.

Courts following Thayer's rule might never have occasion to declare unconstitutional legislation unconstitutional. Judges might confidently believe, on excellent grounds, that an enactment exceeds Congress' legislative authority and is therefore unconstitutional, but they might simultaneously believe that their excellent reasons for regarding the enactment as unconstitutional leave room for reasonable doubt. Thayer understands, of course, that the rule requires greater deference to congressional decisions than would otherwise be warranted. But that is not my present concern.

My point is that the rule requires justification. Judicial review (as Thayer himself appreciates) is grounded upon the idea that the Constitution is law that courts are bound to apply and enforce. This implies a very strong presumption that courts should nullify legislation that they regard as unconstitutional. Thayer would seem to be claiming that in some, but not all, cases federal courts should not straightforwardly apply and enforce

---

24 *Id.* at 155.
25 Thayer does not adequately explain why different treatment is to be accorded state and federal legislation. He asserts that the courts have a duty to maintain the "paramount authority" of the national over the state governments (*Id.* at 154), but all he adds is that the federal legislature is, whereas state legislatures are not, "co-ordinate" with the federal courts. *Id.* at 155.
26 *Id.* at 144.

the federal Constitution, and thus that in those cases this presumption is rebutted. His conception of a federal court's responsibility when reviewing legislation from one of the state legislatures shows that he understands what it means for the courts to apply and enforce the Constitution. He accordingly owes us an explanation of how the presumption in question is rebutted – how courts can *legitimately* refrain from applying and enforcing the Constitution generally, with regard to congressional as well as state legislation.

An answer might make either of two possible claims. It might claim that there are *constitutional* grounds for judicial deference to the legislature in such cases, or it might invoke *extra*constitutional grounds. The difference is significant. Whereas an answer of the first type would raise issues of constitutional interpretation, an answer of the second type would raise issues of principle regarding judicial fidelity to the Constitution.

Thayer appears to recognize that the burden of proof lies on his shoulders, and he attempts to sustain it both by offering evidence that his rule reflects the standard view[27] and by suggesting substantive grounds for the rule. The latter arguments, citing the rule's merits, are presented in quotations from others' writings. But Thayer appears to endorse their points, so I shall proceed as if they represent his considered judgement. The main issue for constitutional theory is not what Thayer himself believed but the character of such reasoning.

I shall now review the suggested arguments in the order in which they are suggested in Thayer's paper:

A. Utilitarianism

Thayer submits that unless the courts limit nullification to violations of the Constitution that are "plain and clear, . . . there might be danger of the judiciary preventing the operation of laws which might produce much public good."[28]

This argument is offered tentatively, perhaps because it is incomplete. After all, courts nullifying federal legislation may prevent public harm as well as public good. A complete argument of this type would need to show that following his rule would do more good than harm, perhaps even that it would do more good, on the whole, than any feasible alternative, including less deferential rules.

But the argument might be bolstered. To avoid circularity and vacuity,

---

27 Thayer's claim that his rule was firmly established is systematically appraised and rejected in C. Black, *The People and the Court* 195–203 (1960).
28 Thayer, "Origin," *supra* note 21, at 140 (quoting Kemper v. Hawkins, Va. Cas. p. 60 [1793]).

let us interpret "public good" as general welfare. It might be held that a reasonably accurate measure of the general welfare is provided by an indirect majoritarian decision process such as that provided by a popularly elected legislature. If so, it might be held that a policy of judicial deference to a popularly elected legislature would promote the general welfare.[29]

Let us then suppose that Thayer's rule can be supported by utilitarian reasoning. This does not appear to count as a legal, or specifically a constitutional, argument. How can it legitimately guide a court's approach to judicial review? How can it legitimately limit a court's application and enforcement of the Constitution? An answer might be based on constitutional or extraconstitutional considerations. After all, either the Constitution implies that utilitarian reasoning may permissibly guide a court's approach to judicial review or it does not.

There is a clear textual basis for claiming that the Constitution acknowledges the validity of utilitarian reasoning, though not to the exclusion of all potentially competing considerations. The preamble says that the Constitution is meant to "promote the general Welfare,"[30] among other things. The values cited in the preamble might be understood to have a bearing upon constitutional interpretation. It might be held, for example, that the Constitution as a whole should be interpreted so as to promote those values. This reasoning would not justify the promotion of the general welfare without regard to the other values cited, but it would legitimize the use of utilitarian arguments, among others, in large scale constitutional interpretation.

But this would not tend to show that the utilitarian argument for Thayer's rule has a constitutional foundation. From the assumption that the Constitution as a whole is supposed to promote a certain value, and that the Constitution as a whole may be interpreted accordingly, we cannot reasonably infer that the same is true of specific aspects of the Constitution. That would amount to what logicians call "the fallacy of division." Besides, institutions do not work that way. Law, in particular, promotes various values *indirectly*.

If a utilitarian argument for Thayer's rule is to be regarded as constitutional, what needs to be shown is that the Constitution implies a utilitarian condition *on the exercise of the judicial power*. Consider the par-

---

[29] The argument provides no apparent basis for deferentially reviewing federal legislation while rigorously reviewing legislation of the several states. The same is true of other arguments considered here, but I shall ignore that hereafter.

[30] I ignore here the differences and possible conflict between promotion of the general welfare when that is limited to the population of the United States and promotion of welfare more generally.

allel case for legislation. Suppose we ask whether the failure of a statute to promote the general welfare is a constitutional ground for nullification of the statute. Thayer's answer would be no: the Constitution provides no utilitarian condition on the exercise of the legislative power. But the same applies to adjudication: we have no reason to believe that the Constitution implies a utilitarian condition on the exercise of the judicial power. If that is true, then a utilitarian argument for Thayer's rule cannot be regarded as based on the Constitution.

If the first suggested argument for Thayer's rule has no foundation in the Constitution, then the argument is extraconstitutional.[31] We return to our original question: How can such reasoning legitimately guide a court's approach to judicial review?

The general problem is this. Legitimate legal arguments vary among jurisdictions, but are usually thought to be limited. Judicial review itself assumes that there are limits to the judicial power to nullify legislation. Some reasons are relevant (the statute is unconstitutional); others are not (the statute is unwise). But if some arguments with no foundation in the Constitution are to be regarded as a sound basis for some judicial decisions (such as whether a court should adopt Thayer's rule), then those limits on legal arguments are threatened. Must courts then be guided by other extraconstitutional and even extralegal arguments – without restriction, in all judicial contexts? If not, then what is the basis for selecting some and rejecting others?

The first argument for Thayer's rule does not begin to answer such questions, but perhaps we have delved deeply enough to suggest some conditions on, and thus some obstacles to, its successful completion. Let us turn, then, to another suggested argument for Thayer's rule.

B. Respect for the law

Thayer next posits that the courts should insure "due obedience" to the federal legislature's authority. If its authority is "frequently questioned, it must tend to diminish the reverence for the laws which is essential to the public safety and happiness."[32]

This suggests that, by rigorously enforcing the Constitution, courts might undermine respect for federal legislation, which in turn might undermine public safety and happiness. The argument assumes both that federal rule

---

[31] It is then an argument that a self-styled "interpretivist" should reject. If "judicial activism" in this area involves the use of extraconstitutional norms, then this is an activist argument for judicial deference.

[32] Thayer, "Origin," *supra* note 21, at 142 (quoting Adm'rs of Byrne v. Adm'rs of Stewart, 3 S.C. Eq 466, 476 [S.C. 1812]).

is essential to public welfare and that it is quite fragile. Thayer seems to assume that extreme judicial deference can not only bolster federal authority but is an essential means to that end.

It may be difficult for us to regard the federal government as fragile, but the idea might have seemed more plausible when Thayer wrote, not very long after the Civil War.

In any event, the argument may be understood in either of two ways. We might emphasize its reference to "public safety and happiness" and read it along utilitarian lines. This would introduce nothing new into our deliberations, so I turn instead to an alternative reading. The argument might be understood to presuppose a principle that seems plausible, if somewhat vague: The judiciary shares responsibility to make the system work.

The principle is implausible unless the judiciary's share of the responsibility is limited, for example, to "judicial" functions. Even if our conception of the judicial role is flexible, it is not coextensive with our conceptions of the other governmental branches. Questions that then arise are whether the adoption of such a rule is in fact compatible with the judicial role and, if so, whether its adoption is in fact necessary to make the system work.

For our purposes, however, the most important question is whether the principle that is presupposed by the argument (*e.g.*, that the judiciary shares responsibility to make the system work) has any foundation in the Constitution. It is tempting to suppose so, but I see no clear argument to that effect. Another possibility is that the principle expresses a conception of civic responsibility, which might be classified as moral rather than legal. Implementing the notion of civic responsibility in this way seems less threatening to the idea of limits on law than does similar use of utilitarian reasoning. Whereas application of the notion of civic responsibility is limited to political or similar contexts, utilitarian reasoning is not.

C. *Independence of the judiciary*

Thayer fears that "[t]he interference of the judiciary with legislative Acts, if frequent or on dubious grounds, might occasion so great a jealousy of this power and so general a prejudice against it as to lead to measures ending in the total overthrow of the independence of the judges, and so of the best preservative of the constitution."[33]

This argument is likewise premised on the judiciary's responsibility to

[33]   *Id.*

help make the system work, as well as on fears that ill-considered or even "frequent" judicial nullification of legislation might provoke Congress to use its considerable power to control the federal courts. There is of course some irony in an argument that seems to counsel sacrificing the Constitution in order to save it. Put more sympathetically, however, the claim is that rigorous enforcement of the Constitution might be self-defeating.

This argument may be contrasted with Learned Hand's later justification for judicial review. Both writers emphasize the importance of preserving the constitutional scheme that separates powers and allows one branch of government to limit the effective discretion of another. Both urge judicial deference to the federal legislature. Beyond that, however, they differ profoundly. Thayer appears reasonably confident of the constitutional basis for judicial review, but is concerned that vigorous exercise of the judicial power might be self-defeating. Hand seems deeply skeptical of judicial review's grounding in the Constitution, and argues that it was necessary for the judiciary to assume the power in order to "keep the states, Congress, and the President within their prescribed powers."[34]

D. Representative government

Finally, in a passage whose principal point is to emphasize the degree of judicial deference that is due the federal legislature, Thayer suggests a further argument:

It must indeed be studiously remembered, in judicially applying such a test as this of what a legislature may reasonably think, that virtue, sense, and competent knowledge are always to be attributed to that body. The conduct of public affairs must always go forward upon conventions and assumptions of that sort. "It is a *postulate*," said Mr. Justice Gibson, "in the theory of our government . . . that the people are wise, virtuous, and competent to manage their own affairs." And so in a court's revision of legislative acts . . . it will always assume a duly instructed body; and the question is not merely what persons may rationally do who are such as we often see, in point of fact, in our legislative bodies, persons untaught it may be, indocile, thoughtless, reckless, incompetent, – but what those other persons, competent, well-instructed, sagacious, attentive, intent only on public ends, fit to represent a self-governing people, such as our theory of government assumes to be carrying on our public affairs, – what such persons may reasonably think or do, what is the permissible view for them. . . . The reasonable doubt [of unconstitutionality] . . . is that reasonable doubt which lingers in the mind of a competent and duly instructed person who has carefully applied his

---

[34] L. Hand, *The Bill of Rights* 15 (1958).

MORAL ASPECTS OF LEGAL THEORY

faculties to the question. The rationally permissible opinion of which we have been talking is the opinion reasonably allowable to such a person as this.[35]

This passage can be understood to serve two functions. On the one hand, it is designed to clarify the rule of judicial deference to the federal legislature. According to the clarified rule, congressional acts may be nullified when, and only when, they are unconstitutional beyond "that reasonable doubt which lingers in the mind of a competent and duly instructed person who has carefully applied his faculties to the question."

On the other hand, it suggests a further ground for the rule. Thayer suggests that the Constitution embodies "a theory of government." He does not state the theory, but it appears to include the following elements: the theory assumes (1) "that the people are wise, virtuous, and competent to manage their own affairs," and (2) that they do so through representatives who are "competent, well-instructed, sagacious, attentive, [and] intent only on public ends." This appears to anticipate the notion that our government embodies or is committed to political principles which, because they favor "self-government" – or the closest practical approximation, government by elected representatives – argue against interference by an unelected federal judiciary. Although the point is not clearly made, it is nonetheless worth pursuing for its continuing importance.

This fourth suggested argument for Thayer's rule is similar to Alexander Bickel's contention that judicial review is "counter-majoritarian" and "undemocratic."[36] Bickel puts the point by saying that, because judicial review "thwarts the will of the representatives of the actual people of the here and now," it is "a deviant institution in the American democracy."[37] These points are understood to provide reasons against judicial nullification of legislative decisions. As judicial review is established in the system, those points are understood to provide reasons for limiting such interference with the operations of representative government.[38]

But what kinds of reasons are they supposed to be? Are they provided by the Constitution? If not, we might ask, once again, why we should suppose that they should be taken into account in the deliberations of

[35] Thayer, "Origin," *supra* note 21, at 149 (emphasis in original).
[36] A. Bickel, *The Least Dangerous Branch* 16–17 (1962). *See also,* Rehnquist, "The Notion of a Living Constitution," 64 *Texas L. J.* 695–769 (1976).
[37] Bickel, *supra* note 36, at 18.
[38] Thayer's reference to "the theory of our government" is problematic. The quoted passage implies that he treats essential elements of the theory as fictions. He does not believe that the elected legislators are generally "fit to represent a self-governing people," and one suspects that, for similar reasons, he does not believe that the people are fit to govern themselves.

courts that are charged with the application and enforcement of constitutional law.

Consider the following facts: *First,* Thayer suggests that the power of judicial review can be inferred from the Constitution; Bickel claims that judicial review is neither implicit in nor contrary to the Constitution.[39] As both writers appreciate, the practice is well entrenched within the system. So, neither writer claims that judicial review is excluded by the Constitution and both acknowledge that it is established practice. *Second,* both writers understand that the Constitution neither prescribes nor permits pure popular government or even unrestricted representative government. The Constitution prohibits a variety of decisions that might be made by elected representatives. The constitutional system has various counter-majoritarian features. As both writers recognize, the constitutional system is not unqualifiedly committed to representative democracy. In sum, even if judicial review clashes with principles of representative democracy, that would not show that it clashes with the principles of the system that we have.

Perhaps the idea is that the Constitution is somehow committed to an *ideal* of representative democracy, despite its counter-majoritarian features. This raises a question that is rarely addressed in the literature of constitutional theory: What kind of reasoning is capable of justifying the attribution of *normative* political principles, including political ideals, to the Constitution? What would make a theory of that kind true? Political principles are often attributed to the Constitution, but on what basis is never made clear. For that reason, it is unclear what inferences might be drawn from, or what applications might be made of, those principles within the context of constitutional interpretation.

Compare Bork's conception of the Constitution. Although Bork refers to "the seeming anomaly of judicial supremacy in a democratic society," he says that the anomaly is "dissipated . . . by the model of government embodied in the structure of the Constitution."[40] That model is "Madisonian," and "one essential premise of the Madisonian model is majoritarianism. The model has also a counter-majoritarian premise, however, for it assumes there are some areas of life a majority should not control."[41] Bork claims that both "constitutional theory" and "popular understanding"[42] provide an adequate basis for judicial review by giving

---

[39] It is unclear whether Bickel means that the Constitution is indeterminate on this issue, and also whether he believes that judicial precedent nonetheless imposes an obligation to engage in judicial review.

[40] Bork, "Neutral Principles and Some First Amendment Problems," 47 *Ind. L.J.* 2 (1971).

[41] *Id.* at 3.   [42] *Id.*

courts the task of clarifying the boundary between majority power and minority freedom.

Because it acknowledges that the system limits representative government, Bork's "Madisonian model" seems descriptively more accurate than Bickel's "majoritarian" model. This might lead one to infer that Bork's model is superior. But these "models" are not purely descriptive. They are meant in part to show why the constitutional system merits respect. And such a model's descriptive accuracy need not improve its qualifications *as an ideal.* Even if the majoritarian model is descriptively less accurate than the Madisonian model, some might think that it nevertheless embodies a superior ideal. They might argue that pure representative government is better than a Madisonian system because it is inherently fairer or better serves the general welfare.[43]

III. CONCLUSION

The relatively brief career of the "interpretive model" for judicial review suggests the difficulty of containing the practice of constitutional interpretation within the narrow confines of textual glosses and psychohistory. Legal theory resists the notion that interpretation might be both controversial and sound, for its ideal of law is black letter. Anything short of certainty is dubious law. But interpretive practice in law, as elsewhere, seeks both hidden and wider meanings. A good deal of "noninterpretive" review turns out to be interpretational after all.

There are limits to the range of legal and specifically constitutional meanings, and so the imaginative practice of constitutional interpretation obliges us to consider the various grounds upon which norms can properly be attributed to the Constitution. But the reasoning behind doctrines like Thayer's rule, which aspire to regulate constitutional adjudication, appears not to respect those boundaries. Is that a sign that civic responsibilities lie just beyond the law? Or does it reflect undisciplined theory-mongering, constitutional infidelity masquerading as "judicial restraint"?

We end, as promised, with questions.

[43] This might be Bickel's view.

9

Basic rights
and constitutional interpretation

This paper considers some strategies of constitutional interpretation. It suggests an approach aimed at promoting judicial decisions that are morally defensible as well as legally justifiable.

Section 1 raises the problem of interpretation in connection with the *Dred Scott* decision.[1] Section 2 suggests how interpretive claims can be surprising yet innocuous even in controversial cases such as *Griswold v. Connecticut.*[2] Section 3 considers interpretation based on "original intent," which it reinterprets sympathetically. Section 4 grounds the recommended approach on a right to be free from morally indefensible coercive regulation. Section 5 returns to *Dred Scott,* and Section 6 suggests both an interpretive argument and the moral limits of the recommended approach.

1.

The Supreme Court made one of its most controversial decisions in *Dred Scott v. Sandford.*[3] The case originated in 1846 when Dred and Harriet Scott each began proceedings in the Missouri courts to establish that they and their children had been emancipated from slavery. Given their histories and Missouri precedent, their claims were neither novel nor implausible, and the prospects for a favorable outcome must have seemed good.

Dred Scott had been owned as a slave in Missouri by Dr. John Emer-

"Basic Rights and Constitutional Interpretation," *Social Theory and Practice* 16 (1990): 337–57. This is a slightly revised version of a paper presented to the Georgia State Conference on Human Freedom, April 6, 1990. An earlier version was presented to a conference on "The Legacy of the 'Rights of Man' for the 1990s" at the Society for the Humanities, Cornell University, October 20, 1989. I am grateful to Greg Alexander for suggestions and comments.

1 *Dred Scott v. Sandford,* 60 U.S. (90 How.) 393 (1857), specific page references to which will be in the text preceded by "S." ["Sanford" is misspelled in the original case report.]
2 Page references to the *Griswold* opinions [381 U.S. 479 (1965)] will be given in the text preceded by "G."
3 My account relies on Don E. Fehrenbacher, *The Dred Scott Case* (New York: Oxford University Press, 1978) as well as Supreme Court opinions in the case.

son, who took Scott with him in 1833 to a U.S. Army post in Illinois. They lived in that free state for more than two years. In 1836 Emerson took Scott with him to another army post, in the upper part of the Louisiana Territory, where slavery had been prohibited by Congress. They lived there for another two years. In 1838 Scott married Harriet Robinson, also a slave. Emerson married Eliza Irene Sanford, and the couple moved to Missouri, taking the Scotts with them.[4]

Missouri court decisions had determined that slaves who had been taken to live in states or territories that forbade slavery, as the Scotts had been, were thereby emancipated. However, the Scotts did not seek to establish that status through the courts at first. After Emerson died, in 1843, Scott tried to purchase their freedom from Emerson's widow. After she refused, the Scotts went to court.

A decision for the Scotts was rendered by the Missouri trial court in 1850. But Irene Emerson appealed, and in 1852 the Missouri Supreme Court, with new members, renounced its own precedents and reversed the lower court's decision. Scott sued in federal court. The federal court trial went against him in 1854, and he appealed to the U.S. Supreme Court.

The case came before that Court during a period of increasing, sometimes violent, conflict over the spread of slavery. The Court addressed that issue by declaring that Congress lacked authority to prohibit slavery in federal territories. This nullified the compromise of 1820, which admitted Missouri as a slave state but prohibited slavery "forever" in much of the western territories. The decision greatly increased the area into which slavery might be extended as well as the number of prospective slave states.

My main interest here is with a different aspect of the decision. In the Scotts' Missouri suits, the defendant had been Irene Emerson. In Dred Scott's federal suit, the defendant was her brother, John Sanford, to whom the Scotts had presumably been sold. As the Scotts were residents of Missouri and Sanford was a resident of New York, Scott sued Sanford under the Constitution's "diversity" clause, which gives to federal courts jurisdiction over cases involving citizens of different states. In its decision, the Supreme Court held that the federal judiciary lacked authority to hear Scott's complaint under the diversity clause because Scott *could not be* a citizen, *even if he were emancipated.* According to Chief Justice Taney, an African-American simply could not become a citizen of the United States, because the Constitution was committed to the proposition that

---

[4] A daughter, Eliza, was born to the Scotts en route to Missouri. They had another daughter, Lizzie, seven years later.

African-Americans "had no rights which the white man was bound to respect" (S, p. 407).

As a statement of political morality, the proposition is outrageous. In its context, it embraced the notion that African-Americans are not persons, for most rights acknowledged by the Constitution are not limited to citizens. They are rights that any human being could rightfully demand that the government respect.

Nevertheless, Taney's was not an implausible interpretation of American law at the time. We may like to think of our constitutional system as committed to respect for the rights of all human beings, but in fact that view of our system has only recently become even plausible.

It is true that in 1776 the Declaration of Independence had asserted that "all men are created equal" and have "unalienable rights" to "life, liberty, and the pursuit of happiness." But the spirit of that Declaration did not dominate the Constitution of 1789, not even after the Bill of Rights was added, two years later. Although the Constitution did not refer to slavery by name, it secured the slave trade for a period of years, extended the reach of slave law into free states to facilitate the capture of suspected fugitives, and enhanced slave state representation by three-fifths of the number of their slaves. Nor was this an aberration from an otherwise egalitarian Constitution. The subordination of others was not as obviously sanctioned by the Constitution, but its failure to secure basic rights was tantamount to acquiescence. Two examples will suffice. The states continued to deny women basic rights,[5] and national policy towards aboriginal Americans amounted to eviction and eradication.

So Taney's assertion that under the Constitution African-Americans "had no rights which the white man was bound to respect" was shocking, and could be questioned as a reading of the law, but it was by no means incredible. That aspect of his opinion raises issues that I want to consider here. I would like to suggest that intellectually responsible interpretive strategy should discourage, rather than be neutral towards, reaching such a conclusion.

Even if Taney's reading of American law was wrong, a morally comparable conclusion might sometimes be sound. We must touch upon the question, if law can systematically be used as an official instrument of slavery and genocide, what should our attitude towards it be?

---

[5] Even after ratification of the Fourteenth Amendment in 1870, the Supreme Court refused to apply its equal protection clause against sex discrimination. This policy was established in *The Slaughter-House Cases,* 83 U.S. (16 Wall.) 36 (1873), and *Bradwell v. Illinois,* 83 U.S. (16 Wall.) 130 (1873), and continued until *Reed v. Reed,* 404 U.S. 71 (1971).

2.

The interpretive issues raised in the *Dred Scott* case were not different in kind from those that must usually be dealt with in constitutional cases. To suggest this, I shall take a circuitous route back to that decision. First I shall comment on another controversial Supreme Court decision, *Griswold v. Connecticut*. Justice Goldberg's concurring opinion contains the germ of an important idea, and this makes *Griswold* a convenient place to review some complications and strategies of constitutional interpretation.

In *Griswold*, the Supreme Court decided that a Connecticut statute prohibiting birth control measures violated a right of privacy that is implicit in the Constitution. The Court's opinion, written by Justice Douglas, has not been treated kindly. Mention of *Griswold* to a law student is apt to evoke sarcastic reference to Douglas's claim that "specific guarantees in the Bill of Rights have penumbras, formed by emanations from those guarantees that help give them life and substance" (G, p. 484).

In fact this colorful language alludes to innocuous points of constitutional law. It concerns the least controversial class of rights that the Court has found implied by the Constitution. Of course, privacy is not mentioned in the Constitution. As Douglas noted, however, judicial recognition and enforcement of implied rights is warranted by the Ninth Amendment, which says that "The enumeration in the Constitution of certain rights shall not be construed to deny or disparage others retained by the people." The Court had found good reason to recognize several such rights. The rationale for enforcing the subclass of implied rights that he called "peripheral" (the "emanations" mentioned earlier) is that otherwise rights that are explicitly mentioned "would be less secure" (G, pp. 482–83).

Freedom of association is a good example. Not mentioned in the Constitution, it is recognized by the Court as implicit in the First Amendment and needed to secure explicit First Amendment rights.[6] It serves in turn as the basis for, and has been secured by the enforcement of, further peripheral rights, such as the right to keep one's associations private, which has itself been protected by enforcing the rights of an association's officers to keep its list of members private.[7]

Douglas described the relevant impact of all these rights as "penum-

---

6 The First Amendment says, "Congress shall make no law respecting an establishment of religion, or prohibiting the free exercise thereof; or abridging the freedom of speech, or of the press, or the right of the people peaceably to assemble, and to petition the Government for a redress of grievances."
7 As in *NAACP v. Alabama*, 357 U.S. 449 (1958).

bras," specifically "zones of privacy" into which government may not intrude. He then reasoned that laws are constitutionally permissible only if enforcement measures for them are permissible. To sustain the Connecticut statute, Douglas said, the Court would have to approve of police searching "the sacred precincts of the marital bedroom for telltale signs of the use of contraceptives" (G, p. 485). He thought it evident that the right of privacy prohibits such an intrusion and concluded that the statute was constitutionally impermissible.

Now, even if we grant Douglas's claim about a privacy right, his explicit reasoning is incomplete. There might well be circumstances in which issuing warrants authorizing police to inspect bedrooms of married couples would be constitutionally permissible.[8] Further argument seems needed to trace the boundaries of the privacy right, to show that they enclose the case. Douglas simply added that a married couple's use of contraceptives would be covered by the right, in view of the importance that the law accords to marital relationships and their special qualities.

Douglas's failure to describe precisely the right of privacy exposed his opinion to somewhat more criticism than would normally accrue to a novel decision. But, though critics demand and lower courts may welcome precision, it is not unusual for courts to identify principles in broad terms without describing them precisely, and to let them be clarified incrementally in subsequent cases.

Consider the following example, involving a constitutional doctrine that is never formulated fully and precisely. The Ethics in Government Act of 1978[9] provides for judicial appointment of an independent counsel to investigate misconduct in the Executive Branch of the federal government. While under investigation by a counsel so appointed, Lt. Colonel Oliver North challenged this provision as a violation of the constitutionally mandated "separation of powers."

That is a plausible argument. The Constitution does not explicitly give us a separation of powers principle, so one must be inferred. But that is not unusual. Other important principles, such as federalism, are not given by the text but are identified by interpretation. The first three articles of the Constitution confer legislative, executive, and judicial powers respectively upon a Congress, President, and Supreme Court, and thus seem to impose a separation of powers. As only the President is specifically instructed to "take Care that the Laws be faithfully executed," it is reasonable to infer that enforcement of federal law is an Executive Branch responsibility. It then seems plausible to suppose that federal prosecutors

---

[8] The government might also acquire indirect evidence that the law has been violated, so it might be possible to enforce the statute without inspecting bedrooms.

[9] 28 U.S.C. Sections 591–98.

should be appointed by and answerable to the President. That would rule out independent counsels.

But the constitutional challenge is problematic, for the separation of powers is complex. The three branches of the federal government are given some linked as well as some separate powers. For example, the President has a role in the legislative process, Congress participates in presidential appointments, and it also performs judicial functions.

A separation of powers principle might be formulated in general terms; it would then be subject to possible overriding by other constitutional principles, such as "checks and balances." Alternatively, a separation of powers principle might be formulated so as to track precisely the explicit provisions of the Constitution. Either way, any separation of powers principle that we could infer from the constitutional text alone would be incapable of answering the specific question raised by North's challenge to the independent counsel provision of the Ethics in Government Act. This is a commonplace occurrence in constitutional adjudication. If a separation of powers challenge is to be decided on its merits, further interpretation of the Constitution would seem necessary.[10]

3.

How should such interpretation proceed? The most familiar approach to constitutional interpretation involves appealing to "original intent." This would seem applicable in the North case, for we have evidence beyond the constitutional text that the "framers intended" to constitutionalize a separation of powers principle.[11]

I want to pursue this in order to suggest that the original intent approach, as usually conceived by legal theorists, involves fundamental difficulties, but that we can salvage the idea by following actual practice and understanding it differently.

The theory of interpretation by reference to original intent calls on judges to identify and follow the intentions that some people had some time ago. There are of course some practical obstacles to implementing the theory, such as limited historical information. But the approach is supposed to promote judicial neutrality and fidelity to the Constitution. My misgivings concern its very conception. As a theory of constitutional meaning, the criterion is radically ambiguous and initially implausible. A

---

[10]   I am here ignoring the fact that constitutional adjudication relies greatly on interpretive precedents.

[11]   See *Encyclopedia of the American Constitution* (Levy ed., New York: Macmillan, 1986), s.v. "Separation of Powers."

brief review of these difficulties will lay the groundwork for an alternative approach.[12]

The intentions of those who gave us the Constitution are not a promising criterion of meaning for the constitutional text. The words that we
use have meanings that are determined by conventions of our language,
and the corresponding public meaning of a text that we produce can
accordingly differ from what we had in mind. Someone who wishes to
interpret the Constitution by reference to what people once had in mind
needs to explain why it should be read in that peculiar way – why its
originators' intentions should supplant the public meaning of the text.

If we had good reason to follow original intent instead of public meaning, we still could not do so unless we determined whose intentions count.
In a constitutional context, "original intent" usually refers to "Framers'
intent," but they did not make it law; ratification by nine states accom-
plished that. Why should we follow the intentions of those who drafted
the law instead of those who made it law? If the two sets of intentions
diverge, we need good reason to follow one set of understandings rather
than another. The ambiguous notion of original intent does not tell us
whose intentions should be followed.

Any serious attempt to use original intent has also to determine which
states of mind are to be counted. Some theorists assume that we should
be guided only by specific applications that the founders contemplated.
But that too seems arbitrary. One who favors a new piece of law may be
expected to have some specific applications in mind, but it is at least as
likely that she also intends it to solve some problem or to achieve some
other desired end. If we are to follow original intent, it would seem at
least as appropriate to be guided by general intent as by intended applications. This becomes important when the founders' general intent turns
out to be frustrated by the specific applications that they had in mind. It
can then make a great deal of difference which intentions courts follow.

Here is a possible example. Raoul Berger[13] objects to the Supreme
Court's decision in *Brown v. Board of Education*.[14] He argues that the
Fourteenth Amendment did not outlaw racial segregation in public schools,
because its originators had no intention of doing so. Berger believes,
however, that the Amendment was intended to secure basic civil rights
for African-Americans. Now, it is arguable that the Supreme Court in
Plessy v. Ferguson[15] held, in effect, that these two intentions – the general and the specific – were compatible, and that the Court changed its

---

[12] I discuss these problems in "Constitutional Interpretation and Original Meaning,"
     Social Philosophy and Policy 4 (1986): 75–101 [reprinted in this volume].
[13] In *Government by Judiciary* (Cambridge: Harvard University Press, 1977).
[14] 347 U.S. 483 (1954).   [15] 163 U.S. 537 (1896).

mind when deciding *Brown*. The Court finally recognized that in this society equal protection could not be secured while government embraced the doctrine and practices of white supremacy.

Let us put aside these problems for a moment and ask why one might be tempted to follow original intent instead of text meaning. A negative reason is to keep courts from straightforwardly interpreting constitutional language such as "equal protection," "due process," and "just compensation," whose interpretation would necessarily involve judgments of political morality. One of the prime virtues claimed for reliance upon original intent, as it is usually conceived by such theorists, is that it enables a court to avoid making "value choices."[16] Instead, a court is supposed to make a purely historical, value-free, factual estimate of what was going on in some persons' minds at a certain time. Some theorists believe this preferable because they equate law-making with the exercise of moral or political judgment and assume that moral or political judgment need not be exercised in the process of legal interpretation. Those assumptions seem false.

To isolate the question at issue, we must ignore the fact that such provisions have already been subjected to judicial interpretation and that courts may properly rely upon interpretive precedent.[17] We can then observe that application of the just compensation clause, for example, requires a court to identify criteria of justice in compensation for private property that is taken for public use. Courts interpreting this kind of provision face a problem of political morality.

Besides, negative rationales for an original intent approach give us no reason to regard it as a sound basis for constitutional interpretation. I have yet to discover a promising argument to that effect. But it may be helpful to consider an example or two of the reasons offered.

It may be said that courts should follow original intent because it is their duty to implement the will of those who made the law. But this begs the question at issue. The one thing with authoritative legal standing that is given by those who make law is a text that has been enacted or ratified into law. The text is made into law by the intentional acts of those who are competent to do so. Courts have a duty to implement the results of those intentional acts. That much is clear, and it offers no reason to be-

---

[16] See, for example, Robert Bork, "Neutral Principles and some First Amendment Problems," 47 *Indiana Law Journal* 1 (1971).

[17] Original intent theory cannot accommodate this routine aspect of judicial practice. Alone among champions of the theory, Henry Monaghan appreciates the problem, but he offers no solution to it; see his "Stare Decisis and Constitutional Adjudication," 88 *Columbia Law Review* 723 (1988).

lieve that some *other* intent takes priority over the public meaning of the legal text.

Another suggestion is that we are bound by a "social contract" to respect the Constitution as it was originally intended. This is puzzling. On the one hand, there seems to be no general agreement, among all of us who are called on to respect the Constitution, that it should be interpreted by original intent rather than by the public meaning of the text. On the other hand, if all who are called on to respect the Constitution were to be regarded as parties to a continuing contract, the relevant intentions would not be those of the originators alone but whatever understanding we *all* have in common. And that is not what is meant by "original intent."

I have rehearsed these difficulties in order to suggest the following points. As it is usually conceived by theorists, interpretation based on original intent is burdened by fundamental difficulties, with no prospect of solutions. Moreover, the standard theory does not seem to square with standard arguments referring to "original intent." A purely historical claim about the founders' intentions assumes that there was a consensus on the point at issue. But this essential element of the argument is almost always missing, even though we generally have good reason to suppose that the various founders had differing intentions. Such arguments rarely try to show, for example, that a given intention regarding a particular aspect of the Constitution was in fact shared by a supporting majority within the Constitutional Convention or among the ratifiers.

There are two possible explanations for this gap between theory and practice. Either references to original intent have the character described by the theory and are simply unsubstantiated, or they must be understood differently. I suggest the latter.

Original intent arguments often cite a piece of reasoning by respected figures, such as Madison or Hamilton.[18] Such slim grounds might be adequate if the argument is *not* meant to show that there was probably an intentional consensus among the founders — if it aims at something different. What the standard arguments often seem to do is this. They recall a relevant political insight which offers a *plausible justifying rationale* for the constitutional arrangement in question.[19] Given a rationale, as I shall suggest, we can decide the specific interpretive issue.

I believe that this is how original intent arguments often work, and that such an interpretive practice is defensible. Before explaining further,

---

[18] Note how often the *Federalist Papers* are relied upon for guidance, when we lack reason to believe that they represent an historical consensus.
[19] A similar point can be made about "legislative intent."

I shall illustrate the approach by applying it to North's separation of powers challenge to the independent counsel provision of the Ethics in Government Act.[20]

The standard rationale for a constitutional separation of powers is the importance of diffusing governmental authority in order to forestall dangerous concentrations of power.[21] Much the same rationale is standardly given for checks and balances, as the two doctrines go hand in hand.[22]

Given this, we can address North's challenge by asking which interpretation of the Constitution would better serve that purpose – one that allows or one that disallows an independent counsel. The obvious answer seems to be confirmed by experience. A dangerous concentration of power is reduced by limiting Executive Branch control over those who are given the job of investigating possible misconduct in it. North's preferred arrangement would invite abuse. That gives us good reason to regard the statutory provision as constitutionally permissible.[23]

4.

I want now to suggest why constitutional interpretation should be guided by justifying rationales. To do so I return to *Griswold* and Justice Goldberg's concurring opinion (G, pp. 486ff).

Goldberg followed Douglas in citing the Ninth Amendment, but he used it differently. Douglas had noted that the Ninth Amendment justifies the enforcement of peripheral rights, which are needed to secure rights that are explicitly recognized by the Constitution. Goldberg seemed to go considerably further by claiming that the Ninth Amendment justifies the enforcement of "fundamental" rights, which are neither specified in the Constitution nor derived from specified rights in the manner of peripheral rights (G, p. 492).

Goldberg characterized fundamental rights as follows: a "fundamental" right "is of such a character that it cannot be denied without violating those 'fundamental principles of liberty and justice which lie at the

---

20 I shall continue to ignore complications stemming from the courts' reliance on interpretive precedent.
21 The specific division of labor between elected law-makers and unelected federal judges is often justified by principles of representative government. This would have been implausible when the franchise was limited to a subclass of white men.
22 See *Encyclopedia of the American Constitution* (Levy ed., New York: Macmillan, 1986), s.v. "Checks and Balances."
23 *North v. Walsh*, 656 F. Supp. 414 (D.D.C. 1987), held that North raised the challenge prematurely. In *Morrison v. Olson*, 108 S.Ct. 2597 (1988), a similar challenge was rejected.

base of all our civil and political institutions.' "[24] He evidently thought that a relevant right of privacy was implied by such principles.[25]

How should we understand the notion that our civil and political institutions are grounded on "fundamental principles of liberty and justice"? It might mean that those institutions are committed to respecting certain moral requirements. That idea is interesting, but I shall focus here on what I take to be a more modest, included point: any call for respect of our civil and political institutions presupposes that they satisfy some basic moral requirements. In other words, someone whose conduct is regulated by a system of law has a right to be treated by the government in a morally defensible way.

I believe this is a reasonable claim and that it has implications for constitutional interpretation.[26] It helps to explain why original intent arguments are justifiable when they are understood as I have suggested. Courts should interpret the Constitution so that it most effectively serves the rationales that provide the best justification of its actual provisions. This approach would maximize the likelihood that decisions reached are morally defensible. It would then maximize the likelihood that decisions will respect one's right to be treated by the government in a morally defensible way.

The propositions I have endorsed are unfamiliar as they stand, but I believe that they express familiar ideas. I think that judges generally presuppose something of the sort.

Here is what I mean. A judge's job is not an intellectual exercise. It is a matter of helping to decide real controversies involving human beings. What is typically done by the courts in the name of the law affects significant human interests most directly. Many of those who come before the courts do not do so voluntarily.[27] We cannot assume that, if they had a choice, they would approve of the law that determines their fate.[28] So what is typically done by the courts to people in the name of the law cannot, in truth, generally be justified by reference to a "social contract." What is typically done requires substantive moral justification.

A plausible justification cannot merely show that what is done is required by the law of the land.[29] Such an argument would fraudulently

---

[24] G, p. 493, quoting *Powell v. Alabama*, 287 U.S. 45, 67.
[25] Douglas likewise suggested that the right of privacy was recognized, not created, by the Constitution; G, p. 486.
[26] I believe it has similar implications for legal interpretation generally.
[27] Many defendants in civil as well as criminal suits may participate only in order to avoid default or contempt judgments.
[28] Most people whose lives have been regulated by law have lacked significant political rights, and many of those with the franchise have lacked effective representation.
[29] See my "Derivability, Defensibility, and the Justification of Judicial Decisions," *The Monist* 68 (1985): 325–46 [reprinted in this volume].

"justify" the enforcement of chattel slavery when genuine justification is impossible.

I do not mean that a judicial decision can be justified only when no injustice is done to any of the parties. It may sometimes be possible to justify doing an injustice to an individual as the lesser of two evils. And a decision that cannot be justified directly, on its merits, may still be justifiable indirectly. Either the laws that are applied must themselves be morally defensible, or there must be adequate justification from another source for enforcing laws that are not themselves morally justifiable. It is routinely assumed, for example, that adherence to principles of representative government justifies the enforcement of bad and even unjust laws.[30]

Here is where the Constitution becomes directly relevant. Judges and other officials who try to justify what is done to people in the name of the law by reference to the Constitution assume, in effect, not only that respect for the constitutional system requires the decision that is rendered, but also that the virtues of the system as a whole compensate for moral deficiencies in the laws that are applied, and thereby render morally regrettable judicial decisions morally defensible. This is typically taken for granted by legal theorists and officials. But the assumption can be problematic in a case like *Dred Scott*.

5.

John Sanford responded to Dred Scott's suit in federal court by challenging the court's jurisdiction. The diversity clause of the U.S. Constitution gives federal courts authority to deal with "Controversies . . . between Citizens of different States" (Art. III, section 2, par. 1). Sanford argued that Scott

was not a citizen of the state of Missouri, as alleged in his declaration, being a negro of African descent, whose ancestors were of pure African blood, and were brought into this country and sold as slaves. (S, p. 400)

The trial court rejected this argument, treating residence in the state and the legal capacity to own property as a sufficient basis for citizenship under the diversity clause.[31] But the jury's verdict favored Sanford. When Scott appealed, the Supreme Court endorsed Sanford's jurisdictional argument. I want to comment on that aspect of the Court's opinion.

The interpretive question faced by the Court was whether those Afri-

---

[30] It may be argued, however, that the enforcement of unjust law cannot be justified unless the system of representative government satisfies some further, substantive moral requirements.

[31] Fehrenbacher, *The Dred Scott Case*, p. 277, citing U.S. court records in St. Louis.

can-Americans who were not slaves could sue under the diversity clause. The issue turned on citizenship, a privileged status under the Constitution.[32] Only citizens are eligible to become President or members of Congress, for example. Most important here, the Constitution lays down that "The Citizens of each State shall be entitled to all Privileges and Immunities of Citizens in the several States" (Art. IV, section 2, par. 1).

In light of the privileges and immunities clause, Taney drew a distinction between the kind of citizenship that a state is competent on its own to confer and citizenship under the Constitution. He understood the Constitution to have given the federal government exclusive power to make someone "a citizen in the sense in which that word is used in the Constitution of the United States"; I shall call this "federal" citizenship.[33] A state may regard anyone it likes as one of its citizens – even an African-American. But, Taney argued, no state was capable of conferring federal citizenship, to which accrued the guarantees of the privileges and immunities clause. Taney thought it obvious that African-Americans could not be federal citizens, because the Constitution could not be understood to guarantee them the privileges and immunities of, say, *white* men in *slave* states. Those states would not have agreed to an arrangement which obliged them to treat African-Americans

who were recognized in any one State of the Union, [as having] the right to enter every other State whenever they pleased, singly or in companies, without pass or passport, and without obstruction, to sojourn there as long as they pleased, to go where they pleased at every hour of the day or night without molestation. (S, p. 417)

Such an arrangement

would give them the full liberty of speech in public and in private upon all subjects upon which [the state's] own citizens might speak; to hold public meetings upon political affairs, and to keep and carry arms wherever they went. And all of this would be done in the face of the subject race of the same color, both free and slaves, and inevitably producing discontent and insubordination among them, and endangering the peace and safety of the state. (S, p. 417)

That specter seems to have haunted Taney.

Now it might be true that in 1857 the slave states would not have accepted such an arrangement. But Taney's argument was supposed to concern what they would have accepted in 1789, when conditions were different and little thought was probably given to the legal status of free African-Americans.

---

[32] It was assumed that slaves could not be citizens. The question was whether the same applied to African-Americans who were not slaves.

[33] S, p. 405; for an interesting discussion, see Fehrenbacher, pp. 356–57.

Taney's reading of the privileges and immunities clause seems in tension with its language, which says that "The Citizens of each State shall be entitled to all Privileges and Immunities of Citizens in the several States." To accept his reasoning, we must suppose that "The Citizens *of* each State" refers, not to those who are recognized *as* citizens *of* the several states *by* those states, but rather to a class of individuals whose federal citizenship was determined, once and for all, in 1789, by assumptions that were then prevalent among white men. Taney's reasoning thus assumed that original intent[34] took precedence over the public meaning of the constitutional text.

Taney argued that the founders regarded African-Americans not as part of "the sovereign people" but "as a subordinate and inferior class of beings, who . . . had no rights or privileges but such as those who held the power and the Government might choose to give them" (S, pp. 404–5). He claimed that African-Americans

had for more than a century before been regarded as beings of an inferior order, and altogether unfit to associate with the white race, either in social or political relations; and so far inferior, that they had no rights which the white man was bound to respect; and that the negro might justly and lawfully be reduced to slavery for his benefit. He was bought and sold, and treated as an ordinary article of merchandise and traffic, whenever a profit could be made by it. This opinion was at that time fixed and universal in the civilized portion of the white race. It was regarded as an axiom in morals as well as politics, which no one thought of disputing, or supposed to be open to dispute; and men in every grade and position in society daily and habitually acted upon it in their private pursuits, as well as in matters of public concern, without doubting for a moment the correctness of this opinion. (S, p. 407)

One need not minimize the depth or prevalence of racism during the revolutionary period to regard this picture as exaggerated. Contrary to Taney's contention, antislavery sentiment and abolitionist societies were at the time neither unknown nor insignificant.[35]

But Taney's factual claims were more extreme than his argument required. In order to substantiate his reference to original intent, he needed to show it likely that there was then a consensus[36] that African-Americans were to be excluded from the constitutional protections.

Taney's strategy was to claim that the law and opinion of 1789 permitted no distinction between free and enslaved African-Americans. He cited the slave trade and fugitive slave clauses of the Constitution as if

---

[34] Taney appealed to original intent along the lines recently suggested by original intent theorists, not as recommended above. In any case, his argument relied upon doubtful historical claims.
[35] Fehrenbacher, *The Dred Scott Case,* p. 18.   [36] It need not have been "universal."

their tacit reference to slavery somehow precluded a distinction between free and enslaved African-Americans (S, p. 411). He cited state laws as if officially sanctioned racism likewise precluded such a distinction (S, pp. 408–9, 412–6). But the evidence was, at best, inconclusive.

Taney's most interesting argument concerned the Declaration of Independence. He acknowledged that its claim "that all men are created equal . . . endowed . . . with certain unalienable rights . . . among them . . . life, liberty, and the pursuit of happiness,"

would seem to embrace the whole human family. . . . But it is too clear for dispute, that the enslaved African race were not intended to be included . . . for if the language, as understood in that day, would embrace them, the conduct of the distinguished men who framed the Declaration of Independence would have been utterly and flagrantly inconsistent with the principles they asserted. (S, p. 410)

Impossible, says Taney; those "were great men . . . high in their sense of honor, and incapable of asserting principles inconsistent with those on which they were acting" (S, p. 410). It is noteworthy that Taney regarded deviation from principles publicly espoused as a serious moral fault, more serious than enslaving others and rationalizing the arrangement with racist doctrines.

Taney's strategy of argument had extreme implications. The Constitution linked some rights to citizenship, but many rights were not so limited. From the right of habeas corpus (Art. I, Section 9, par. 2) to the right against cruel and unusual punishment (Eighth Amendment), the Constitution set limits on what the government might do to *persons.* Taney implied that no such protections applied to African-Americans. By equating the legal status of free African-Americans with that of slaves, he implied that African-Americans could not be persons in the eyes of the law.

6.

The rhetoric of Taney's opinion suggested that its logic was conclusive, that an alternative interpretation could not reasonably be endorsed. Such hyperbole is not unusual. As usually happens when law requires interpretation, however, alternative results are reasonable and neither interpretation is logically compelling.

On the one hand, it was reasonable initially to assume that identical criteria determined citizenship under the provisions that made rights conditional upon citizenship, such as the diversity and privileges and immunities clauses. But laws in some states restricted severely the activities of African-Americans, regardless of their citizenship in other states, thus denying them privileges and immunities that supposedly accrued to their own citizens. Judicial rulings had not found these laws in violation of the privileges and immunities clause.[37] Legal practice thus strongly suggested that free African-Americans were not to be counted as citizens "in the sense in which that word is used in the Constitution of the United States." If so, and if citizenship under the diversity clause must be understood similarly, then free African-Americans could not qualify (as plaintiffs or defendants) under the diversity clause either.

On the other hand, it seemed necessary to recognize degrees of federal citizenship. White women, children, and men without property were classified as citizens although they had a smaller share of rights and lacked political power.[38] This means that African-Americans might qualify for citizenship even though they too enjoyed a smaller share of rights.[39] Furthermore, the Court had already shown that citizenship under the diversity clause need not be identical with citizenship under the privileges and immunities clause. The Court had denied that corporations counted as citizens under the privileges and immunities clause, but it accorded them rights under the diversity clause.[40]

If there are grounds for either interpretation, how decide the question? I have suggested that the Constitution should be interpreted so as to respect, as far as possible, one's right to be treated by the government in a morally defensible way.[41]

To apply that criterion here, one need not pause over rationales for the diversity clause. To deny a class of individuals access to the courts is to deprive them of recourse to whatever justice the law makes available. To deny them citizenship is to mark them off as meriting significantly less legal solicitude and less official respect than their privileged neighbors.

But what if the law of the land were incapable of the morally preferable interpretation? What if there were negligible grounds for supposing that African-Americans might qualify for citizenship under the federal Constitution?

[37] See Fehrenbacher, *The Dred Scott Case*, pp. 68–72.
[38] Taney recognized this, S, p. 422, though he initially linked citizenship with political power, S, p. 405.
[39] "In some respects . . . a [free] black man's status was superior to that of a married white woman, and it was certainly far above that of a slave. He could marry, enter into contracts, purchase real estate, [bequeath] property, and, most pertinently, seek redress in the courts." Fehrenbacher, p. 349.
[40] In *Bank of Augusta v. Earle*, 13 Peters 519, 585–87 (1839), and *Louisville, Cincinnati and Charleston R.R. v. Letson*, 2 Howard 497, 555 (1844), respectively, cited by Fehrenbacher, *The Dred Scott Case*, p. 72, n. 85.
[41] I am not suggesting that we can realistically imagine Roger Taney reasoning in that way. My purpose is to suggest how constitutional ambiguities may *justifiably* be resolved.

I want to mention this problem, however briefly, because the literature of jurisprudence typically embodies a crucial degree of moral complacency. Serious injustices – sufficient to throw into question the relative weight of an official's obligation of fidelity to law – are almost always treated, generation after generation, as if they could only have been problems of the past. But the future's past is the present.

If the law to be interpreted is incapable of receiving any measure of genuine justification, the interpretive approach I have suggested would seem impossible to apply successfully. As a result, it might be impossible to justify particular decisions. The injustices that would be done by implementing the law might then outweigh any merits retained by the legal system as a whole.

In that event, a court should find itself facing a crisis in which it is doubtful that one can in good conscience administer the law that one has pledged to uphold.[42]

---

[42] Except, perhaps, when doing so realistically offers the prospect of preventing greater injustice by preventing the application of such law on subsequent occasions.

10

Critical analysis
and constructive interpretation

This paper concerns two problems of legal practice – interpretation and the justification of judicial decisions. Largely because of Dworkin's work, legal theory now addresses without skeptical presumptions the issue of interpretation, and his "constructive interpretation" is the most important entrant in that field.[1] But legal interpretation (in the relevant sense of discovering the determinate meaning or implications of existing law) is not an end in itself but serves adjudication, which impinges on important human interests. For our purposes, judicial decisions should be viewed not as propositions of law but as things that are done to people in the name of the law.[2] And the things that judicial decisions do[3] to people, such as depriving them of life, liberty, or valued goods, require moral justification.

Many of those who come before courts do so under duress and have lacked a reasonable opportunity to affect the political process. We cannot assume that they would approve of the law that determines their fate or that they are committed in any way to the law that is applied against them. What is done to them in the name of the law requires substantive moral justification. And the fact that something is required by law does not itself provide such a justification.[4] So interpretive legal theory is, or should be, concerned with the justification of judicial decisions. The issues to be addressed include not only logical support for legal propositions but also the moral defensibility of their practical implications.

Ancestors of this paper were presented at Brooklyn Law School, Cornell University, the Graduate Center of the City University of New York, the University of Kansas, McGill Law School, Tulane Law School, and a joint symposium of the Canadian Philosophical Association and the Canadian Society for Social Philosophy. I am grateful to Greg Alexander, David Dyzenhaus, Stephen Massey, and Roger Shiner for comments.

1   Ronald Dworkin, *Law's Empire* (Cambridge, Mass.: Harvard University Press, 1986). "Constructive" is the generic name Dworkin gives to interpretation of social practices; he calls its legal application "law as integrity." I ignore that detail here.

2   For simplicity's sake, I assume that judicial judgments are implemented. Joel Feinberg has reminded us, moreover, that legal judgments themselves have important expressive functions.

3   Or cause to be done.

4   See my "Derivability, Defensibility, and the Justification of Judicial Decisions," *Monist* 68 (1985) 325 [reprinted in this volume].

One reason for the importance of constructive theory is its ambition to provide guidance for interpretation that promotes the justifiability of judicial decisions. Because what counts as law is not automatically limited by moral criteria, it is reasonable to expect the achievement of that ambition to encounter serious obstacles. Statutes can be morally indefensible and common-law doctrines can suffer grave moral defects, so the soundest interpretive theory may be incapable of ensuring that each legal requirement enjoys some measure of moral justification.

The theory that I here dub "critical analysis" appears in prominent writings associated with the critical legal studies movement (CLS).[5] The features that it shares with constructive interpretation suggest the possibility that critical analysis might provide the foundation for a distinctive approach to legal interpretation. That caught my attention because CLS has been linked with the notion that indeterminacy pervades the law, a view that precludes interpretation in the relevant sense. Besides, interpretive legal theory needs all the help it can get. Promising theories of legal interpretation are rare.

Section I explains the need for interpretive legal theory. Section II examines constructive interpretation and argues that it fails to justify a crucial class of decisions, including some that may not be justifiable. Section III considers critical analysis as a possible basis for legal interpretation, with constructive interpretation as a point of reference.[6]

I. THE NEED FOR INTERPRETIVE THEORY

Many theorists seem skeptical about the possibility of legal interpretation. This is not limited to those who regard the law as pervasively indeterminate, for many theorists who accept that there are legal rules with clear enough meaning hold that such meaning is more limited than the scope of the rules. They hold, in effect, that when interpretation is needed it is impossible. Courts can then decide cases only by changing the law.

A. Open texture

If law's determinate meaning is limited to what is clear and uncontroversial among competent lawyers, that must result from something dis-

5 See, e.g., Duncan Kennedy, "Form and Substance in Private Law Adjudication," *Harvard Law Review* 89 (1976) 1685, and Roberto Unger, *The Critical Legal Studies Movement* (Cambridge, Mass.: Harvard University Press, 1986). For a broader sample of important CLS writings, see *Critical Legal Studies*, ed. Allan C. Hutchinson (Totowa, N.J.: Rowman & Littlefield, 1989); another CLS collection is *The Politics of Law*, Revised Edition, ed. David Kairys (New York: Pantheon, 1990).
6 I consider these as approaches to interpretation, not as theories about the nature of law.

tinctive about law. For the general idea that a subject matter is determinate only where experts confidently agree about it implies that facts of all kinds are creatures of confident consensus, unmade by dissensus or uncertainty. And that is simply implausible.

The most widely accepted basis for such an idea about law is H.L.A. Hart's theory that law is "open textured."[7] From the fact that competent language users are uncertain or disagree about some applications of a word (e.g., whether a wheelchair counts as a vehicle), Hart infers that corresponding legal propositions (e.g., whether bringing a wheelchair into a park violates the park's prohibition against vehicles) are neither true nor false. Hart speaks only of law, and he could not plausibly generalize to other subjects. For we do not generally assume, nor would it seem true, that where linguistic conventions are imprecise (where competent language users are uncertain or disagree about the applications of terms) the corresponding states of affairs are indeterminate. But Hart fails to explain why dissensus and uncertainty render law indeterminate.

So this theory about law requires justification. And there is reason to doubt it. Suppose the government uses its power of eminent domain and condemns my home to make way for a public highway. The constitution of my state says that "private property shall not be taken for public use without just compensation."[8] In the absence of strong reason to the contrary, we must suppose that this requires what it says – just compensation. The constitution does not define just compensation, and we may be uncertain or disagree about it.[9] According to open texture theory, if uncertainty or disagreement is widespread among competent language users, the provision lacks determinate meaning until a court confers such meaning on it. But that does not seem right.

Suppose a judge has to decide whether I have received just compensation. If she were interpreting the clause without aid of interpretive precedent or if she questioned past interpretations, she might reasonably believe that the answer to the legal question (How interpret the just-compensation requirement for this sort of case?) depends on the answer to a moral question (What constitutes just compensation?). Uncertainty or disagreement about the moral question does not show that it has no

---

[7] *The Concept of Law* (Oxford: Clarendon Press, 1961), pp. 121–32.

[8] New York State Constitution, Art. 1, § 7. Compare the U.S. Constitution, Amendment V.

[9] Does it depend on whether one's ownership is just as well as lawful? If so, one must determine when ownership is just. If it doesn't (or if my ownership is just) we must determine the value of my house for the purpose. Should it be based on market price or replacement cost? How determine the former without a sale in a competitive market? How determine replacement cost? And so on.

right answer. And we have as yet no other reason for concluding that there is no sound answer to the legal question.

When judges are uncertain about the law, they seem to reason about its meaning. Their interpretive arguments are subjected to appraisal by others. Unclear law is treated not as indeterminate but as subject to analysis. Disagreement does not discourage but rather spurs interpretive reasoning. These facts suggest that lawyers and judges try to interpret law and believe that interpretation is possible even when there is dissensus or uncertainty. Their practice might be misleading; they might be deceiving others or even themselves. But we lack reason to believe this. We cannot dismiss the possibility of legal interpretation, and theory is needed.

B. Original intent[10]

The most familiar interpretive legal theory is that courts should read statutory and constitutional texts in terms of what the lawmakers had in mind. Original-intent theorists believe that interpreting law by reference to that historical state of affairs respects the separation of powers that is required by both democratic principles and our constitutions. These theorists equate law making with the exercise of moral judgment, which they assume need not be exercised in the process of legal interpretation.

The standard theory of original intent is misconceived. First, the intention of one who drafts or votes for a law is not an initially promising criterion of meaning. The words we use have meanings determined by social conventions. Original-intent theorists fail to explain why the meaning of written law is determined by lawmakers' purposes and the applications that they contemplate instead.

Second, the just-compensation example seems to show that the desire for value-free interpretation is unrealizable.

Third, the theory is ambiguous. A drafter or adopter may intend a law to serve an identifiable purpose and intend it to have certain specific applications because he assumes that they would serve that purpose. But he may be mistaken, so his two intentions may clash. Original intent would then offer inconsistent guidance for interpretation.[11]

Fourth, original-intent theory presumably implies that a law which is

[10] I criticize original-intent theory in "Constitutional Interpretation and Original Meaning," *Social Philosophy & Policy* 4 (1986) 75, and suggest a reconstruction of original-intent practice in "Basic Rights and Constitutional Interpretation," *Social Theory and Practice* 16 (1990) 337 [both reprinted in this volume].

[11] As the disjunction "drafter or adopter" may suggest, the theory is ambiguous in other ways, too.

drafted or adopted by several persons has determinate meaning only if there was an intentional consensus. But law makers can and often do have differing intentions. Now, it would be implausible to attribute an intention to a legislature or one of its enactments when, for example, most members intended the enactment to serve a different purpose or to apply differently. Reflection on such considerations would lead one to conclude that an intent can be attributed to a legislature only when a substantial proportion of the legislators[12] have the same intentions about its content. That condition does not always obtain when law is meaningful.

The standard *theory* of interpretation based on original intent seems overwhelmed by such difficulties. But legal *practice* may fare better. Judicial opinions and legal commentaries often reason from framers' or legislators' intent. But these arguments often do not square with the standard theory. Because that theory regards original intent as an historical state of affairs, it requires there to have been an intentional consensus. Evidence is rarely offered to show that there was probably an intentional consensus on the point at issue. And we know that those who enact law often have differing intentions and that some who vote for a bill give it little thought. We have good reason to doubt that enactments are generally accompanied by an intentional consensus regarding the full meaningful content of the written law. But if original-intent arguments were purely historical, strong evidence that there was a relevant consensus would be needed. This crucial element is almost always missing from original intent arguments without, however, weakening their persuasive force.

There are two possible explanations for this gap between original-intent theory and practice. Either judicial references to original intent are unsubstantiated or they must be understood differently. I suggest the latter. What an original-intent argument often seems to do is identify a *plausible justifying rationale* for the legislative or constitutional provision in question.[13] Given that, we can often decide the specific interpretive issue. I believe that is how original-intent arguments often work.

Construed in this way, original-intent arguments make sense and have some hope of being sound. But then they are neither purely historical nor value free; they involve judgments of political morality. And they approximate constructive interpretation.

---

[12] Perhaps a number sufficient to enact the legislation, counting only those who voted for it, wishing it to be enacted.

[13] Note how often the *Federalist Papers* are relied upon for guidance, when no evidence is offered that they reflect a consensus among constitutional framers or ratifiers.

II. CONSTRUCTIVE INTERPRETATION[14]

Legal interpretation is presented by Dworkin as a special case of a widely applicable approach: To interpret a social practice, we must view it in the best light. A practice is seen, if possible, as serving values that make it worthwhile. The rules of the practice are reinterpreted as needed to more effectively serve those justifying values.

Dworkin suggests "that the most abstract and fundamental point of legal practice is to guide and constrain the power of government" by reference to prior legislative, judicial, and other authoritative decisions.[15] This mode of deciding cases promotes procedural fairness and predictability. Dworkin also believes that, when past decisions are understood as committing the government to acting even-handedly, on principle, legal practice promotes "political integrity" and true political community for a heterogeneous population. Past decisions are interpreted by reference to the moral principles that provide their best justification.[16]

Dworkin's theory is meant to be both normative and descriptive: It is supposed to give *guidance* for interpretation so that judges will be able to decide cases in the way that existing law *requires* them to be decided. An interpretation must closely fit the legal facts. But Dworkin's theory is not purely descriptive. He wishes to explain how law can provide some genuine moral justification for judicial decisions. The question I shall raise is whether constructive interpretation succeeds – whether it ensures that all of the decisions it authorizes enjoy, as a consequence, some measure of justification, however slight.

Value-guided interpretation, such as Dworkin's theory requires, offers some promise of respecting this moral imperative. The constructive approach interprets law in terms of principles that are capable of providing moral justification for what is done to people. Within the constraints imposed by the descriptive aspect of genuine interpretation, this would seem to maximize the capacity of interpreted law for justifying current decisions. That improves the likelihood that applications of law will be justifiable.

Still, the normative ambition of constructive interpretation is difficult to achieve, and several features of Dworkin's theory render it more manageable. First, Dworkin holds that law enjoys a measure of justification whenever, but only when, constructive interpretation is possible. As he

---

[14] I consider Dworkin's theory (and other problems for it than those discussed here) in "Reconstructing Legal Theory," *Philosophy & Public Affairs* 16 (1987) 379.

[15] *Law's Empire*, p. 93.

[16] These rationales need not be laid down in written law or endorsed explicitly by courts.

appreciates, a community's law can be so outrageously immoral as to provide not even the slightest justification for its application.[17] In that extreme case, constructive interpretation is inapplicable.

Second, Dworkin does not claim that the relevant law is always justifiably enforced. There can be good justification both for and against enforcement. All things considered, a legally required decision might be morally unjustifiable.[18] His theory aims only to account for defeasible justification.

Third, Dworkin believes that law can have moral force even when it is morally deficient. This corresponds to the notion that citizens can have an obligation to obey such a law. If the specific law being applied is morally deficient, some special justification is required for enforcing it. Constructive interpretation must therefore have recourse to indirect justification of what is done in particular cases.

According to Dworkin, common-law decisions can be justified only by invoking moral principles. He does not assume that the common law is morally perfect. Rather, he assumes, crucially, that *nonideal* principles are capable of justifying decisions. This enables him to believe that judicial decisions can be justified under morally deficient common-law doctrines.

That assumption is not implausible. In a parallel way, we may assume that we have a genuine right to compensation for economic losses that others have culpably caused us, without supposing that the system of property under which we owned what was lost is morally perfect. Even so, I am skeptical.

Here is the sort of legal situation that constructive interpretation seems clearly intended to cover. Suppose that prevailing precedent in personal-injury law firmly embraces the doctrine of contributory negligence. The victim of another's negligence is entitled to compensation, but only if she has not contributed to the loss by her own negligence. This may be regarded as a plausible principle, for it requires compensation justly in many cases.

Suppose, however, that Alice was very careless and as a result Barbara suffered greatly; but Barbara was slightly careless and would otherwise have suffered slightly less. Then Barbara has no valid legal claim to any compensation from Alice. Dworkin's theory implies that a judgment denying Barbara compensation enjoys some measure of justification. Its moral force has two possible sources. One is the doctrine of contributory negligence itself. But I do not see how the fact that this principle justly re-

---

[17] *Law's Empire,* pp. 101–8.
[18] *Law's Empire,* pp. 108–13 (on the "grounds" and "force" of law).

quires compensation in *other* cases[19] confers some measure of justification on its application in this case. For this case is just the sort of situation that led jurists to reject the doctrine.

Nonideal principles such as contributory negligence have implications that are morally unproblematic in some cases. But these applications do not seem to confer any measure of justification upon the problematic applications. The problem for constructive interpretation is to explain how justification is conferred on applications that embody the *defects* of nonideal principles.

If nonideal principles cannot do the required work, can the principle of political integrity fill the moral gap? I do not see how. "Political integrity" is a name for the special virtue of a system in which courts view past authoritative decisions as commitments to principle. Widespread acceptance of this value is supposed to promote the most desirable form of political community, in which each member accepts a responsibility of equal concern for all other members, and the constitutional foundation of such a community is regarded as most likely to generate a genuine obligation to obey the law.[20] Suppose these claims are sound, and general acceptance of political integrity would have those desirable consequences.[21] I do not see how *that* helps to justify decisions representing the morally deficient aspects of the law. Those consequences do not seem *relevant* to the problem of justifying (say) the judgment denying Barbara compensation.

Now consider the statutory context. Dworkin seems to hold that unjustifiable statutes can justifiably be enforced. He does not explain how, but he suggests that a decision which cannot be justified directly, on its merits, may still be justifiable indirectly.

Here is an example.[22] Half a century ago, Mr. Daniels was a street trader and Mrs. Tarbard operated a pub in the South London neighborhood of Battersea. Mr. Daniels purchased a bottle of R. White's lemonade from Mrs. Tarbard at her pub. Carbolic acid was in the lemonade, and Mr. and Mrs. Daniels suffered accordingly. Carbolic acid must have combined with the lemonade in R. White's bottling plant, for the bottle remained sealed until used by Mr. and Mrs. Daniels. They sued the manufacturer of the lemonade as well as Mrs. Tarbard.

Judge Lewis applied the negligence test for manufacturer's liability, found that the evidence had not established negligence, and held the

---

[19] This is the main if not the only basis that it has for being considered the sort of principle that can be included in the constructive interpretation of a body of law.

[20] *Law's Empire*, pp. 190–1.

[21] I see no reason to suppose that any community has ever satisfied those conditions.

[22] *Daniels and Daniels v. R. White & Sons, Ltd., and Tarbard* ([1938] 4 All E.R. 258).

manufacturer free of legal liability. But the Sale of Goods Act made Mrs. Tarbard liable to Mr. Daniels because she sold him "goods of unmerchantable quality." Judge Lewis acknowledged that Mrs. Tarbard was "entirely innocent and blameless in the matter," but he held her liable for Mr. Daniels' loss.

We may assume that Judge Lewis believed not only that his judgment against Mrs. Tarbard was required by law but also that his rendering it was morally defensible. The latter belief bears scrutiny. He might have believed that the decision against Mrs. Tarbard was fair to her though regrettable. But his remarks suggest that it was unfair to Mrs. Tarbard, and our analytic purpose is served by considering this possibility. If he believed that his judgment was morally defensible although unfair to Mrs. Tarbard, then he must have believed it could be justified indirectly. He might have believed that imposing strict liability on retailers was justifiable despite regrettable applications. For present purposes, however, let us suppose that he had strong reservations about strict liability and regarded the statute as unfair. If so, he must have believed that unfair statutes can (sometimes) justifiably be enforced. A justification of his judgment against Mrs. Tarbard would then rest on some broader claim about, say, the virtues of that legal system or of respecting law.

In his discussion of *Daniels*, Neil MacCormick suggests some such arguments:

1. "it is good that judicial decisions be predictable and contribute to certainty of law, which they are and do when they apply known rules identified in accordance with commonly shared and understood criteria of recognition";
2. "it is good that judges stay within their assigned place in the constitutional order, applying established law rather than inventing new law";
3. "it is good that law-making be entrusted to the elected representatives of the people, not usurped by non-elected and non-removable judges";
4. "the existing and accepted constitutional order is a fair and just system, and accordingly the criteria of recognition of laws which it institutes are good and just criteria which ought to be observed."[23]

Considerations like these are often advanced for compliance with law, especially when the relevant laws or their applications are morally prob-

[23] *Legal Reasoning and Legal Theory* (Oxford: Clarendon Press, 1978), pp. 63–4.

lematic. They might be used to argue that the judgment against Mrs. Tarbard is justifiable; but I am skeptical.

Dworkin once presented the most important element of such arguments as follows:

> The constitution sets out a general political scheme that is sufficiently just to be taken as settled for reasons of fairness. Citizens take the benefit of living in a society whose institutions are arranged and governed in accordance with that scheme, and they must take the burdens as well, at least until a new scheme is put into force either by discrete amendment or general revolution.[24]

This conventional picture of political obligation is plausible if we assume conditions such as the following: The objectionable laws are aberrations, and the objectionable applications are otherwise randomly distributed results of honest error or of the unavoidable characteristics of rules, such as under- and overinclusiveness.

But such an argument cannot be applied widely enough to serve its purpose. Such an argument is implausible when applied, for example, to someone who suffers injustice systematically under the law. The fact that benefits and political rights are enjoyed by others would not seem to justify enforcement of unjust law against its usual victims.

In some cases, justification seems quite problematic. Consider *Thomas Sims's Case*.[25] Under the Fugitive Slave Act of 1850, Sims was taken prisoner and held for a hearing before a federal commissioner. The Act provided for summary hearings in which alleged fugitive slaves could not testify. Upon hearing a claimant's evidence, a commissioner was empowered to authorize him to transport the prisoner to the slave owner's locale.

Petitioners sought a writ of *habeas corpus* for Sims on the ground that conferring judicial authority on commissioners violated the federal Constitution. The Massachusetts court rejected this argument. Chief Justice Shaw explained that he was bound by precedents validating the Act, and he defended the Fugitive Slave Clause as necessary for the constitutional settlement and as proper because it served the interests of the states.

Dworkin has suggested that decisions for slave owners under the Fugitive Slave Act might enjoy some measure of justifiability.[26] The problem is how any plausible expansion or revision of Shaw's reasoning could justify the court's sending Thomas Sims to slavery.[27] As an African-

---

[24] *Taking Rights Seriously*, p. 106 ("Hard Cases").
[25] 61 Mass. (7 Cush.) 285 (1851).
[26] In " 'Natural' Law Revisited," *University of Florida Law Review* 34 (1982), p. 186.
[27] It has been suggested that the arrangements could be justified as mere extradition hearings, to be followed by regular trials in the claimants' locales (see Allen Johnson, "The Constitutionality of the Fugitive Slave Acts," *Yale Law Journal* 31 [1921–2]

MORAL ASPECTS OF LEGAL THEORY

American (slave or free), Sims was arguably not a beneficiary of the constitutional accommodation. He was barred from the political processes that led to and followed from the Constitution. Neither benefits for others nor their political rights tend to confer any measure of justification for enforcement of the Fugitive Slave Act.[28]

I am not arguing against the possibility of indirect moral justification of judicial decisions. I do not assume, for example, that the *Daniels* judgment was morally indefensible. But neither do I assume the contrary. The burden of proof falls on those who wish to claim that what is done to people in the name of the law enjoys some measure of moral justification. Dworkin's arguments do not seem to sustain this burden.

III. CRITICAL LEGAL ANALYSIS

CLS appears to embrace a less favorable view of our law. One might therefore suppose that its approach to interpretation – if it has one – would be more sensitive to the problem of justifying what is done to people in the name of the law.

Critical scholars perceive a definite deep structure in the law. They hold that law contains some reasonably determinate rules that represent reasonably determinate underlying values. They regard those values as pregnant with further implications. This suggests that the values might provide the basis for further interpretation.

The underlying values are held to have a certain character. In any branch of law, such as contracts, property, or torts, some established rules are seen as reflecting one particular moral position, usually called "individualism," and other rules as reflecting a rival view, called "altruism."[29] It is claimed, for example, that rules holding people to contracts reflect individualism whereas rules relaxing contractual rigors reflect altruism.[30]

161). It is unclear how this warrants excluding testimony from prisoners or how realistic it was to suggest that alleged fugitives would receive fair hearings in slave owners' courts.

[28] I do not consider the possibility that political integrity might justify the application of unjust statutes because it is unclear how it might help in a statutory context. In *Law's Empire* Dworkin suggests that indirect justification in a statutory context relies upon fairness in the distribution of political power. My point is that such fairness as could have been found in the contemporary system is irrelevant to justifying what was done to Sims in the name of the law.

[29] The terms vary. Individualism is sometimes opposed by "communitarianism." In a constitutional context the poles may be seen as "liberalism" and "civic republicanism."

[30] As both enforcement of and refusal to enforce a contract are advantageous to one party and disadvantageous to another, this analysis needs justification. Enforcement requires one party to serve another's interests, so it could be thought to reflect altruism instead of individualism; nonenforcement benefits one party at some cost to the

The opposing views have parallel structures. Each holds that we as individuals have a certain degree of responsibility for what happens to others[31] and rights to others' consideration, perhaps even to their positive help. They differ about the extent of those rights and responsibilities. Individualism maintains that it is legitimate to pursue one's own interests with less regard for others than altruism requires, and it accordingly holds that one has a narrower right to others' aid or concern.[32] Altruism maintains that we have a greater responsibility for what happens to others, a greater obligation to share one's resources and to make sacrifices for others' sake, and thus a greater right to others' consideration and positive assistance.

According to critical analysis, the law is in tension between these views. Individualism is dominant in our society, but an altruistic tendency is ineradicable. Thus law has a deep bi-polar structure.

Can critical analysis ground a normative approach to legal interpretation? That possibility is suggested by the fact that individualism and altruism are seen as providing rationales for rules of law. Interpretation might be based on those values – extrapolating further from them – as in constructive theory.

There are several obstacles to developing a theory of interpretation from critical analysis. (1) It is unclear that the underlying moral positions have the requisite relation to rules – that they account for rules by *justifying* them. (2) If those values are to ground interpretations of the law, conflicts between them (or their respective rules) must be resolved in particular cases. For this to be possible, we must reinterpret the values, for they are defined in contradictory terms. But by specifically identifying the underlying values, critical analysis resists such a move. Furthermore, it seems to maintain that we lack the means for effecting a principled resolution of the conflict. (3) It is doubtful that critical scholars *want* their analysis to serve as the foundation for legal interpretation. It seems intended for a different purpose.

(1) Critical analysis presents us with a puzzle: What is the relation supposed to be between either of the polar moral views and the rules it is said to explain? Compare critical analysis with constructive interpre-

---

other, so it could be thought to reflect individualism instead of altruism. If a given rule is to be associated with one position to the exclusion of the other, that must depend on other factors. Thus Kennedy suggests that individualism embodies the ideal of "self-reliance," whereas altruism represents a notion of interdependence.

[31] And that we may justifiably *be held accountable by law* for what happens to others. The descriptions offered of the polar positions typically ignore the possibility that some moral rights and obligations should not be enforced by law.

[32] As noted above, critical analysis associates "self-reliance" with this view. I focus on the relevant moral principles, but that may not do justice to the analytic theories.

tation, which tells us that the relevant values provide the best systematic, coherent justification of past authoritative decisions. Now, one may be unhappy with this prescription; for it provides no litmus test. Different well-informed, reflective judges might reasonably reach different conclusions when attempting constructive interpretation. But at least the theory gives us a clear idea of the relation that principles must have to past political decisions in order to qualify for an interpretive role. Critical analysis, by contrast, does not clearly tell us what relation is supposed to obtain between legal rules and the underlying moral positions. We need to know this in order to understand and test its analytic claims. And if the underlying values do not account for rules and particular decisions by justifying them but have a different relation to rules, it is unclear that we should wish to or could use them as the basis for further interpretation.

One reason to suspect that the underlying values do not necessarily justify their respective rules is that critical scholars suggest more serious reservations about individualism than about altruism. They might well regard it as incapable of truly justifying rules and decisions under them. In addition, individualism and altruism may be meant to play a role within the law different from that of justifying rules. Critical scholars suggest that acceptance of the underlying values has causally contributed to the development of the law. The law serves as a repository of past political decisions, and we should expect to find within it rules representing the moral views that helped to shape them. It is plausible to suppose that law has been shaped by differing views about the rights and responsibilities that may legitimately be enforced, views that might well differ as individualism and altruism do.[33] In that case, critical analysis offers a *genetic* theory of law – an historical, causal account of legal development. And a theory that explains why decisions have been made neither promises to justify them nor clearly offers guidance for interpretation.

(2) There is another bar to finding interpretive guidance in critical analysis. The conflict between individualism and altruism is supposed to be irresolvable. This explains why, according to critical analysis, judges cannot simply apply the law. Whenever judges reach for law, they find conflicting rules, alternative grounds of decision, some reflecting a wider conception of other-regarding obligations, others a narrower conception. Critical scholars maintain that those conflicts cannot be resolved without

---

[33] This represents only part of the explanation for the bi-polar analysis of law as is found in CLS writings. Critical analysis has other sources, such as a predilection for Hegelian dialectics and the idea that humans are torn between social and antisocial dispositions reflecting our simultaneous need for and vulnerability to others.

a "meta-principle."[34] And they hold that no meta-principle is available, so a judge must simply *decide* which way to go. That is why, according to critical analysis, judges cannot neutrally apply the law. That is why adjudication is said to lack legitimacy.

This does not mean that judicial practice is totally unpredictable. Individualism is regarded by critical scholars as the dominant view in our society, one that most judges can be expected to share. A judge who is uncertain about the law can be expected to interpret narrowly its requirements of assistance for others and to interpret broadly its recognition of a right to be free from legal intervention.

Ironically, this suggests a resolution of the conflict that critical analysis finds within the law. If individualism is the dominant tendency, one might imagine that a faithful interpretation of the law would systematically favor individualist interpretations. But I think that this would be unacceptable to critical scholars. I cannot imagine their endorsing an approach to adjudication that would reinforce individualism. Besides, as I mentioned earlier, critical scholars might well regard individualism as incapable of truly justifying rules and decisions under them. In Dworkinian terms, individualism "fits" well but fails adequately to justify the relevant decisions and rules.

The reverse applies to the opposite strategy, resolving such conflicts in favor of altruism. Critical scholars may favor altruism and may believe that it more adequately justifies the decisions and rules it has engendered. But, precisely because they hold that individualism dominates the law, critical scholars are committed to holding that altruism does not fit enough of the law to provide overall guidance for genuine interpretation.

Can one escape between the horns of this dilemma? Part of the problem is that critical scholars understand law as filled with clashing rules reflecting moral views that are *logically* incompatible. Individualism and altruism are defined so as to represent contradictory positions on issues such as the extent of one's responsibility for what happens to others. This aspect of the conflict seems avoidable. An alternative interpretation of the same body of law might depict the value conflict as a clash between (say) the principle that one may legitimately be held accountable in law for what happens to others and the principle that coercive state action should be minimized. These clash in practice, but they are not logically incompatible. Individualism and altruism could then be seen, not as the values underlying law, but as differing conceptions of the appropriate

---

[34] See, e.g., J. M. Balkin, "Taking Ideology Seriously," *University of Missouri–Kansas City Law Review* 55 (1987), p. 421, and Clare Dalton, "An Essay In the Deconstruction of Contract Doctrine," *Yale Law Journal* 94 (1985), pp. 1025–6.

resolution of the conflict. To interpret the law, one would seek the most reasonable resolution (in general, in the branch of law, or in the particular case).

Critical scholars are mistaken if they assume that conflicting principles must necessarily be contradictories. Consider a conflict between one's obligations as a teacher and as a parent. It may be impossible for me both to stay with my sick child and to teach my scheduled class. What I should do will depend on the facts, such as whether my child requires personal attention and, if so, whether anyone else is available to provide it. It will also depend on what inconvenience my students will suffer if I do not appear. If my child is either an infant with a life-threatening condition or a capable teenager with a minor illness, the right decision may be clear. Other decisions will be more difficult. But we have no reason to assume that conflicts between obligations (or principles generally) necessarily resist rational resolution. Nor need we assume that their resolution requires recourse to "meta-principles."[35]

If we had adequate reason to analyze law in bi-polar terms, with principles like the ones suggested substituting for individualism and altruism, we might have the basis for a distinctive approach to legal interpretation. The result, however, would not clearly be distinguishable from constructive interpretation.

(3) Critical scholars can be expected to resist my suggested reinterpretation of the underlying values. For one thing, they specifically identify individualism and altruism as those values. Furthermore, the rhetoric of critical scholarship does not seem to encourage interpretation beyond bipolar analysis. Why should that be?

One possible reason is this: Critical scholars wish to liberate the bench and the bar from what they regard as a deeply entrenched assumption that law must continue to develop largely along individualistic lines. They emphasize the availability of alternative directions in decision making. They wish to persuade judges that they have opportunities to reform the law as they decide cases. It would seem as if they wish judges to try, where feasible, to do justice *directly* in the cases that come before them, rather than rely on law to work justice indirectly. They suggest, for example, that adjudication should favor the less advantaged, because it is reasonable to assume that their disadvantages cannot be justified and will otherwise be intensified.

Conventional wisdom counsels otherwise. It says that courts should assume that justice will be done, if not directly then indirectly, when

---

[35] My impression, however, is that philosophers have not attended sufficiently to the question whether the rational resolution of a conflict between principles requires appeal to a further principle.

courts apply the law as it stands. This assumes not only that law is by and large determinate (which critical scholars may mean to deny) but also that justice can effectively be done indirectly, and thus that the law merits respect. But our discussion of constructive interpretation suggests how difficult indirect justification may be.

The problem facing judges is not merely to apply the law but to render decisions that are morally defensible. Suppose, as commonly happens, the law requires interpretation. Theories of interpretation tell one how to apply it. But interpretation is problematic; one cannot be confident of success. One might reasonably have even less confidence in the moral claims that are conventionally made on behalf of adherence to existing law. Critical analysis can be understood to suggest that one often has much stronger reason to expect success if one tries to do justice directly than by trying to interpret and apply existing law.

Thus, critical scholars avoid the issue that is addressed, in effect, by constructive justification – how to show that there is at least some measure of justification (however slight) for every judicial decision that is required by law. They do so either by maintaining (perhaps unsoundly) that deep value conflicts prevent law from requiring decisions one way rather than another in particular cases; or else by advocating that judges use their opportunities to do justice directly as they decide cases (perhaps on the ground that differing decisions are unlikely to be justifiable anyway).

Neither position is adequately defended or even articulated. But our examination of these two theories about adjudication suggests that the *moral* problem facing interpretive theory is more important than the literature implies. It is in fact almost totally neglected. The simple reason, I believe, is that legal theorists generally assume (as Dworkin quite clearly does) that judicial decisions that are required by law, and thus the things that are done to people in the name of the law, normally enjoy some measure of moral justification. That assumption seems to me unwarranted. It is quite possibly wrong. It demands very careful scrutiny.